DAILY LIFE IN
THE FRENCH REVOLUTION

DAILY LIFE IN THE
French Revolution

Jean Robiquet

TRANSLATED FROM THE FRENCH BY
James Kirkup

THE MACMILLAN COMPANY
NEW YORK, NEW YORK

FOURTH PRINTING 1971

The Macmillan Company
866 Third Avenue, New York, N. Y. 10022

Printed in the United States of America

28586

CONTENTS

ILLUSTRATIONS

DAILY LIFE IN
THE FRENCH REVOLUTION

CHAPTER ONE

THE PARIS OF 1789

---

*Paris at the time of the Revolution – Narrowness of the streets –
Division of districts – Slowness of communication – Traditional meeting-places: the Tuileries, the Palais Royal – The
lively appearance of the crowds – General optimism*

PARIS AT THE TIME OF THE REVOLUTION

In order to understand the daily life of those who witnessed
the Revolution, we must carry constantly in our mind's eye a
picture of the outward appearance of Paris in 1789.

It is a difficult task, because the great reconstructions made
during the First and especially the Second Empire profoundly
changed the capital. Accustomed as we are to its modern
aspects, how are we going to conjure up the city as it was
known by Danton or Camille Desmoulins?

How is it possible to imagine the Jardin des Tuileries without the Rue de Rivoli, and bounded, on the side of the Terrasse
des Feuillants, by conventual buildings, while the Place du
Carousel was cluttered with hotels and stalls and the Butte des
Moulins still existed only two hundred metres from the Palais
Royal? And everywhere there were alleyways, yards, steps and
stairs, gates that were closed at dusk, culs-de-sac where it was
easy to lose one's bearings, a city at once mysterious and foreign
to us, and one in which only those born to the Paris streets
could find their way without too much trouble.

NARROWNESS OF THE STREETS

Excepting for the boulevards, the quais and the Rue Saint-
Antoine, the larger thoroughfares were rarely wider than today's

Rue Saint-Honoré, on the Right Bank, or the Rue des Saints-Pères or the Rue du Bac on the Left Bank. And there were so many streets where it was difficult for two carts to pass, murky little lanes, a few examples of which still remain in Saint-Germain-des-Prés, around Saint-Séverin or the Panthéon. The Paris of the Revolution still persists today in those places, where we can obtain some idea of the curious structure of the capital in the late eighteenth century.

DIVISION OF DISTRICTS

The contrasts between the various quartiers or districts were striking, for each had its own atmosphere, its peculiar population. Whereas the nobility and the rich bourgeoisie occupied the Faubourg Saint-Germain, the Marais, the Temple and the Arsenal districts, there was quite a different air about the less strait-laced quartiers of the Théâtre-Français (the Odéon), Bonne-Nouvelle and the Palais Royal. And the change of climate was accentuated in the purely working-class zones: in Saint-Paul, where the masons lived, in Croix-Rouge, where the furniture and building industries were centred, in the Rue Saint-Denis and the Rue Saint-Martin where were to be found milliners, haberdashers and the makers of fashionable fancy Parisian goods.

The peculiar character of local inhabitants became more pronounced as soon as one entered the suburbs. To the north, the suburbs of Montmartre, Saint-Lazare and Saint-Laurent depended mainly on the sale of cloth. To the west, Chaillot had ironworks and cotton mills; the suburb of Roule, with its ragpickers in the area known as 'la Pologne' (Poland), on the site of the present Boulevard Haussmann, was one of the poorest quartiers in Paris (though its fortunes have risen since then). Finally, to the east, on each bank of the Seine, the suburbs of Saint-Antoine and Saint-Marcel contained, respectively, many furniture workshops, including Réveillon's famous wallpaper factory; dyeworks, tanneries, breweries and the Gobelins tapestry works.

So there were many small towns in the large one, many trades whose workers, leading the same lives, performing the same tasks, rarely went outside their local area. Calls were made on neighbours; Sunday would be celebrated at the nearest little tavern; and one usually married someone from the same district. People bothered very little about what was going on outside their own quartier.

The distinguishing feature, therefore, of revolutionary Paris was this extreme compartmenting, caused chiefly by the difficulties of transport and traffic between one district and another. And this is probably also the explanation of very many phenomena which today fill us with astonishment: the great differences between the reactions of politics on daily life, the ignorance of certain events which throw one section of the city into a turmoil and are not even heard of in the rest of the capital; the careless indifference of housewives going on with their shopping at the local market while fighting is going on in the Tuileries and people are being massacred at Petite Force.

SLOWNESS OF COMMUNICATION

None of the swift communication media that we know today existed then: our numerous means of speedy transport, our mass-circulation dailies, telegraph, telephone, radio and TV and all those systems for disseminating news and turning a whole city into an uproar still did not exist.

News was spread by word of mouth, and it is perfectly understandable that with their barriers and boundaries the various districts were often a long time in getting to know even the most sensational reports.

TRADITIONAL MEETING-PLACES: THE TUILERIES, THE PALAIS ROYAL

Nevertheless there was a certain number of meeting-places in Paris where those eager to hear the latest news could satisfy their curiosity: the Jardin des Tuileries, which, after being simply a fashionable parade-ground, was soon to become the

3

open-air anteroom of the Assemblée; the Place de la Grève, the traditional setting for funeral cortèges, processions of the National Guard, mass gatherings and revolts;[1] and above all the Palais Royal, the forum of the Revolution, the centre of café life, restaurants, all kinds of entertainments, but also the stamping-ground of agitators, scandalmongers, soapbox orators always ready to jump on a chair or a table and save the nation between two cups of mocca.

Certainly when the Duke of Orleans, five or six years earlier, had reconstructed his private grounds and rented out his galleries to tradesmen to make a pleasure-garden, he had never guessed that he was playing such a dirty trick on his cousin the King of France. There was no political club more dangerous to the future of the Crown than that noisy fairground of news and notions.

Since the spring of '89, it had begun to play its part. Though it enchanted Parisians, it filled provincials with astonishment. One of these, the Marquis de Ferrières, seems to have been somewhat overwhelmed by an evening at the Palais Royal:[2]

> You simply cannot imagine all the different kinds of people who gather there. It is a truly astonishing spectacle. I saw the circus; I visited five or six cafés, and no Molière comedy could have done justice to the variety of scenes I witnessed. Here a man is drafting a reform of the Constitution; another is reading his pamphlet aloud; at another table, someone is taking the ministers to task; everybody is talking; each person has his own little audience that listens very attentively to him. Ispent almost ten hours there. The paths are swarming with girls and young men. The bookshops are packed with people browsing through books and pamphlets and not buying anything. In the cafés, one is half-suffocated by the press of people.

Let us leave for the moment the cafés which we shall pay special attention to later, and take a stroll round Paris. Many of the great urban settings – the Place Louis-XV, the Invalides, the Champs-Elysées, the Champ-de-Mars – are to have an important rôle in the events to follow. Prieur and Duplessis-Bertrand will often use them as backgrounds for their *Pictures of the Revolution*, and as historical events as such are not treated in them, we can find all the more to interest us in their scenes of everyday life.

Take, for example, this little painting by Senave in the Musée Carnavalet, showing the Pont Notre-Dame, the Pont au Change and the Quai de Gesvre in 1791. A charming corner in the heart of Paris, it has a swarming population suggesting the proximity of Les Halles. In the background, the Palais de Justice and the Conciergerie, exactly as Marie-Antoinette saw them three years later. The Pont au Change has already been cleared of its double row of houses, whose recent demolition is indicated by a few piles of rubble. In front of the square tower of the Pompe Notre-Dame, some mountebanks have staked their pitch, and the leader of the group, who is holding a puppet, is surrounded by a circle of gaping spectators. In the foreground, there are stalls, a recalcitrant donkey, a pretty girl on a white horse, a lame man on crutches and a pair of prosperous bourgeois taking their dog for a walk. Shop windows, vendors of liquorice water, women selling waffles and pancakes – the whole picture is innocent, gentle and far from revolutionary, and if one did not see, to the left, a platoon of the National Guard marching past with flags flying, one might almost think one was back in the days when the Queen played at being a shepherdess and the most peace-loving of all monarchs' hobby was the locksmith's trade.

THE LIVELY APPEARANCE OF THE CROWDS

This lively, happy atmosphere of the Parisian crowds is one of the first things that strike foreigners when they visit the capital. Listen to what the German bookseller and writer from Brunswick, Campe, has to say: he visited Paris in 1789, and noted the politeness of people in the streets, of coachmen and sentries; but above all he remarked on the vivacity of the passers-by:[3]

> Among the thousands of people who cross the Pont-Neuf, the twenty or thirty thousand that swarm in the Tuileries or on the boulevards, one hardly ever sees a single person walking slowly, phlegmatically, hardly one whose hands and facial features are not in perpetual movement, and if two or more people are walking together, the thread of their discourse is never broken . . .

> This gives the Parisian crowd a distinction that can be found nowhere else: it is more vivacious, more noisy than any other crowd in the world. Everybody is talking, singing, shouting or whistling, instead of proceeding in silence, as is the custom in our parts. And the multitude of street-vendors and small merchants trying to make their voices heard above the tumult of the streets only serves to make the general uproar all the greater and more deafening.

If Paris cannot keep quiet, the reason is temperamental; but it is also probably because she feels she is on the threshold of startling events. The Revolution had barely begun before people thought it was all over. The day after the fall of the Bastille people were falling upon each other's necks in the streets. It was not only the common people who rejoiced; portions of the very best society joined in their enthusiasm. Mme de Genlis, governess of the children of the Duke of Orleans, took her three charges, among them the future King Louis-Philippe, to gaze in the Rue Saint-Antoine at the ruins of 'the frightful monument to despotism' and to shower their praises on those who were demolishing it, men 'whose avenging hands seem to be those of Providence itself'.

The excitement increases still further on July 17, when the King proceeds to the Hôtel de Ville, considering such a fine revolt and the spectacle of a dismantled fortress well worth an after-dinner stroll. At the sight of the King receiving the tricolour cockade from Bailly, a vast throng of people, swayed by fraternal emotions, fell into each other's arms. It was the culmination of all their hopes, the end of all their miseries, 'the dawn of a brilliant future, opening up an era of liberty, abundance, peace and happiness'.

How curious this delusion on the part of the Parisians, who felt they had witnessed the end of a drama that was only just beginning! Each twist and turn of its plot was hailed as the climax. With the taking of the Bastille, they believed that liberty had been established. With the creation of the National Guard, they believed that order had been established. The day after the night of August 4, they believed they were all equal, and when they brought from Versailles the baker, the baker's wife and the baker's man, they imagined that they had banished for ever the spectre of famine.

Nevertheless, according to some witnesses, life in the capital was still far from being a bed of roses. One could encounter there now a number of strange figures who had not been there in former times: the workless come from the provinces and who were compelled to work in the quarries of the Butte Montmartre.

A special kind of virago, too, began to invade the streets. One evening when the sedate Campe had gone to admire the sunset over the Place Louis-XV and had given himself over to 'the voluptuous delight of sublime sentiments' at the spectacle of the fiery orb's descent, he found himself suddenly assailed by three frightful old hags who tried to snatch both his kisses and his purse. As he protested against this behaviour in a very strong Teutonic accent, they finally let him go, taking him for an Englishman.[4]

Other misadventures befell those aristocrats who had stayed on in Paris. The first exodus took place on July 15, and another, much larger one, after the October Days:

'Don't try to pass the barriers without your passport!' writes the Count de Quélen,[5] father of the future archbishop, to his friend the Président de Saint-Luc. 'I got nabbed the other day, when I wanted to go to the Bois de Boulogne.

From a pile of manure too high-smelling to investigate I was presented with the sharp end of a bayonet by the alguazil, who forced me to turn back. After proceeding full speed astern, I reached the city gates where a band of self-appointed guardians of the peace stopped me again and asked what I had to declare, to which my reply was: "That I am without liberty. Is it dutiable? Have I to pay for it?" – "No. You may pass." I returned to the city unable to believe in the liberty and the rights of man which had been proclaimed by the most august assembly in creation. And so, if we can't avoid something, we must put up with it. I drink, eat, sleep just like a pig in a sty, a beast that has no more right to its litter than I have to my bedchamber. *Res miranda!*'

Malcontents unwillingly have to admit that the regular day and night patrols keep the streets fairly peaceful, but they add that the richer districts are emptying, that trade is slack, that money is becoming more and more scarce and that soon only paper will be in circulation. 'Paris is one great nightcap,' sighs the Countess de Seneffe on January 9, 1790. 'No balls. Everyone stays at home. It has even been decided that there shall be no more concerts.'[6]

In the same year, the air of uneasy uncertainty seems to have increased. There were indeed actual revolts, like the sacking of the Hôtel de Castries, following the duel in which the duke had wounded Charles de Lameth. Other less tragic incidents, like the one Mme Cressonier de Beauplan recounts to her friend the Baron de Blaisel, wittily reproduce the atmosphere of the streets:

A man nearly made me jump out of my skin this morning when he shouted like a mad thing, right in my ear: 'Père Duchesne's bloody patriotic seventh letter!' That word *bloody* was pronounced with such energy that, forgetting a lady of quality ought not to use bad language, I shouted back: 'Well damn me, what a way to talk!' Whereupon a small crowd of people round us burst out laughing very heartily, as I did myself, though I was blushing all over. That, my dear Baron, is what is known as baying with the pack![7]

After a few months, we see politics creeping into schools and colleges. At the Collège des Quatre-Nations, the scholarship pupils, roused to revolt against their clergymen teachers who had sworn the constitutional oath, armed themselves and one fine evening invaded the principal's apartments. There was a terrific uproar in the neighbourhood. A detachment of the National Guard had to be despatched to deprive the insurgents of their arms and powder and send them packing to their dormitories. But the next day the day-students tried to avenge their teachers. A fresh outburst of violence, and again the law had to be called in. The combatants were finally separated by being given a half-holiday.[8]

GENERAL OPTIMISM

As we can see, all this was not very serious. The Paris of the beginning of the Revolution is striving hard to keep smiling, and is still the capital of optimism. Because two hundred thousand voices chanted the Ça ira on the day of the Federation people thought everything was going well, that victory was certain. Everyone retained these high hopes, even after the escapade at Varennes, when they saw Louis XVI accept the new Constitution.

By making this gesture he was forgiven everything and a few days later he was greeted by a prolonged ovation at the Opera, when he appeared with the Queen and one of the cast of *Castor and Pollux* brought out, at the top of his voice, the following lines:

> The entire universe demands thy return . . .
> Reign (*bis*) over thy faithful people!

How could this faithful people not believe in its good fortune, how could it not be convinced that, once again, everything was over bar the shouting?

It was not until the great upheavals of 1792 that these

9

illusions finally vanished. But we must not anticipate events. We are still only at the prologue in 1789, a time when nine out of ten citizens refused, as did the author of the *Tableaux de Paris*, to admit the hypothesis of 'a revolt degenerating into sedition'.

One thing alone was in the minds of everybody: the benefits expected from the Assemblée de Versailles. As they arrived from their provinces, the deputies were regarded as so many celestial envoys who would create a new nation.

As Paris had eyes only for these men, let us try to get acquainted with these agents of providence and surprise some of them, not in their official capacity, not in their public life but in the amusing unexpectedness of their daily existence.

CHAPTER TWO

THREE DEPUTIES AT THE STATES GENERAL

The life of a deputy at Versailles – A rural abbé far from his parish – A nobleman deputy organizes his household – A deputy from Tiers who is a good husband and father

THE LIFE OF A DEPUTY AT VERSAILLES

The States General did not know the grandest occasions only. Beside the historic sittings like the Serment du Jeu de Paume or the night of August 4, there were many rather dull, rather monotonous days which gave the deputies opportunities to relax a little.

These intermissions were welcome. When one arrives from some remote corner of France and is suddenly transported to a place like Versailles, however conscientiously one fulfils one's mission, nevertheless at certain times one's private interests clamour for attention. One has to make one's way in a new setting, see to it that one has board and lodging, bother one's head with a thousand petty details: in short, one has to adapt oneself.

Whether the deputies belong to the nobility, the clergy or the Third Estate, nearly all of them are in the same boat. And nearly all of them are haunted by the same thought: how are things at home? What's the latest news from the castle, the parish? How are the wife and children? So that the great preoccupation for all of them is the receiving and the writing of letters. Never before, perhaps, had people written so much to each other, because never before had they had so much to write about.

Such letters, exchanged at such a time, are mines of precious information. But it must not be thought that politics takes the first place in them. Much more often such correspondence treats of familiar matters: the price of a room or a dinner, the state of the writer's health or of his pocket. They are packed with advice about the linen-cupboard, the wages of servants, the care of the garden or the upkeep of the home farm. And though this chit-chat affords us a view of the Revolution through the wrong end of the telescope, we are able to reconstruct its essential atmosphere and become acquainted with the actors in it.

They reveal themselves to us as they really were: good, decent provincial Frenchmen, for the most part rather bewildered by the adventure chance has dragged them into, very proud of the rôle they play, but never forgetting that somewhere, perhaps very far away, there is a little corner of France where people are thinking about them, a church whose gilded weather-cock seems to follow them with its eyes.

It must be admitted that many of them are only fairly obscure deputies. We would never find their portraits in Déjabin's collection. But the eye-witness accounts they give us are all the more significant because the celebrity of a great name does not tend to put out of focus the perspective of the little pen-sketches with which their correspondence is studded.

A RURAL ABBÉ FAR FROM HIS PARISH

Though he belonged to the clergy, the first order in the kingdom, the Abbé Emmanuel Barbotin, parish priest of Prouvy, near Valenciennes, for example, was a somewhat obscure person.[1] Certainly he had nothing of the starving priest about him, reduced to an 'unseemly' pittance like many of the country clergy. He was a great tithe-owner, well-off indeed, and the successful director of a kind of agricultural business. He had been elected representative at the assembly of the bailiwick of Quesnoy, then deputy for Hainaut at the States General. We find him sending his substitute in the parish of Prouvy, R. P. Englebert Baratte, letters in which accounts of the day's happenings are mixed up with much more personal questions.

The abbé goes into great detail about his settling-in at Versailles. After 'a great deal of heat and dust and fatigue, etc', he and his colleagues arrived at the royal town on May 8, 1789, 'all of us in good health'. He then goes on:

> Our first necessity was a good dinner. After that we had to look for a lodging, which we did not find that day. After a great deal of rushing about we are finally lodged, in rather cramped quarters I must say, but clean and convenient, in a healthy district near the Palace itself. For this we each have to pay sixty *livres* a month. We still have made no arrangement for our meals, but it seems we shall have to pay very highly for them, since the first dinner we had here on our first evening cost one *louis* for the four of us. At night, we follow the Paris style and all we have for supper is a crust of bread, which is very good here, and a few glasses of beer.

This Paris-style supper would probably surprise many much less frugal Parisians, but we are dealing here with a worthy ecclesiastic well accustomed to long periods of abstinence, and for whom a second Lent presents no terrors:

> As for luncheon, better not to mention it: we cannot cope with so much food; we must tighten our belts and accustom our gullets to the waters of the Seine, which does not appear to incommode me up to now. My very worst wine is worth infinitely more than what I am obliged to drink here.[2]

Despite this change in his way of life, the abbé's health remained good. All he complains of is a touch of eczema on his right hand, which was soon cured by drinking an infusion of fumitory. He also complains that the bed-bugs prevent him from enjoying good sound sleep. And above all he inveighs against the rain that had been falling for three weeks and which often compelled him to stay in his lodging.

On the other hand, as soon as the sun comes out, he seizes the opportunity to go out with his colleagues and do some sightseeing in Versailles and the neighbourhood. Thus on June 21, the day after the Serment du Jeu de Paume, a small group of deputies took him with them for a little outing, 'at least six leagues'. They went to Marly to see the Machine; they visited the château there and the one at Louveciennes, 'occupied by the infamous Du Barry . . .' I imagine the beautiful hostess cannot have cared for such a visitation.

All in all, apart from the high cost of living, his stay in Versailles seemed quite enjoyable to the Abbé de Prouvy: 'Otherwise, there can be no more gracious place to stay in than Versailles: as long as one has plenty of money, all goes smoothly.'[3]

But his cheerfulness diminished when, after the October Days, the Assembly was moved to Paris. Having to settle in all over again! And the noise, and the people! The din of the immense city displeases him as much as it pleases others: 'I am in a district,' he writes, 'where my lodging is surrounded by streets on all sides, in which vehicles do not stop running from six in the morning until three the next morning. So sleep is usually out of the question . . .'[4]

Amid all his worries, the abbé does not forget his little farm at Prouvy. To his substitute, R. P. Baratte, we find him sending all kinds of advice about selling in good time the oats, the wheat, the flax, bundles of faggots; he tells him when to bleach linen, to whitewash the barns, the bakehouse, the pigeon-cote; he instructs him when to plant colza instead of flax, and, as a complement to the harvest, and one whose importance he emphasizes, 'the garnering of good Christian souls, if there be any such'. He is concerned that there should be enough butter for the month of October. He wishes to know the amount and the quality of the harvest. He insists on the different grains being sorted as cleanly as possible.[5]

With the arrival of winter, he is pre-occupied by another question: his wine-cellar, and writes:

> If the red wine is ready to be tapped, it must not be allowed to stand and spoil. If you haven't already changed the cask, the wine must be clarified. In order to do this, you must first broach the cask and put in the cock, draw out the bung, and, if the cask is full, draw off at least one bottle, beat the whites of six eggs with a pint of wine, pour it all back into the cask, stir it in with a stick for five to ten minutes, bung it up well again, let it stand seven or eight days and then tap.[6]

Here we have an abundance of advice from a man whom the adversity of the times has reduced to drinking water! Perhaps as a kind of consolation the fragrance of his new wine warms his heart even at a distance. But we must not imagine that these material cares made him forget the duties of his ministry or his obligations as a Christian.

To fulfil these, he went to spend Whitsuntide at the abbey of Vaux-de-Cernay, where he was so well received that he went back there at the end of June and on August 15. On the 25th of the same month, dedicated to Saint Louis, 'the King's birthday and our parish anniversary too', he spent the whole morning in church praying for his flock in Prouvy.

Nothing concerning their welfare – births, marriages, deaths too – is overlooked in the letters to Father Baratte. As if the poor fellow was not already sufficiently occupied with his farming and coopering tasks, he also has to devote his spare time to teaching the children their catechism, and here are the instructions he is given on the subject:

> As you are often out on Sundays and saints' days, I imagine you will hardly be in a position to teach the catechism. I would beg of you, if you are unable to do so on those days, to teach it from time to time during the week, if only for half an hour before or after your mass; and see

to it that the children attend school regularly. I would ask you to pay especial attention to those who have already taken their First Communion . . . As far as I know you will have no First Communion services this year, because the oldest are still too young; so you must pay special attention to those who took their communion last year. It is in childhood that the eternal truths of our religion are engraved most readily on the spirit, when they can act freely upon hearts devoid of lustful passions; and we are living in a time when religion needs to be upheld by our preaching and even more by our practice. Do not think ill of me for preaching to a preacher, for after all I am still the parish priest of Prouvy and the more cause I have to fear for my parishioners and for religion in general, the more I love them.

Then, in the same letter, without transition: 'By now you must surely have had the pig stuck, for it must not be left to put on useless fat.'

The good man's whole candid soul lies revealed in that ingenuous juxtaposition.

A NOBLEMAN DEPUTY ORGANIZES HIS HOUSEHOLD

Charles Elie, Marquis of Ferrières-Marsay, like the Abbé Barbotin, was not destined to play in the Constituent Assembly, though he was a greater public figure in Poitou than his pious colleague was in Hainaut.[7]

Dividing his leisure time between his château at Marsay in the Mirabelais region and his house at Poitiers, this disciple of the philosophers had published three essays: *Theism* (1785), *Women in the Social and Natural Orders* (1785), and *Vows* (1787), a mordant satire on monastic vows, one which had earned him the reputation of being an intellectual, which in turn had led to his being elected by the nobility of Poitou as their representative at the States General.

Compelled by this new distinction to live first in Versailles and then in Paris, he was to keep up an abundant correspondence with his wife Henriette de Monbeille d'Hus for the next three years. To whom but to his lawfully wedded spouse could the gentleman-writer have given so many details about his daily life – that wife who, in the social as well as in the natural order of things, held the first place in his thoughts?

Like the majority of deputies, the Marquis de Ferrières deplored the transfer of the Assembly to Paris: 'It rains every day here,' he writes. 'The streets of Paris are rivers of mud. I miss Versailles; I had grown attached to the place. Now I dare not go out in the evenings for fear of being run over by carriages in the streets, and spend the time rather sadly seated beside my fire.'[8]

This lack of taste for solitude soon made the marquis decide to send for the marquise to join him in Paris. Nothing more natural on the part of a philosopher opposed to monastic vows. But it is important to have servants who will be able to look after them properly. And this is why our deputy asks so many questions in his letters: would the cook at Poitiers be able to dress her mistress? Would she also make the beds and sweep the floors? 'If she is not agreeable, I'd rather have the little chamber-maid; she would be able to help you with the washing and could surely manage to do some cooking, if only to make the soup, because here we have the joint brought in from the restaurant.'[9]

Having made her arrangements, Mme de Ferrières finally arrived in Paris and spent two winters there. It was only in the summers of 1790 and 1791 that she returned to Marsay and her husband, left behind in Paris, started writing to her again.

It was a very prosaic correspondence however, in which domestic affairs formed the bulk of the contents. In August 1790, the marquis declared that he was highly satisfied with a certain Toinon who was apparently an excellent servant and gave him every attention. He ate beans, haricots, cucumbers, very little meat. And so the price of living was not too high, especially as he messed together with a deputy representing the nobility of Béziers who shared expenses with him. In the preceding month, provisions, butter, coals, vegetables, fish and desserts had cost one hundred and eighteen *livres*, and bread thirty *livres*. Total: one hundred and fifty *livres*, not counting butcher's meat and wood. Whereupon the deputy concludes: 'This makes at the very most four *livres* each a day. Add to this lodging, three *livres*. We don't do badly: the food is wholesome, and that's the main thing.'[10]

The next year, Toinon was replaced by a girl called Marguerite, who appears to have been goodnatured and an excellent hand at making vegetable soups. The staff also included a man-servant who, strangely enough, was called Baptiste. Unlike his master, he was no vegetarian, and 'did for himself' in the cooking line. When guests are invited to dinner, he eats meat three times a day. He is fond of coffee and generally manages to sneak a cup from under Marguerite's nose. In short, he is a jolly fellow who 'does very well for himself', spends his free afternoon at the marionettes in the Place Louis-XV and has no serious shortcomings except when he goes down to the wine-cellar. On August 26, 1791, the marquis writes: 'I bought half a barrel of Bordeaux, a good, pure wine, which a fellow-deputy let me have. Baptiste had the job of taking it down to the cellar and in the process got very merry.'

Doubtless the faithful major-domo imagined that the old Bordeaux would not suit the tastes of his master, who was on a diet. The slightest departure from this would give the marquis a temperature, one of those little erratic fevers that come and go, die down and then flare up again; it became a sort of *leitmotif* in the conjugal correspondence.

In an attempt to rid himself of it, M de Ferrières would admit only two remedies: infusions of centaury – not the centaury of Paris which has neither strength nor aroma, but the good old centaury of Marsay, which is carefully dried, and

which the marquise sends in little packets of white paper –
and purges with Seidlitz water. The latter is the *ultima ratio*.
He often had to resort to it. It was a fascinating subject for
letters, even when the happenings of a particular day might
have suggested other themes.

In June, the month of the flight from Varennes, our deputy
was purging himself and thus reducing his fever. In July,
when the bloody affair of the Champ-de-Mars took place, he
started on a new bottle of Seidlitz water. In August, while
the King of Prussia and the Emperor were drafting the principles of their coalition, he had a third go, and this time found
relief:

> I am feeling better. My pills are giving me a good clear-
> out and are dispelling that caked bile which could have
> caused the obstruction.

The poor marquis! It would have been better for him if he
had taken himself in hand a little sooner, if he had not over-
done the eating and drinking and had avoided certain dinners
such as the one he told us about, in one of his very first letters,
written after leaving M de la Châtre's:

> A light repast: six courses, more like hors d'oeuvres than
> anything, and including black puddings, sausages, pâtés, a
> couple of joints of meat, two roast fowls, four kinds of sweet,
> two mixed salads . . .

This 'light repast', enjoyed on April 26, 1789, heralded the
new parliamentarian's first entry into political life. It may
have had disastrous results for his stomach, but at least we are
indebted to the marquis' account which proves that what is
said to have been a famine in the land had not yet reached
general proportions.

It makes us think, when we read again that phrase of Taine's:
'Since the spring of 1789, there had been famine everywhere,
and it grew like a rising tide from month to month.'[11]

19

A DEPUTY FROM TIERS WHO IS A GOOD HUSBAND AND FATHER

Was there much difference between the manner of living of a representative of the Third Estate and a deputy of the nobility? The letters from Louis-Prosper Lofficial, lieutenant-general of the bailiwick of Vouvant, with a seat at La Châtaignerie and sent to the Assembly by the seneschal court in Poitiers, would seem to prove the contrary.[12]

He came from the same electoral constituency as the Marquis de Ferrières. Like his colleague, Lofficial was married; like him, he kept thinking of his wife and writing to her often.

As soon as he arrived at Versailles, he took lodgings in the Rue des Bourdonnais, number 12, sharing with another deputy, and a day's food cost him only one crown. In the month of August, when the Assembly allowed each of its members expenses of eighteen *livres* a day, this canny bourgeois calculated that he would only have to spend one half of his allowance. Save a penny, save a pound! It didn't mean that just because you had money you should squander it. Lofficial pushed this principle so far that he reproached his wife with having bought an extra watering-can and particularly with having purchased some 'very cheap cloth' to make shirts for her son Jacques, when his old ones could have lasted at least another two years. All these 'bargains' are simply ruinous![13]

We must not be surprised, therefore, to find the old boy constantly preoccupied about his property. A week before the fall of the Bastille, what are his main concerns? He wants to know 'if it has rained at La Châtaignerie as at Versailles'. If so, 'the hay must have got a good dousing . . . It'll be lucky if it's not ruined!'[14]

Afterwards, having given an account of the events of July 14, he writes that he is worried about the elms he planted the year before on his estate at Montigni; he gives orders for them to be pruned and trimmed, and then inquires after the lucerne. One feels that his mind is far away from Paris.

His mind, and his heart also, for, despite his love of

economizing, he already is beginning to think, like so many others, of bringing his wife and two children to Versailles, the latter being Jacques, a lad of twelve, and Marie-Thérèse-Mariette, one year his junior. The manservant from La Châtaignerie, faithful Falour, would also be of the party. He could be given an old dresscoat which his master had left behind, and he would take a seat on the top of the stagecoach, the place usually reserved for servants. From Angers to Paris this would cost thirty-six *livres*, but a Versailles servant would demand at least sixty *livres* a month, and one would not be able to rely on him. A few spare shirts were to be put in the luggage, and above all table things, so that they could take their meals at home. Another wise economy.[15]

In the midst of his exposition of all these plans, Lofficial remembers to ask if Jacques had obtained a prize on speech day at the Collège de Beaupréau. As he receives an affirmative reply, the happy father instructs his wife to give the laureate a crown of three *livres*. As for Mariette, who, it appears, 'lacked concentration', she had to make do with only twenty-four *sous*.

Why was this projected family reunion delayed until the autumn? On account of political exigencies or local obligations in Poitou? The letters refer to it only after the holidays are over and Jacques has gone back to school. But then we are treated to a thousand and one pieces of advice: Mme Lofficial must not forget to bring a fur-lined cloak, a muff, fifteen or eighteen of the best towels, four or five sets of silver tableware. As the house at La Châtaignerie will remain empty all winter, she might ask their friend Dupouet to sleep there, to keep a fire going in the stove in order to keep the furniture in good condition, as well as the books – a precious library that has just been rearranged – and to light fires from time to time in the bedrooms; otherwise, everything will go mouldy with the damp.

Unfortunately the Assembly's exodus to Paris soon upset their plans. An annoying thing happened: Lofficial left behind at Versailles a sarcenet sample that his wife had sent him hoping he could match it with the same stuff, of which she needed two and a half ells. Feeling guilty about this and wanting to get back into his wife's good books, the poor fellow buys a ring and sends it to La Châtaignerie.

What an excellent husband, and what an indulgent father! Probably none of his letters shows him in a more favourable light than the one of November 3 in which he recommends gentle treatment for Jacques and Mariette. In the boy's case, there is no trouble: he is satisfactory in every way. But one feels that his sister is a handful. Mme Lofficial had to complain about her, and to patch matters up the father embarks upon a lengthy moralizing letter, well in keeping with the spirit of the times:

> The mistakes that children make proceed less from inborn viciousness than from the capricious nature of their age. Always keep this truth in mind, my dear one, and soon you will feel more satisfied with your daughter . . . Her natural merit may have tended to vanish sometimes, but are we ourselves entirely without blame in this respect? Might we not have alienated her sweet nature by too harsh a reprimand, by attaching too much importance to trivial misdeeds and by depriving her of that fond attention which we must always give our children? There is still time to grow attached to your daughter . . . Show her you have confidence in her more and more as she is growing up; speak to her only in a friendly way, and kindly; let your demands on her appear rather evidences of your trust and satisfaction than imperious orders. Converse with her in a tone of equality and kindness, but let your conversations always be useful and instructive. Finally, let her learn to look upon you only as a mother who loves her and never as a woman whose every command must be obeyed.

We do not claim that this little paternal sermon in which the rhetoric of Fénelon borrows the literary style of M Bouilly is a work of extreme originality. But at least it proves to us that Lofficial was a good man.

CHAPTER THREE

DAILY LIFE IN THE PROVINCES

The state of the harvest in 1789 – First signs of discontent in the country – The Great Fear at Clermont-en-Beauvais – The panic at Creil – The country people and the new régime – The prestige of the National Guard

---

THE STATE OF THE HARVEST IN 1789

A writer whose severe criticism of Taine is legendary, nevertheless recognizes that he was one of the first to discern that the history of France was 'not only political but economic, not only Parisian but provincial'.[1] It is by virtue of this principle that the author of *The Origins of Contemporary France* endeavoured to find premonitory symptoms of the Revolution in a kind of 'spontaneous anarchy' which he declared swept the country and especially the rural districts just before 1789.

We must beware of generalizations. At all times there have been popular movements, even at periods when the monarchy was at the height of its power and brilliance. The country's difficult situation could not but make this type of crisis all the more acute after the year of lean oxen in 1788 and on the eve of the great national consultation, an assembly that occupied everyone's thoughts. But to conclude from this, after citing a few isolated cases (grain-stealing in Normandy, uprisings in Languedoc or in Brittany) that France was then in the throes of revolution, that property was everywhere being invaded, that disorder and insecurity reigned, is to claim something quite different from the truth.

In fact, eye-witness accounts of many contemporaries tell quite another tale. When the English doctor Rigby was travelling through the countryside in 1789, he was astonished by the fertility of the soil and the healthy appearance of the inhabitants. 'Not an acre which is not cultivated with the most ingenious thoroughness; one would never imagine that there had been a famine; everybody seems to be well nourished.' And he concludes, not without a note of sadness: 'In England the peasants are certainly not as well off as here; at any rate they appear to be much less happy.'

In the biggest cities and in the humblest hamlets and bailiwicks the meeting of the States General is looked forward to with immense hopes. The composition of the famous *Cahiers*[2] naturally gives rise to somewhat heated discussions. Not only are the interests of the three orders frequently in opposition, but in many regions the peasants already feel that the bourgeoisie will defend their cause only half-heartedly. In the claims they formulate, the landowners of Ménil-le-Horgne, in the bailiwick of Commercy, write to the Garde des Sceaux[3] that 'the poor country communities have been passed over'. Many of their brethren think the same.

Yet few of them dare complain, for the peasant soul possesses great reserves of patience. And then the worries of getting in the harvest dominate all other considerations in the lives of these good people. What will the harvest be like after the abominable spring of 1789? Uneasiness is felt almost everywhere, the clergy order prayers to be given and at Evreux, on Sunday, August 2, there is a solemn procession praying heaven to bring back fine weather and to ripen the crops.[4] This is the most pressing wish in country districts.

After all, the harvest was not as bad as had been expected. Later, those of 1790 and 1791 were almost good.

Let us not concern ourselves here with trying to find out what political effects the first great events of the Revolution had on the various provinces of France. Municipal elections were held, and a militia or National Guard set up. It appears that except for certain turbulent centres like Strasbourg, Mauberge or Troyes the change from one régime to another was effected without any great violence. The account of those days in the little town of Meulan, told by Raoul Rosière,[5] offers us an example of these apparently peaceful change-overs.

A curious phenomenon that shattered the country's nerve during the summer of 1789 is more relative to our subject. I mean the 'Great Fear' which suddenly descended upon country districts at harvest time, and the full extent of whose gravity was indicated by a royal proclamation that was displayed on the walls and read to the leaders of the parish:

From the King's hand.

His Majesty is informed that troops of brigands scattered throughout the land are persistently deceiving the inhabitants of various communities, persuading them that, without going against the will of His Majesty, they may attack the château, steal the archives and commit other excesses against the habitations and property of their masters, the noble Lords of the Realm. His Majesty finds Himself compelled to make known that such actions of violence arouse His indignation . . . It is not without the greatest grief that He observes the troubles afflicting His Kingdom, troubles instigated some time ago now by men of ill will and who begin their dastardly deeds by spreading false rumours round the countryside, in order to arouse alarm and incite the inhabitants to take up arms . . . His Majesty invites all loyal citizens to oppose with every means in their power the continuation of a disorder which has reached the proportions of a scandal and is a disgrace to the fair name of France, being contrary and utterly opposed to the benevolent views that animate the hearts of the King and the representatives of the Nation in their endeavours to advance the happiness and prosperity of the Kingdom.

Given from Our hand at Versailles, August 9, 1789.

Signed: 'Louis.' And, lower down, 'Le comte de Saint-Priest'.

What, then, is this Great Fear which seems to fill the public authorities with such alarm, at a time when so many other subjects ought to be claiming their attention? A sort of collective folly; a people that frightens itself and sees brigands where there are only persons suffering from hallucinations.

THE GREAT FEAR AT CLERMONT-EN-BEAUVAIS

We are fortunate in possessing two documents, the one official, the other private, concerning the events which took place at that time in the region of Beauvais. And by a strange coincidence the two pieces suggest conclusions that are almost identical about the great rural panic.

The first is a report which Duguey, chief of police at Clermont, addresses to Blossac, commissioner of police at Soissons, on July 28. In it he tells that the night before some poachers had been involved in a quarrel with gamekeepers on the estate of Estrées-Saint-Denis, which is four leagues from Clermont. The inhabitants of that parish, unable to get away from the idea that their crops are being damaged or stolen, hastened to give the alarm. The neighbouring parishes too sounded the tocsin and the next morning, at seven o'clock, the mounted police were out, accompanied by a detachment of the Royal Bourgogne troops. While chief of police Duguey was saddling his horse, express couriers from Lieuville and Estrées-Saint-Denis arrived telling him that everything had been devastated in those areas. As he sped across the village all he could see were women taking to their heels and others bolting their shutters. The whole world was shaking with fright and gloomy foreboding, for it had already been given out that four thousand brigands had arrived in Clermont along the Nointel road.

The chief of police kept telling himself that the news was hardly credible, but all the same he was in a very excited state when he set off with sixteen troopers and ten mounted citizens who were determined to lend him a hand. Scarcely had he left the town than he met the Duke of Bourbon's master of the hunt riding to tell him that the danger was entirely imaginary, that no corn had been cut and that the whole thing boiled down to a quarrel between gamekeepers and poachers which had attracted a crowd of inquisitive onlookers.

This was reassuring for Clermont, but it did not last for long, because another rumour began to spread: armed bands were reported coming from the direction of Paris and Beauvais. At once it was assumed that everything was lost; there were some attempts at forming a defence force and they all swore they would die together until it became apparent that the so-called agressors were law-abiding inhabitants of the neighbouring parishes who, armed with forks and axes, were coming to the aid of their fellow-citizens. After such a palpitating alarm, one can imagine the rejoicings that followed! The people of Clermont subscribed to offer a *vin d'honneur* to their gallant defenders, and when they had drunk their fill they were taken hunting in the forest of Neuville where a wholesale slaughter of pheasants went to prove that from now on aristocratic privileges were a thing of the past.

THE PANIC AT CREIL

Let us examine now the story of a peasant girl living in the region of Creil and for whom the Great Fear of 1789 was the first revelation of a new order. Later she was to experience much excitement of the same kind, as we shall see further on.

Marie-Victoire Monnard[6] was the eldest of a family of fifteen children living in the hamlet of Vaux, a gun-shot from Creil. She was no weakling. She could give a hand in the fields and when her father decided to go to the market at Pont-Sainte-Maxence to sell twenty-two pigs he put her in charge of them. Her father himself was a great character. If he had to cross a river with a donkey that was afraid of wetting its hooves, he would hoist the beast on his shoulders in the most carefree way, never bothering about what the critics of La Fontaine's miller might say.

One day the peaceful inhabitants of Creil were roused by an alarm-bell as those in Clermont had been. The men armed themselves with scythes, pitchforks or spits and began running across the fields; the women put oil to boil on their hearths, filled buckets with ashes and carried big stones upstairs in order to scald, blind or crack the skulls of the enemy, while others made for the bridge which they barricaded with carts. It was the wife of the bridge-keeper, a strong and courageous woman, who organized the resistance: 'I envied her strength and bravery,' sighs little Marie-Victoire. 'I wished I could have taken her place so as to be in the thick of it, but she ordered all the children to go home, which I didn't like at all.'

Her disappointment was all the greater when her mother shut her up in a hayloft with three of her eldest sisters, left them a large loaf and a quarter of a Brie cheese to see them through the rigours of a siege and took refuge herself with the remainder of her children in the church steeple at Creil.

Round the church there was the greatest confusion. Distraught women arriving from Pont-Sainte-Maxence related that their husbands had been slaughtered before their very eyes. The four little Monnard girls discovered a peephole in the hayloft from which they could look out on the surrounding countryside. They were not tall enough to see out of it, and so they took turns standing on each other's backs and were able to watch men from several of the surrounding villages searching the fields but without encountering any of the famous brigands. 'Weary of supporting one another on our backs,' the youthful siege-victim goes on,

we began to eat our bread and cheese which, if my mother had been there, would have had to last us four days; at the end of three hours there was nothing left. After being cooped up there all that time, we wanted to get out; I was the first to go down, very quietly. My sisters followed me; I opened the door a little and, all of a tremble, peeped out to see if I could see the enemy. When I saw no one, we went back home where we found our mother who likewise had seen nothing of the men we had been so panic-stricken about.

In both cases, the episodes are identical: a minor incident to start with, a crowd gathering somewhere in the countryside and giving rise to fears of an attack; the alarm bell alerting the villages, the arrival of armed allies who are mistaken for the enemy, people who are afraid of their own shadows . . .

It also resembles somewhat a tale by Dumas the Elder which we all loved as children; the kingdom of Punch and Judy is invaded by a large army, but the defending hump-backed general gets the idea of taking down all the mirrors in his capital and having them set up in the fields, where he waits until his adversary, seeing his own reflection in the glass, throws away his arms and takes to his heels . . .

All over France similar ridiculous episodes were reported, all about the same time. In Angoulême a duststorm seen in the distance on July 28 at three in the afternoon gave the impression that the brigands were attacking. The people took up arms, everyone was called up and twenty thousand men hastily mobilized spent the night in fruitless patrols. The next day their number had doubled and the provincial government was already proposing to send out a real army.[7] There had been sinister rumours indeed. The forest of Braconne was said to be full of marauders; Ruffec, Verneuil and La Rochefoucauld were reported to have been burnt down . . . Nevertheless, however much the men searched the countryside, investigating copses and thickets, not a single brigand was to be found. And finally they came to the conclusion that the cloud of dust which had alarmed the whole town must have been raised on the highroad by the Bordeaux mailcoach.

Nevertheless the gravity of this panic persuaded Angoulême to take definite steps towards the formation of a citizen's army. And for the same reason many places, large and small, adopted the same policy: they organized themselves on a military footing. In towns and rural districts the National Guard was born.

But now the affair begins to take a strange turn. Because the nobility had not performed its traditional rôle, which was to assure the safety of the peasants, all these little local forces lost no time in turning against their masters. They called for the abolition of privileges which were not justified by services rendered. And so the Great Fear, an episodic phenomenon, soon began to have serious consequences. We may say that it has a great part in any explanation to be offered of the night of August 4.

THE COUNTRY PEOPLE AND THE NEW RÉGIME

The year 1790 is the one in which the new régime is organized in France. The country people soon realized that it would bring them considerable advantages: the suppression of outmoded tax systems which would be replaced by new ones that they would often forget to pay; the right not to have to address their masters as 'Monsieur le marquis' or 'Monsieur le comte', the right to extend their little plots of land by annexing parts of the castle estate; and no longer would they find their cabbages and lettuces eaten by the hares and other game that were kept there. From now on the rôles are reversed; it is Tom, Dick and Harry who eat the hares, and they are not slow to appreciate the benefits of such a fortunate permutation . . .

In addition, they are able to play a part in village life, to aspire to elective functions if they can only sign their names or even if they cannot. Labergerie, deputy at the Assembly, would state one day in debate that 'out of forty thousand municipalities, there are twenty thousand in which the municipal officers can neither read nor write'.[8]

How will the country Frenchman use politics, the new toy that has been put in his hands? The records of the deliberations of the commune of Pieux, a town in the Manche territorial subdivision, can give us some idea, but we shall glance through them very quickly, because this example, picked out of thousands, offers us nothing sensational.[9]

In 1790, on February 26, the election of the municipal officers took place in Pieux; these members of the town council are subjected to a fresh election on November 20 and 21. The revenue from the parish livings is evaluated as well as the total amount from taxes. On November 30, the eleven communes of the canton assemble to nominate a justice of the peace. The only event connected with the history of France as a whole is the celebration, on September 17, of a solemn service in honour of the victims of the massacre at Nancy. From this we can see that lower Normandy is on the side of Lorraine.

In 1791, the religious question comes up: on February 6, there is the oath-taking by civil priests as ordered by the Civil Constitution of the Clergy. On July 31, a priest named Lecointe takes the oath, at the end of high mass, 'witnessed by the whole town council wearing the national colours in the form of sashes'. On September 18, the said priest is invited to sing a *Te Deum* 'to thank Heaven for inspiring the King to accept the Constitution'. Three months earlier, on June 20, the energetic citizens of the canton had gathered at Pieux to designate those electors who would be given the task of going to Saint-Lô to nominate the future members of the Legislative Assembly. But this time the name of the King had not been mentioned; there had been no *Te Deum* and we cannot but approve the involuntary tact of the inhabitants of the Manche: for this was the day of the flight from Varennes.

The records of many communes are very much alike, for the same questions were everywhere being asked: everywhere there was the need to adapt provincial life to the new legislation, to control supplies, to establish the basis of taxation, to proceed with the elections, to see one's way clear in a snowstorm of complicated paperwork: these were the thorny problems facing town councils who did not automatically assume the wisdom of experience with their tricolour sashes.

THE PRESTIGE OF THE NATIONAL GUARD

But they all understood that what was really needed was a National Guard which would parade magnificently at celebrations and would also, if necessary, protect elected members of the town council. The smallest towns as well as the big cities were very proud of their militia, and wanted to see them well turned out. For example, the inhabitants of Evreux, watching their National Guard take the oath on November 20, 1789, in the castle courtyard, deplored to a man that such valiant soldiery did not have drums. What is an army without drums? You might as well say a ball without a band. And so our Evroicians were carried away by a generous impulse. Officers and civilians subscribed and Paris was requested to rush to them eight big drums which the young men would be taught to play in order to inspire heroism in the hearts of the population.[10]

As we are in a country that loves music so much, how could one fail to mention the cathedral bells? They are in very poor condition, but the closing of the convents will allow them to be replaced and these transfers of bells occupy a large place in communal deliberations. The bells of the Abbaye du Parc, the bells of the parish of Saint-Pierre, the bells of the Abbaye de Conches, all of them take the road to Evreux. Some are taken to Rouilly on the river Andelle to be melted down into coins. Others perambulate from parish to parish, from Saint-Pierre to Bacquepuits, from Saint-Thomas to Coudres or to Sacquenville. Never before did those weighty individuals travel so much outside Holy Week. Never before were 'bell politics' so widely practised.

These were the sort of petty questions that made up the life of a town council in the majority of communes until September 1791. But then people's minds suddenly suffered a change. The news of the flight and the arrest of the King spread like wildfire into the smallest hamlets, creating a veritable panic. Fresh departures of emigrants left many a French château empty, and only then did peasant France begin to realize she was really in a state of revolution.

CHAPTER FOUR

LIFE IN HIGH SOCIETY

---

*Established and new salons – Public and private art ex-
hibitions – The French Academy: Abbé Barthélemy's
reception – Président de Gourgue's ball at Bordeaux – A
scandal at Montpellier*

ESTABLISHED AND NEW SALONS

Social life, which had occupied such a large place in the history
of the eighteenth century, could not just stop with the advent
of the Revolution. A handful of frightened people or those
whose lives had been threatened may have crossed the frontier
on the outbreak of the first troubles; others may have thought
it prudent to shut themselves away in their castles: but this
was not enough to radically change the social physiognomy of
Paris. A few salons closed down, but many others remained
open, most of them already famous before 1789.

Literary men and philosophers still met at Mme Helvetius'
in Auteuil, at Mme de Condorcet or at Mme Panckoucke's
Thursdays. Socialites continued to frequent Mme Beauveau,
wife of the field-marshal, and Mme de Sabran, the gracious
model of Vigée-Lebrun; while the house of Julie Talma in the
Rue Chantereine drew the élite of the artistic world before it
accommodated Bonaparte and Joséphine on their honeymoon.

There existed between the political salons, some of them of
very recent origin, nuances of 'opinion' that were very marked,
even though people still held back from forming parties.
Brilliant talkers, such as Rivarol and Champcenetz, editors of
the *Acts of the Apostles*, met at the house of the Marquise
de Chambonas: future *Feuillants*[1] gathered at Adrien Duport's,

who was a parliamentary adviser and the deputy for the Paris nobility; the Orleanists *chez* Mme de Genlis in the Rue Neuve-des-Mathurins, in an apartment all done out in several shades of blue, decorated with gilded baguettes and eighteen thousand *livres* worth of mirrors, and which with good reason was known as 'the waiting-room of the Palais Royal'. Finally, the patriots went to Mme Bailly's, wife of the astronomer-mayor, and particularly to Mme Necker, whose Thursdays saw gathered together such names as Sieyès, Parny, Condorcet, Grimm, Mme de Staël, Talleyrand and whose 'little suppers', of a more intimate character, boasted, every Tuesday, twelve to fifteen guests.[2]

In 1791 and 1792 salons with rather more advanced notions began to open: those of Lucile Desmoulins, of Mme Roland, Mme Dodun or Louise de Keralio, wife of the advocate Robert.

PUBLIC AND PRIVATE ART EXHIBITIONS

Another place where high society met was at exhibitions of paintings. There were great crowds at the Salon in 1789 to which Durameau had sent his sketch for the *Etats Généraux*, the Chevalier de Lespinasse a view of the *Halle aux Blés* and David *Les amours de Pâris et d'Hélène*.

Private exhibitions of the work of painters and sculptors are not, as one might imagine, a phenomenon of the present day, but flourished everywhere at the end of the eighteenth century. Thus it was that on October 31, 1790, Houdon exhibited at his own house his statue called *l'Écorché*, cast in bronze and destined for the Académie des Beaux-Arts. This was a very solemn Paris occasion, happily attended by the German writer Gerhard de Harlem, who had come all the way from Oldenbourg to visit the capital:

'In fact,' he writes, 'one sees very little of the cast itself. The artist seems to regard the occasion simply as an opportunity to display his works in a blazing light to the gaze of high society.' But the same traveller admired the maquettes of the *Washington* and of the *Monument à Gesner*, the *Frileuse*, the busts of *Molière*, *La Fontaine* and the actor *La Rive*. A similar visit to the studio of David, at the Louvre, gave him a preview of that painter's *Brutus* and the *Serment des Horaces*, which were to be exhibited at the Salon of 1791.

The meetings of the French Academy were also well attended by lovers of literature. Another German traveller, Joachim Campe, whom we have already encountered on the terrace of the Tuileries, describes rather amusingly the reception of the Abbé Barthélemy, author of *Le Jeune Anacharsis*, for which Marmontel, permanent secretary of the *Académie Française*, had sent him a card on August 25, 1789.[3]

Though he arrived an hour and a half before the seance was to begin, the hall was already packed:

> We had the greatest difficulty in moving and finding a place to stand: but I am expressing myself badly, for it was impossible for us to settle in one spot. The whole of that great mass of humanity, standing on tiptoe, was subjected to endless oscillations which were kept up by the incessant shoving of new arrivals. We were all held up by one another and indeed lifted and carried by the pressure of bodies, and the smaller of us were indeed standing on air most of the time. If one of the walls of the hall had given way, the whole assembly would have fallen flat on its face. It was very hot, the sun blazed through the high windows and everyone was stewing in his own juice long before the illustrious entry of the Forty Immortals* irradiated the hall.

There follows a passage in praise of French women who were able to endure the most fearful tortures out of love of literature:

> These martyrs of the mind and of knowledge, at each ingenious expression with which the members of the Academy strove to ornament their speeches, were oblivious of the

* The forty elected members of the French Academy (Translator's note).

painful position in which they found themselves . . . The patches on their faces melted with the heat of the hall or with the ardour of their sympathy: their cheeks were on fire, their eyes sparkled . . . Their hands never ceased applauding and from their delectable lips there constantly burst forth phrases like: 'Ah! Bravo!', 'Ah! how beautifully expressed!' and 'Ah! Charming!'

One can almost imagine oneself at one of those Academy galas which still rejoice the hearts of present-day Parisians: at the reception of a Paul Valéry or a Léon Bérard. But on this occasion, alas, it was only the Abbé Barthélemy. How was it that the severe charms of the young Anacharsis managed to rouse the ladies to such a pitch of enthusiasm?

PRÉSIDENT DE GOURGUE'S BALL AT BORDEAUX

While Paris still had its distractions, social life did not languish in the provinces either, or at any rate not as long as the general situation there was still more or less tolerable. Receptions were still being given in most of the larger cities, and at times fresh political upheavals would spice these formal occasions with rather picturesque incidents.

At Bordeaux, for example, in the first months of 1789, there was a ball one evening at the home of the president of the Parliament, Michel de Gourgue, who would soon be marrying off his daughter. The fun was at its height when there appeared four strange-looking individuals dressed in the style of Pourceaugnac and swagged with noble orders. Although they had no invitations, they asked to be admitted, saying they were deputies of the nobility. The master of the house allowed them in and was the first to laugh at their jokes. But the quartet disappeared only to return almost immediately disguised as deputies of the Third Estate. They brought also a change of manners and language to their entertainment:

> While speaking in the manner of the people they said
> the most witty things which made our company regret that

they hadn't thought of doing a take-off on the clergy . . .
We were unable to guess the identity of the four who took
part in this clever masquerade.[4]

We must admit that the youth of Bordeaux, at the beginning
of the Revolution, was not down in the mouth about it.

Of a more intimate and serious nature were the little *soirées*
in Marseilles which Barbaroux remembers with such pleasure
in his memoirs. Young men of like opinions would gather on
Sunday evenings together with charming society ladies to
gossip, recite verses, discuss a thousand and one questions
and, like all true southern Frenchmen, to grow intoxicated
with the charm of words:

> We never left before midnight, and indeed sometimes
> dawn would still find us talking about Plato, Horace, Newton,
> the characters of cats and dogs, the former so beloved of
> Crébillon, so detested by Buffon; we would discuss public
> events which at that time were not yet called assassinations,
> and hold forth on friendship, that divine abstraction that
> is everywhere adored but is no better known these days than
> the other godly attributes.[5]

A SCANDAL AT MONTPELLIER

In another large southern town, Montpellier, social life remained
as brilliant as ever during the winter of 1789–1790, if we are
to believe Pierre-Louis Pascal Jullian who was studying law
there at the time. Two groups of amateur actors, one composed of members of the nobility, the other of bourgeois and
tradespeople, rivalled each other in the presentation of plays.
Many salons remained open and provided their usual hospitality, notably that of the comte de P——, who was still
giving very fine balls. But during one of these there was an
incident which people found very disturbing. At the height
of the revelry the leader of the people's party, whom Jullian
does not name, but who might well have been Cambon,

arrived with fresh news and exhibiting 'his usual impudence of manner'.

'Are you aware, monsieur le comte,' this individual asked, 'that your precious authority is b——d and that the only thing for you to do now is b—— off?'

The guests were indignant and wanted to throw the foul-mouthed intruder out of the window, but the count prevented them, saying:

'I shall take my leave when service to my King no longer requires my presence here and when I am recalled by His orders.'[6]

The retort was not lacking in style, but all the same the scene created a scandal and the ball ended on a note of disquiet.

Very soon the ferment in Paris was to reach most of the big towns, cutting short all the pleasures of elegant society . . . And that evening, perhaps, the smart set in Montpellier had danced their last minuet.

CHAPTER FIVE

PARIS THEATRES AND CAFÉS

The golden era for cafés: fashionable establishments in the Palais Royal and other districts – Trends in the theatre – The popularization of the Comédie Française and the Opera

THE GOLDEN ERA FOR CAFÉS: FASHIONABLE ESTABLISH-
MENTS IN THE PALAIS ROYAL AND OTHER DISTRICTS

This summer of 1789 was a golden era for cafés, an era when the sun shone, faces were flushed with argument and the thirst for liberty parched everyone's throats as much as it inflamed their breasts!

We have already noted, as we followed the Marquis de Ferrières at the Palais Royal, what temptations this paradise offered to lovers of British beer, bavaroises and ratafia. There was not a single arcade or gallery which did not sport some celebrated signboard. At the corner of the Perron passage there was the entry to the famous *Caveau* in front of which there were always throngs of people until two in the morning. Nearby there were the *Chartres* or the *Conti* cafés, the *Grotte Flamande* with its superb beer, the *Italien* with its porcelain stove in the form of a ball.

In the Rue des Bons-Enfants there was the *Café de Valois*, where the Feuillants would come to read the *Journal de Paris*, while the Jacobins, with Chabot and Collot d'Herbois predominant, would frequent the *Café Corazza*. And we must not forget the curious *Café Mécanique*, where the mocca was pumped up to the waiting cups through the hollow central leg of each round café table – an early example of central heating – nor, above all, the veteran, the doyen, the most illustrious of them all, the *Café de Foy*, which, it was said, was to the Palais Royal what the Palais Royal was to Paris. It was the most popular establishment of them all, with its fine gilded salons and its pavilion in the garden. It was Jousserand, the proprietor of the *Foy*, who drew the attention of his clients to a certain brandy from Andaye (*sic*) but which may well have come from Suresnes, and to a certain liqueur from the West Indies which, according to some malicious tongues, was manufactured no further away than the Faubourg Saint-Germain . . .[1]

But hospitable as was the domain of the Duke of Orleans, he did not have the monopoly of restaurants and cafés. Every corner of Paris had its own favourites: on the Left Bank, the *Café Zoppi*, the final incarnation of the celebrated *Procope*. In the Rue de Tournon, there stood the *Café des Arts*, rallying-point for extremists from the Odéon district. In the Rue de Sèvres, the *Café de la Victoire* attracted the more moderate elements. After crossing the Place Dauphine, passing the *Café Conti* and, on the way down to the Pont-Neuf, the *Café Charpentier* whose proprietor was Danton's father-in-law, you would find, on the Place de l'Ecole, the *Café Manoury*, the daily and (more often) nightly port-of-call of Restif de la Bretonne.

On the Right Bank, at the *Régence*, they still adored La Fayette, while in the Rue du Roule, at the *Café de la Monnaie*, he was burnt in effigy. At the Tuileries, on the Feuillants' terrace, the windows of the *Café Hottot* had been bricked in, to prevent the tricoteuses from squinting at the palace. And how many more establishments there were, from the *Café de Jean-Bart et du Père Duchesne* (singular conjunction!) to the delightful *Café des Bains Chinois*, run by Mme Baudray; from the *Café de la Porte Saint-Martin*, frequented by quiet, respectable folk, to the *Café Godet* in the Boulevard du Temple, whose proprietor, a captain of the National Guard, was one day involved in a quarrel with a light-infantry officer, got a bullet in his stomach and had his stock and fittings stolen by a band of fanatics.

There were cafés for all tastes and to suit every pocket and every opinion, for each of them sported its own colours. Whether aristocrat or Jacobin, a man was judged henceforth by the type of café he went to for his cup of mocca, just as in Athens in days gone by 'one judged whether a citizen professed the ideas of Aristotle or of Zeno according to whether he frequented the Lyceum or the Porch'.

The conflict of ideas exposed many café-keepers to certain professional risks. When a discussion got heated, cups and saucers would fly through the air. But at least they gained a regular clientele, and the period was a profitable one for them.

Not for nothing had thousands of National Guardsmen, far from their homes and most of the time without anything to do, been poured into the Paris streets; the café on the corner soon became their canteen. Whether one wore a fur cap or a cockaded hat, the habit of taking 'a little glass of something' soon caught on, and civilians were not slow in following this self-indulgent example.

The women too followed it. Until then they had only very rarely been seen inside the cafés. But now, they felt, why shouldn't they visit them? The Rights of Man, of which their husbands and lovers were so proud, surely deserved to have a counterpart applying to the 'stronger sex'. And this was all the better for a certain kind of trade which was to become indispensable to the life of the capital.

Thus, with the arrival of a new era, the cafés are to know prosperous times. Of all the conquests made by the Revolution, they will probably be the only one enjoyed by everyone. Governments may change, but the great vogue of these delightful establishments devoted to doing nothing, to idle gossip and where everyone feels at home while at the same time being part of a crowd, will never diminish. In years to come, as in the past, they will remain one of the great attractions of Paris.

TRENDS IN THE THEATRE

Why did the Revolution not bring the same kind of prosperity to the theatres? In that domain, it must be admitted that its influence was execrable, and the idiocy and banality of the productions dished up to the public from 1790 to 1795 were unsurpassed.

And yet never had the public shown a more passionate desire for spectacle and drama. Comedies, occasional pieces, Jacobin buffooneries, parades or civic ballets – the public applauded everything with equal fervour. Sometimes, four thousand persons, standing on seats and benches, would begin to dance on the spot, taking hands to form an immense human chain, and following the rhythm of the choruses would chant at the top of their voices the same patriotic refrain.[2]

In such a fevered state of affairs, the most inept rubbish could be passed off as a masterpiece. Neither the Jacobins of the deepest dye who took their seats at the theatre with their pipes in their mouths and their manes of hair like a fox's coat, nor their often slovenly female companions were of a mind to enjoy anything but the most vulgar spectacles. A play was judged a success if it was adorned with common slang expressions or stupid declamations.

But the French stage did not immediately fall into this degenerate condition. At the start of the Revolution, the public was content to find in the works it was shown – the revival of Voltaire's *Brutus* and in particular the *Charles IX* of Marie-Joseph Chénier – more or less transparent allusions to recent events. Tremendous cheers greeted on November 4, 1789, tirades evoking the massacre of Saint Bartholomew's Eve or predicting the destruction of 'fearsome Bastilles', the punishment of evil kings.

'The murders done by kings shall never go unpunished!' At a single stroke, the Théâtre-Français had been booked solid; all the boxes had been reserved for eleven performances and in five evenings the actors had touched fifteen thousand *livres*.[3] The drama, produced later in smaller theatres, thanks to the suppression of privileges, enjoyed the same success with 'the greasy coat-collars of the boulevard'. It was an enthusiastic public, but only moderately well educated, if one judges by the notices which the managements found themselves forced to hang in the foyers: *Ladies and gentlemen, you are requested to remove your hats and to commit no nuisance in the boxes.*

The next year, the new productions were even worse. When the German Harlem came to spend the autumn of 1790 there, he spent his evenings listening to *Socrate ou le Régime des anciens temps* by Collot d'Herbois and the *Rigeurs du Cloître* (Rigours of the Cloister) by Fiévée which were given by the Théâtre de Monsieur. He also saw *Le Baron de Trenck* and *l'Autodafé ou le Tribunal de l'Inquisition*, which Gabiot had produced at the Ambigu, as well as the last play done at the Théâtre-Français: *Nicodème dans la Lune ou la Révolution pacifique*, by Beffroy de Reigny, known as le Cousin Jacques. It would be saying too much to state that the visitor retained a very enthusiastic impression of these elucubrations.

THE POPULARIZATION OF THE COMÉDIE FRANÇAISE AND THE OPERA

But the crisis was only beginning. With the advent of the Terror it took on its full dimensions. Then on stages large or small one would see presented every evening plays worthy of Charenton and whose sole attractions were either their crapulous liberty or their demagogic verbiage. Does the reader require a few examples? Well, take first of all this comedy of manners entitled *L'Epoux républicain*. A husband, dissatisfied with his wife, denounces her to the Revolutionary Committee and has her guillotined. As the curtain falls, the whole house bursts into tumultuous applause and the author, in a curtain speech, tells the audience: 'I am sure that there is not a single husband among you who is not prepared to do as my republican husband has done.' What must the poor wives and sweethearts have thought of these final lines?

A grandiose spectacle next: *Le Jugement dernier des Rois*, a work by Sylvain Maréchal. On an island inhabited by savages who nevertheless know the virtues of revolutionary principles there arrive all the kings of Europe, in chains. Only one –

43

Louis XVI – is missing from the collection, but he has a cast-iron excuse because he has just been guillotined. As they are all most fearfully hungry, they are thrown a crust of bread; each king makes a dive for it and the episode turns into a free-for-all. Pope Pius VI throws his tiara at the head of Catherine II who retaliates with her sceptre and smashes the pontifical cross; the king of Spain loses his cardboard nose. But at the height of the dust-up the island's volcano erupts and engulfs all these top names. This settles the question of the monarchy once and for all.

It would be tedious to continue with outlines of a whole junk-heap of productions one as idiotic as the other: anti-clerical masquerades called *L'Abbé mis au pas*, *La Papesse*, *A bas la calotte!*, inane literary compositions like *Le Mariage de Jean-Jacques Rousseau* or naïve apotheoses like *The Taking of the Bastille, heroic drama adapted from the Scriptures*. *Le Moniteur* had something to say to the authors of this degraded type of literature:

> It would seem a highly paid conspiracy run by Pitt and Cobourg to make the French theatre sink to its lowest depths, to rob it of its glorious crown, so justly won, and to deprive dramatic art of the powerful means it had to consolidate the Revolution's immediate gains.[4]

It wasn't as if the works of art of the past had been given due respect! But when from time to time they appear on the bills their contents are so mutilated that it is difficult to recognize the old classics. They cut Molière[5] because he used the expression *valet de chambre*; the undesirable distiches were chopped out of Voltaire's *Mahomet*, and, in order to jolly up old Racine, a scene from the *Malade Imaginaire* was coolly inserted into *Athalie*.

That is not the whole story. If any dramatic author should have found favour with the new outlook it was obviously Beaumarchais, who was one of the first to mock at the nobility and undermine the monarchy. Well, *The Marriage of Figaro*, his most audacious work, that delayed-action bomb in which Napoleon was to see 'the Revolution already at work', was banned by a frankly Jacobin city, Marseilles. The objections made about the play were that it depicted personages 'recalling the haughty prejudices, the maxims of despotism and anti-social distinctions'; that it called for 'costumes now justly outlawed'; and in short that it was 'immoral and unworthy of the attention of Republicans'.

After such an enormity, all one can do is throw in the towel. The stupidity of the *sans-culottisé* theatre could scarcely be more clearly demonstrated.

And yet it was this theatre Paris turned to for distraction and comfort in her gravest hours. It was this theatre which sustained the morale of an infinite number of simple souls, greedy for forgetfulness of the cruelty of events, of poverty, worry, and longing to contemplate more entertaining spectacles than bakeries without bread and deserted markets.

Flat and ridiculous though they were, all those plays which were presented every evening brought a little consolation, a little illusion. For this reason much can be forgiven them: they served as distractions from the cares of daily life.

CHAPTER SIX

THE REVOLUTION AND FASHION

*The disappearance of panniered skirts and knee-breeches –
Patriotic jewels and fans – The vogue for the tricolour – The
carmagnole and the red cap*

THE DISAPPEARANCE OF PANNIERED SKIRTS AND
KNEE-BREECHES

'The Revolution was won by long trousers and short waist-
coats,' Norvins wrote in the nineteenth century. And this
statement, albeit a trifle summary, contains a particle of
truth.

During the last years of the *ancien régime*, simpler fashions
and a freer cut announced that fashion was about to change its
style. Could the generation of Louis XV ever have foreseen
that one day people would have the nerve to show themselves
in salons wearing anything but knee-breeches, embroidered
coat and white stockings? Yet such was the frightful example
the youth of the day was setting now. One could see the
arbiters of elegance sporting not only the round hat and the
English-style frock coat but also cashmere pantaloons, often
accompanied by riding-boots. 'The impudence!' the old
dowagers huffed. 'They're not wearing breeches! They are
sans-culottes!' This expression, *sans-culottes* or 'without knee-
breeches', was soon to become widely used, taking on, naturally,
a quite different significance.

The fair sex (the women), for their part, gave up their ample
panniered skirts with the long trains. They began wearing
almost tubular dresses and a bodice in what was known as
the *pierrot* (jester) style; this bodice was a kind of small

close-fitting jacket whose hem rose to a little point at the back. One man who knew women both as a poet and as an abbé, Jacques Delille, had already noticed this detail:

> Cornelia in a *pierrot* and Caesar in a waistcoat – I fear
> Such would the ancient Romans have worn if they were
>   here.

He might also have noticed that heels had become less high, hairdos less extravagant: those pompadour puffs, laborious scaffoldings on which were piled sometimes an entire garden, a menagerie or a galleon in full sail – constantly threatening to become entangled with the chandeliers – were declining into a well-deserved eclipse. The Parisiennes of 1789 seemed to want to escape from the tender tyrannies of fashion, to free and emancipate themselves, but, with a very typically feminine contradictoriness, as soon as the Revolution got going, they began dressing themselves up as orderly officers, adopting a kind of uniform outfit. Within a few weeks, the tricolour was everywhere: it was all the rage, not only in the galleries of the Palais Royal, but also in the swankiest society sets.

Not a single article of attire that did not borrow its tones of toytown gaiety. Dresses *à la Circassienne*, merrily striped with the national colours, made red-white-and-blue shoes a 'must' for every woman who wished to be both fashionable and patriotic; her hat would be decorated with a great cockade, and, pinned in the folds of her *fichu*, she would display a huge bouquet composed of daisies, cornflowers and crimson poppies. The names then given to the smarter toilettes were also highly significant. We had a dress style called *à la Camille française*, created by Mme Teillard, and even more stunning, the *Constitution Cut* which the Goncourt brothers have described for us so minutely:

> A hat in the shape of a half-helmet of black gauze, a *fichu* of lawn shirting which was caught up in a nacarat sash whose colours were those of the national flag, and a skirt of

47

very finest printed cotton, scattered with a pattern of wee red-white-and-blue posies.[1]

The fashion houses launched also the Patriotic Woman's Négligée, which was composed of a royal-blue coat, a red collar piped with white, two little starched ruffles edged with red, white cuffs and a white skirt. The universal tricolour had only one rival: pure scarlet, which, after the tragic affair of July 23, was gaily dubbed *Foulon's blood-red*.

Alas, how far we have departed from the palette of Versailles, from tints known as *the Queen's hair* and *the Dauphin's caca*!

PATRIOTIC JEWELS AND FANS

With all this upheaval in the world of fashion, jewellery became much simpler. After the first great impetuous outpouring of precious donations to the Patriotic Fund from the jewelcases of ladies of fashion, few women still ventured to trick themselves out with rings and expensive necklaces. These were replaced by rocamboles, trinkets of gilded copper, wedding-rings engraved with the words Nation, Law and King; earrings were made of glass imitating rock-crystal and above all there were the very popular trinkets made out of bits of stone from the Bastille – rings, medallions, pendants, amulets – all worn with pride, as if a small fraction of the prison constituted the finest proof of a liberated people. Mme de Genlis' medallion is doubtless the masterpiece in this genre. On a polished fragment of the famous stone she had engraved, in brilliants, the word Liberty. Above it, the sun of July 14, and below it the moon exactly as it was on the eve of that great day. All round it was a garland of laurels made from emeralds and tied with a cockade of small gems in the three national colours.[2] And to think it was all because she was the mistress of the Duke of Orleans!

The feminine arsenal during the first years of the Revolution also included a large number of fans. But it was adieu to those tender mythologies and gallant pastorals in the manner of

Boucher! Adieu to the ivory, mother-of-pearl or tortoiseshell fan-sticks which made one think, as they were unfurled, of great golden butterflies! Now one had to do with wretched wooden fans, or simple sheets of paper decorated with naïve, highly coloured designs. As far as the subjects of these designs went, they were nearly always of contemporary events, so that one had, as it were, a sort of living chronicle coyly fluttered in the ladies' hands; the States General, the National Guard, Bailly, Mirabeau, La Fayette. There could be nothing nicer than the sight of all these little pictures, held in slender, helpless fingers, beating the air on the terrace of the Tuileries or in a fashionable café. They were useful, too, in helping one to show what side one was on. According to whether one was a patriot or only a demi-convert, one stirred up a little cooling breeze with the aid of Necker or the King himself. But the idols of yesterday were soon abandoned for those of the morrow. One's public is *so* fickle ... Gone, sometimes, with the wind of a paper fan.

THE VOGUE FOR TRICOLOUR

The enchanting series of engravings by Duhamel shows us the evolution of frocks and hats during the first years of the Revolution. It was at the moment of Federation that the tricolour vogue seemed to reach its apogee. It became the obligatory 'note of colour' in even the most insignificant articles of attire and adornment, from gloves to garters. The very children were dressed as walking tricolours, parading the streets disguised as little patriots or little National Guards under the fond gaze of their red-white-and-blue parents. It is the triumph of the cockade, the pretty cockade which came in silk, dimity or patent leather (by means of a new process invented by Beau, the *chapelier* of the Rue Saint-Denis). As for the *chapeaux* themselves, they remained fairly large, with a high crown (the brims rounded like lamp-shades) and amusing garnitures of feathers and ribbons in red, white and blue.

The ladies dressed thus the following year too, but do not

49

imagine from this, dear reader, that questions of fashion impassioned them less than before. In the spring of 1791 proof of this may be found in the correspondence of a young and very well-born couple, the Marquis and Marquise de Mesmon. While her youthful husband was detained in Paris by interminable business affairs, the little marquise was yawning her pretty little head off in her château in the Ardennes, from time to time uttering despairing cries for her departed male. What does he do to soothe her impatience? He trots off to 'a little woman round the corner' and then hastens to write:

> My sweet little thing, I am doing your bits of shopping and shall forget not a thing. I have purchased for you a terribly pretty hat in the latest fashion which is entitled: *To Liberty* – the most *ravissant dernier cri!* – and as the ribbons, my dear, would come off in the rain, I've had ever such a pretty hatband tacked on, all golden, with fringes and everything, the whole thing both beautiful and dependable . . .

And the sweet little thing twitters back:

> Tenderest thanks, my pet, for the kindness you show me and for the dear little hatkin you have bought me. You are indeed the most charming of men . . . Your sweet little thing, who adores you, to distraction, etc. . . .[3]

This would seem to indicate that the tricolour ribbons on a hat entitled *To Liberty*, bought on May 6, 1791, by a real nobleman, were still not getting too bad a press, even in provincial drawing-rooms . . .

The Revolution did not really transform fashion, or more exactly destroy it, until after the triumph of the Jacobins. Then, with all its clientele dispersed or reduced to beggary, the trade which throve on elegance was constrained to shut up shop. No more work for the little sempstresses, nor for the *modistes*, nor for the thousand and one tiny fingers that dealt so swiftly and neatly with all the furbelows and finery and fal-lals. Embroidresses, stitchers and sewers, lacemakers, feather-dressers, hat-shapers, trimmers, furriers and fellers – all these brave, tiny hands were condemned to idleness. And there was the same fearful slump in the industries concerned with male raiment. The tailors, the hatters, the bootmakers dismissed their personnel, and the poor fellows had to turn their hands to manual labour to earn a pittance – moving earth in the Champ-de-Mars, and losing within a few months a professional touch that would never come back again.

This aspect of the crisis was dismaying. 'Perhaps I'm quite mistaken,' wrote one young man who was by no means fond of luxury, 'but I should not be surprised if in twenty years' time there is not a single worker in Paris who can trim a hat or make a pair of pumps.' The author of this statement cannot be accused of partiality: his name was Marat.

THE CARMAGNOLE AND THE RED CAP

Henceforth, revolutionary fashion offered only two novelties: the carmagnole and the red cap. The carmagnole was simply the everyday wear of working people seen in many towns and notably in southern France. The volunteers from Marseilles in 1792 brought to Paris the name they had given themselves, and it caught on. How was it that Carmagnola, the little Piedmontese castle town in the region of Turin, gave its name to a popular song and a civilian uniform? The mystery can only be explained by Italian immigrations and the strange destiny of certain words.

In the form it had during the Terror, the carmagnole consisted of a short woollen or dark cloth jacket, hip-length, with a slight fullness at the back. It was usually worn with trousers of the same material or of drill with tricolour stripes, an ox-blood waistcoat and democratic wooden clogs. Dressed in this way, a patriot was sure to be greeted by flattering murmurs when he went to his club or strolled down the street. Perhaps he might even hear hummed behind him the couplets of the famous song:

> Yes, we shall always remember (*bis*)
> The sans-culottes of the faubourgs (*bis*)
>   Drink to their health!
>   Long live the lads!
>   Let's dance the Carmagnole.
>   Let the sound ring out! (*bis*)
>   Let's dance the Carmagnole!
>   Let the sound of the guns ring out!

As for the origin of the red cap, much nonsense has been written on the subject. Some historians have uncharitably insinuated that the Republic had adopted it from convicts, whose headgear it then was. Others claim that the Swiss troops in revolt from the regiment of Chateauvieux, having been pardoned by the Legislative Assembly and given heroes' welcomes on their return from prison on April 15, 1792, the citizens of the capital adopted the red cap in their honour.

Such explanations overlook the fact that it had been used as a symbol ever since the first year of the Revolution and that popular prints depicted it in every context, whether in imaginary depictions like the one of November 2, 1789, *The Funeral Service of the most high, most powerful and most magnificent Seigneur le Clergé*, or the one of July 18, 1790, entitled *The Illuminations in the Champs-Elysées* or *The open-air Ballroom on the Site of the Bastille*. Three months earlier the same emblem, stuck on the head of a lance, could be seen raised right in the centre of the *Camp fédératif de Lyon*. There was not a corner of France where the *bonnet rouge* was not known. It was an ancient symbol of liberty used by the Romans when they affranchized their slaves, and Paris did not need the example of the regiment from Chateauvieux to adopt a cap which had long been before her eyes before she put it on her head.

One of the first occasions when it was worn officially was

at the funeral ceremony for Voltaire, in July 1791. The Marquis de Villette is careful to note, in his description of the ceremony: 'The clubs, the fraternal societies, the suburban braves, armed with pikes, who have lately begun to be called *bonnets de laine* (woollen caps) . . .' And he expatiates on it thus: 'Ever since France recovered her liberty, this head-dress has become the civic crown of the free man and of every regenerate Frenchman.'

We know the rôle it was to play later in the Revolution. Like the carmagnole, it was never officially adopted – Robespierre and Saint-Just would not wear it; but numberless other Montagnards,[4] from Bourdon de l'Oise to the ex-Capucin Chabot, wore it with enthusiastic pride.

From the year II, we may say, its use became general, not only in the Paris clubs, but also in the lowliest people's societies in the provinces. The bulletins from the Convention are filled with addresses from small provincial towns announcing that their inhabitants no longer wear anything but the famous *bonnet*. And indeed how could they resist wearing it when it is seen everywhere, on flagpoles, on the steeples of churches, on official placards, engraved on letterheads, on waistcoat buttons, rings and earrings?

Its triumph was universal. The most sober-minded citizens adorned themselves with it as with a sacred halo and the Academician La Harpe never gave a lecture at the Lycée without decorating his old monkey-skull with the patriotic headgear.[5]

The Parisiennes, jealous of seeing their menfolk so smart, were determined to keep up with them. They disguised themselves as Bellone, as Amazons out of some New World operetta. The most outrageous of them all was Théroigne de Méricourt, who exhibited herself in public wearing a *chapeau Henry IV* drooping over her ear, a long sword hanging at her side, two pistols in her belt and a riding-whip in her hand; but the riding-whip's handle was formed of 'a golden scent-box filled with aromatic salts in case of faintness and to neutralize the odour of the people'.[6] Perhaps this precaution stood her in good stead on the day when the crowd replied to her eloquence with striking arguments on the terrace of the Tuileries.

As a matter of fact, many no less foolish females deserved the same kind of correction. On the 27th Brumaire of year II, a troup of young beauties wearing the Phrygian bonnet and armed to the teeth presented themselves at the bar of the Conseil de la Commune. Their carmagnoles and their trousers caused a prolonged sensation among the public in the court, but the members of the Assembly had no taste for such pleasantries, and the attorney Chaumette went for them, delivering a broadside which was not without a certain bite:

> You rash women who want to be men, aren't you content with your lot as it is? What more do you want? You dominate our senses; the legislator and the magistrate are at your feet; your despotism is the only one our strength cannot combat because it is the despotism of love and consequently a work of nature. In the name of that very nature, remain as nature intended you, and instead of envying us males the perils of a stormy existence, content yourselves with letting us forget them in the bosoms of our families, where we may rest our weary eyes on the enchanting spectacle of our offspring made happy by your tender ministrations!

The ladies could hardly have been more courteously sent back to their hot stoves nor made to understand in more gentlemanly fashion that the word *sans-culotte* cannot be employed in the feminine.

CHAPTER SEVEN

FRENCH AS SHE IS SPOKE

The pompous style of the Revolution – Egalitarian forms of address – The title citizen – Streets and villages renamed – Children's names

THE POMPOUS STYLE OF THE REVOLUTION

The Revolution could say, as did Victor Hugo later on: 'I put a red cap on the old dictionary . . .' But the former attempt was much less happy than the latter.

There frankly could be nothing more insupportable than the language used by the men of '93. There was nothing in it resembling the light, supple, lively style, all nuance and wit, of the eighteenth century. Not only is bombast the order of the day in court, but it slips into daily talk, even into the gossip of the lesser orders. Because antiquity is admired, people express themselves in pompous terms, like college pedants. Because they are disciples of Rousseau, people borrow whole speeches from *Emile* or the *Contrat Social*, not because of any admirable qualities they may have but because of their maudlin repetitiveness, their exasperating mawkishness. If you put this rhetoric together with the Billingsgate of the Halles, the style of *Le Moniteur* together with the graveyard weepiness of inscriptions on the tombs in the *Père Duchesne*, you will find yourself with a strange mixture: French as it was spoken during the Revolution.

EGALITARIAN FORMS OF ADDRESS

The study of this language belongs to literary history rather than to a record of social manners. Of this metamorphosis in

55

language, we need only remember the egalitarian *tutoiement* (that is, addressing everyone by the second person singular pronoun *tu* instead of *vous*, the more formal style) the obligatory use of the word 'citizen' and the mania for de-baptizing anything that recalled religion or the *ancien régime*.

It is rather quaint to note that long before it entered common usage, the idea of universal *tutoiement* was launched by a woman of quality who was also a blue-stocking: Louise de Keralio, daughter of the Chevalier Guinement de Keralio, member of the Academy of Inscriptions and Belles-Lettres and wife of the Liège advocate Robert. It was she who first suggested that *vous* should be put in quarantine, in an article published on December 14, 1790, in the *Mercure National*, of which she was the editor-in-chief.[1] The project must have caused many smiles at the time. We hear nothing more about it until three years later, when a delegation of the people's societies in Paris submitted it, this time very seriously and accompanied by a wealth of arguments, to the attention of the Convention:

'We distinguished three persons in the singular and three in the plural,' the petitioners declared, 'but in despite of this rule the spirit of fanaticism, haughtiness and feudal mentality caused us to form the habit of using the second person plural when we spoke to a single individual. Many evils resulted from this abuse . . . It panders to the arrogance of the perverse; and adulation, masquerading as respect, banishes the principles of the fraternal virtues . . .'

There was only one conclusion possible: *tutoiement* must be made obligatory: 'Thus we shall have less arrogance, less insistence on distinctions, less enmity between men, more open familiarity between them, more tendency towards fraternity, and consequently more egality.'[2]

The Assembly let itself be convinced. It did not pass any decree, but it inserted the petition in its *Bulletin* with an honourable mention and public opinion did the rest. Did not the use of the second person singular have to recommend it the august example of the Romans? Caesar had said: '*Tu* quoque . . .'

And then what a lark it was for the butcher's boy to be able to address his master or the customers in that familiar way, for the wage-earners of all classes to speak to their superiors – that is, those who paid them – just as they spoke among themselves.

Though it was sanctioned by no law, the reform was applied with impressive rapidity. In less than a week, all Parisians had become bosom friends or at least spoke to each other as if they were. Profiting from this upsurge of fraternal feeling, the writer of vaudeville sketches, Aristide Valcour, soon put on a piece entitled *Le Vous et le Toi*, whose success was prodigious. *Le Moniteur Universal* wrote:

> We invite those citizens who may still feel some repugnance in pronouncing the words *tu* or *toi*, which should be for all men the badge of fraternity, to go to the Théâtre de la Cité and applaud *Le Vous et le Toi*. Probably, like all those who attended the first performance, they will be tutoying their neighbours before leaving the theatre.

Though it was always optional, the new usage was rapidly to become obligatory in practice. A man who stuck to the old ways of speaking lost face, tended to make himself regarded as a suspect, and as novelties in the capital are always exaggerated in the provinces, many towns showed themselves to be even more intransigent than Paris on this point. Witness the decision taken on the 24 Brumaire, year II, by the Revolutionary Committee of the Département du Tarn, and committed to its records. It sums up better than any other official document the whole question of *tutoiement*:

> The Revolutionary Committee, considering that it is of the essence of such an institution to contribute all in its power towards the elimination of abuses caused by the *ancien régime* . . .
>
> Considering that the eternal principles of egality cannot admit of a citizen addressing another as *vous* and being in his turn addressed as *toi*;

Considering that the word *vous* addressed to an individual offends equally the rules of good sense, reason and even of truth in the strictest meaning of the word, since one person is not several;

Considering finally that the language of a regenerate nation should not be that of a people enslaved, but ought to be the symbol and guarantee of its regeneration.

It is resolved:

ARTICLE THE FIRST. The word *vous* in pronouns or used with verbs, when it is a question only of a single individual is from this moment banished from the language of Free Frenchmen and shall on all occasions be replaced by the word *tu* or *toi*.

ARTICLE THE SECOND. In all public or private documents, *tu* or *toi* shall be in all cases substituted for *vous* when a single individual is meant.

ARTICLE THE THIRD. The present resolution shall be printed, publicly displayed and sent to the people's societies and to the authorities concerned in the Départment du Tarn.

From this we can see that the Revolutionary Committee of Albi was much more energetic than the Convention itself. The Midi is always in the van.

THE TITLE CITIZEN

The replacing of the words *Monsieur* and *Madame* by the appellations *Citoyen* (Citizen) and *Citoyenne* (Citizeness) came in a few months before *tutoiement* was made obligatory. This usage was officially decided by a resolution issued by the Paris Commune and dated August 21, 1792. Both measures moreover were inspired by the same principle: that of doing away with the distinctions that had hitherto existed between the various classes of society.

One anecdote, reported by Mercier in his *Nouveau Paris*, allows us to appreciate what exactly people had against two terms that had long been consecrated by popular use:

In a primary assembly, the roll-call was being taken. The president would call *Monsieur* any member with money, while he addressed those with little wealth just by their family name. He addressed a young vine-grower in this manner. 'I was waiting for you to say that!' the latter cried. 'Why don't you call me *Monsieur*, as you did my neighbour? Have you forgotten the new politeness formulated by egality? Please remember that everyone is *Monsieur*; either that, or no one is *Monsieur* at all.'

It was the second solution that prevailed. Obeying the young vine-grower's desires, the highest and the lowest were all classed under the same name. There was soon only one name or form of address for everyone.

Soon the clubs, the meeting-halls and the smallest country courthouses stuck on their walls notices which ran:

THE ONLY TITLE RECOGNIZED HERE IS THAT OF CITIZEN.

The Musée Carnavalet today possesses one of these posters which today have become rather rare. Dare we hint that it constitutes a 'speciality of the house'? This thought is provoked by the memory of the Grand Duke Wladimir of Russia who often visited the museum in the Rue de Sévigné. He would pause in front of the famous poster with a smile, and then, turning to his adjutant, would bark at him: 'Tattichef, call me *citoyen!*' After which His Imperial Highness would be shaken by gales of Homeric laughter. Those were the days when grand dukes still did not believe that the French Revolution was an article for export.

To return to the vocabulary of '93, the official form of address was adopted very quickly. Our classic theatre itself had to drop the word *Monsieur* and two lines from the portraits in the *Misanthrope*:

He says *tu* when addressing those of the highest degree
And the word *Monsieur* is one he never uses . . .

This couplet was replaced by a new version:

The word *citoyen* is one he never uses,
And being addressed as *tu* seems to him outrageous.

From time to time, however, patriots of less deep a dye would, either through malice or inadvertency, let slip the old form of address. On July 22, 1793, a player at the Opéra-Comique who had to make a public announcement made this unfortunate beginning: '*Messieurs . . .*'

'Say "citizens"!' came the roar from two thousand throats.

'Citizens, Mlle Jenny . . .'

'Say "citizeness"!'

'Citizens, citizeness Jenny is indisposed, and we beg of you to accept in her place Mlle Chevalier.'

Then there was a perfect storm of protests. The unfortunate man in vain pleaded to be excused, blamed his absent-mindedness, the force of habit – the spectators threw their seats at him.

Relating the incident next day, the *Journal des Spectacles* followed its account with a few quite judicious reflections:

Is it not true that the words *citoyen* and *citoyenne* which have been proposed to take the place of the old forms of address are insufficient? When one says Citizeness Saint-Aubin, Citizeness Desforges, who knows whether the one is married or the other not? Nevertheless I am given this information when I hear someone addressing the former as *Madame* and the latter as *Mademoiselle* . . . I shall not enter into a discussion on political grounds about whether the title *citoyen* can be applied to all men, but I must say that *citoyenne* does not apply to all women . . .

And the editor, expatiating on the debate, concludes:

Reasonable men ought not to suspect or even condemn a man simply because he calls them *messieurs* or *citoyens*. Alas! Up to now, words have had too much influence altogether and we fear it is too late now to exhort our compatriots to abandon them in favour of concrete realities.[3]

This was the voice of common sense, but our journalist had taken on more than his match. The influence of words over things was to last a long time and the former appellations were to be as vigorously attacked by the men of the Directory[4] as by the Jacobin government. We would do well to read a resolution dated year IV:

> Let those who wish to *monsieur* this and *monsieur* that restrict their activities to those coteries which admit such a usage; but those *messieurs* must not expect to be employed by the Republic.[5]

And this example of administrative prose was written not just by anyone. It was signed by the great Carnot himself.

STREETS AND VILLAGES RENAMED

Let us imagine a Parisian who had left the capital in 1791 and was seeing it again for the first time two years later. How could the poor man find his way in a city where four thousand streets had been renamed according to the immortal principles of the Revolution? Their civil status had been disguised, their name-plates mixed up as one shuffles a deck of cards.

The operation began with those Paris streets bearing the name of the king or the court. There was no longer a Place Royale, which became the Place des Fédérés. Then the Place Louis-XV became the Place de la Révolution, the Rue Bourbon the Rue de Lille. Likewise the Place Louis-le-Grand became the Place des Piques, the Rue Monsieur-le-Prince the Rue de la Liberté, the Rue Madame the Rue des Citoyennes, and the Rue du Roi-de-Sicile, named after the brother of Saint-Louis, was rechristened Rue des Droits-de-l'Homme[6] (Rights of Man Street).

Nor were the great men who had served the monarchy given any less cavalier treatment. Henceforth the Rue de Richelieu was called Rue de la Loi and the Rue Neuve-Richelieu, near the Sorbonne, became the Rue Chalier.

But they had only just started. The great thing was to get

rid of all titles inspired by religious superstition, and that meant doing away with all the names of saints which were to be found at every street corner.

'Saints have done as much harm as princes,' Grouvelle proclaimed in a report to the Conseil Général de la Commune. It was necessary to replace the cult of 'the imbeciles or hypocrites of legend' by that of the friends of Reason. At once, legions of workmen set to work laicizing hundreds of little slabs of stone. The streets named, for example, after Saint Denis, Saint Roch, Saint Antoine became the Rues Denis, Roch and Antoine, while the tiny cul-de-sac named after Saint Fiacre became the Cul-de-Sac Fiacre.

Even less fortunate than the saints, the two angels of the street of that name found themselves liquidated completely. In the Place de la Croix-Rouge (Red Cross Square) the word *Bonnet* (cap) was substituted for *Croix*; this respected the colour though the general significance was somewhat altered. Nothing more logical in a city where even the churches had been given new names: Notre-Dame was called the Temple of Reason, Saint-Gervais the Temple of Youth, and Saint-Laurent, probably appropriated for the solemnization of republican marriages, became the Temple of Hymen and Fidelity.

If we move outside Paris, we find the same curious imagination presiding over the changes wrought in the names of towns, whether large or small, which wanted to change their colours. There were six thousand of these, six thousand which, for quite obvious reasons, could no longer stomach their age-old names. For how could decent patriots live without shame in places like Bourg-la-Reine, Bois-le-Roi and Bourbon-l'Archambault? Quick, rechristen these unfortunate localities with respectable names! And the rest were authorized to free themselves of the word *Saint* which so long had been their shame.

Saint-Cloud without delay became simply Cloud; Saint-Cyr[7] (which aurally, in a rather dreadful pun, might be interpreted as 'Five Wax'), became Cinq-Bougies or Five Candles. But the record in saint-cutting goes to a commune of Deux-Sèvres which did not hesitate to omit twice the unfortunate sound that recalled the French pronunciation of 'Saint' in its name: Saint-Symphorien-sur-Sèvre was diminished to Phorien-sur-Sèvre. This afforded a slight relief for those afflicted by a lisp.

Quite often the old names were replaced by entirely new ones. Saint-Denis became Franciade, Meudon became Rabelais, Montmorency became Emile, in memory of Jean-Jacques Rousseau. Saint-Germain-en-Laye preferred to be known as Montagne du Bon Air; Saint-Malo was known as Victoire Montagnarde; Saint-Lô was dubbed Rocher de la Liberté. About thirty French communes adopted the name of Marat. Others had even stranger notions: Saint-Léonard, a suburb of Angers, was baptized *Fruits Sucrés* (Candied Fruits); Saint-Jean-de-Bournay in Isère, which is far from being a maritime province, became Toile à Voiles (Sailcloth); and Coulanges, in Loir-et-Cher, called itself, in order to annihilate its *anges* or angels, Cou sans-culottes (Neck without breeches) as if the only place for those nether garments was round the neck.

CHILDREN'S NAMES

But let us conclude a list which might soon overwhelm us with tedium. The most one can say in favour of these transformations is that they were even less bizarre than the names chosen for themselves or for members of their families by a large number of citizens:

> Come on, don't let's be backward,
> Let's get rid of our names, boys!
> For Jack and Jim and Dennis and Dick
> Are the stupidest names in the world, boys![8]

Thus a doggerel-writer of the period. And indeed the saints of the Christian calendar were now on the Index and something else had to be found in order to distinguish one's children one from the other. Fond parents chose the names of characters from antiquity, of contemporary celebrities, of revolutionary episodes or great Republican virtues.

In fact, some rather amusing results were obtained. Besides the epidemic of names like Brutus, Lycurgus and Epaminondas there was a blossoming of babes called August the Tenth, Fructidor[9] and Constitution. A *sans-culotte* named his son Marat-Couthon-Pique, and Lebrun called his daughter Civilization-Jemmapes-République. If we may imagine the two young people getting married later, one can envisage some complexity in their expressions of conjugal bliss.

And yet there were even more striking examples: citizen Lacau of the Hautes-Alpes, registering an infant of the female sex, inflicted on her the darling name of Phytogynéantrope, which means, in Greek, a woman giving birth only to warrior sons.[10]

By racking their brains in this way, the good folk of 1793 thought they were bringing about a revival of the ancient world, and making their Republic closer to those of Greece and Rome. But probably they were only making it closer to Charenton.

CHAPTER EIGHT

REVOLUTIONARY LIBERTIES

*Rapid progress to debauchery – Women of the Palais Royal –
A reform project conceived by Restif de la Bretonne – The
Jacobins try to purify Paris – The end of the crisis in virtue*

RAPID PROGRESS TO DEBAUCHERY

Naturalists tell us that the beaver (L. *castor*) – in German *hiber*,
by alliteration *biver* – lived in swarms all round the capital in
former days and especially on the banks of the Bièvre, which
is said to have taken its name from them. We must suppose
that the race had degenerated at the time of the Revolution,
for Paris possessed only *demi-castors*, as good old Mercier puts
it. But we have already seen how numerous they were and
how large a place their earths occupied in the gardens of the
Palais Egalité.

We would do well to go back a little in time for our consideration of this curious colony in order to understand the
indignation of the moralists and the subsequent knock-out
blow the Jacobin government was to feel itself obliged to give it.

The truth is that the victories of 1789 had brought advantages
to only one set of women: the worst. After having governed
for so long and with so firm and sometimes brutal a hand
those ladies who wished to emulate Manon, the police had
discovered more urgent occupations, and the hunt for love,
like everything else, had to all intents and purposes been
liberated.

Nothing could have been more natural: the Revolution had
begun in the streets and the street always is on the side of
those liberties that flourish in it. And then, with men arrogating

65

so many new rights, why should the women too not have their fair share of liberties, and be delivered from a control they had always inveighed against?

Emboldened by this fine reform which moreover came about of its own accord, the goddesses of hospitality no longer had any hesitation in parading their charms. Very soon the Palais Royal and the little streets round about, which had never been noted for sanctity, took on the most outrageous aspect. At the balconies in the Rue Saint-Honoré and the Rue des Petits-Champs, as well as at windows in the Rue de Beaujolais one might observe bevies of young persons who seemed to have a passionate interest in the problems of pedestrian traffic.

Others, feeling a little exercise might be good for the health, would wend their way towards the *Galeries de Bois*, which were still called the *Camp des Tartares*, or would stroll to mingle their plaintive sighs with those of the thirty-two young ladies in the alley of the same name, sung by Restif de la Bretonne. At once club and seraglio, the garden knew no corner where the indefatigable 'strolling sisters' did not come every day to cast their silken nets.

They came from everywhere, from furnished attic rooms, from basements, from backshops or else from the communal dormitories presided over by horrible matrons in the region round the Palais. Creatures of all ages and origins, the youngest twelve and the oldest well above fifty, some had come from their country homes and others from the Faubourg Saint-Marcel: what an extraordinary band they made! There were work-girls who had run away from their workshops, sempstresses weary of plying needle and thread, flower-girls using all their wits and charms to sell, time and time again, the same flower – a thousand tiny hands that were good for nothing but ready for anything. For those who knew their way around, there was a sudden blossoming of the liberal arts, assisted by the universal thirst for sensual pleasure and by the illusion of feeling at last unshackled by convention.

Among these apprentice *grandes cocottes*, chance, beauty and savoir-faire could not fail to create very rapidly rather marked distinctions. Mayeur de Saint-Paul, a former boulevard actor, who appears to know his subject from first hand, enumerates for us three categories of beauties: kept women, courtesans and the rest, whom he calls by a very nasty name.

The first have one or several men whose sole task in the world is to provide for all their needs; when they get together it is exactly like a meeting of a joint stock company.

The second, more brazen, are dressed in the latest fashion, stroll about bare-headed or wearing those ribboned chapeaux which spread their broad blooms over the engravings of Debucourt. These women flaunt their double watch-chains, their lorgnons, their earrings; they enter theatres time and time again, always coming out almost at once, sending their inviting smiles and flashing eyes in all directions, and in short endeavour ceaselessly to attract attention because, belonging to no one they belong to everyone, and their occupation is to hire out their hearts and all the rest as a park employer hires out garden chairs. These women might be said to belong to a limited liability company rather than to a joint stock company.

Finally, the *fille publique* or gay girl, generally accompanied by a 'mother' or by some sluttish servant, likes nothing better than to lounge around the galleries so as not to have to show in the revealing light of broad day her paste brilliants and her bedraggled skirts. She confines her ambitions to third-rate conquests, seeking out the timid foreign tourist, the trembling young shop assistant or gambler on his uppers, or almost. She is a perambulating charity chest for the underprivileged.

WOMEN OF THE PALAIS ROYAL

Any Parisian gentleman who knows his way about has no trouble in finding his level. He knows that neither Bersi the mulatto girl nor the three Teniers, so called because they have as lovers three rich merchants from Amsterdam, nor Latierce, the blonde, nor yet black-haired Saint-Maurice, with her slender waist and neatly booted feet, are in the modest price

range. But let us suppose some provincial arriving unenlight-
ened from Languedoc, Brittany or Dauphiné and coming upon
this Tower of Babel inhabited by the oldest profession. He
might well find himself on the wrong floor.

This is precisely what was feared as the Great Federation
of 1790 drew near, and when the various regions of France
were preparing to send to Paris their numerous delegations.
These would include many bachelors; and even among the
married men there might well be more than one who, under
cover of the drive for national unity, might confuse free speech
with free love – at a price.

Fortunately there were thoughtful spirits who had foreseen
all this, and a few days before the provincial delegations arrived
a progressive publisher had the brilliant idea of sending out a
little pamphlet which would indeed fill a long-felt need.
Designed as a newspaper and destined to have several editions,[1]
it sported the title: *List of emoluments for the ladies of the Palais
Royal, and district, and for the other regions of Paris, comprising
names and addresses.*

The author was careful to point out in his preface that he
believed 'he was performing a patriotic service in his ardent
desire to counsel the large numbers of strangers attracted to
Paris by their love of liberty'. And it must be said that this
'Loose Who' which was trafficked on the boulevards and often
sold in locked boxes, the better to rouse the interest of idlers,
provided the most extraordinarily precise directions: not only
the names and addresses but also the physical peculiarities of
each young lady and the average amount they accepted for
services rendered to out-of-town visitors.

Now then, you country boys, make your choice! Here is a
work of convenient pocket-size which will afford you some
unforgettable moments. If you happen to have twenty-five
livres, Mme Dupéron and her four lady friends will see to
your needs at No. 33 Palais Royal. If you prefer the medium
price-bracket, you could hardly do better than Victorine, whose
favours, which are considerable, you may win with six *livres*

and a bowl of punch. The same tariff prevails at No. 132, where dwells La Paysanne, not nearly as peasant as her name implies, but in all charity we would advise clients that this healthy youngster likes a good night's sleep. Let us pass lightly over the faults of Georgette, who, it appears, is a 'perfect disgrace' after she's been drinking. A more serious omission would be La Bacchante, a superb young filly whose portrait, in oils, was hung at the last Salon, and who is well known among connoisseurs for her daring eyes, her electric body and opulent locks: however, she is scandalously lacking in all notions of egality, for her tariff runs to six *livres* for those brilliant ephebes who have little more than their youth to offer, and twelve for the company of the maturer man. This is the rule of the house . . .

At a period when the ways of antiquity were enjoyed by all and when Paris took pride in emulating the Rome of old, it would seem that gentlemen of advanced years and ancient appearance ought to have merited rather better treatment.

The only rival to La Bacchante it appears was another habituée of the Palais Royal who had pompously christened herself La Vénus, and who, according to certain accounts, was not altogether unworthy of the appellation. The German Friedrich Schulz wrote:

> She is dark, fresh, delicate. She made her appearances, that summer, in an elegant negligée of the finest muslin which lay lightly upon her and allowed one to glimpse, as she moved, the graceful bend of her waist, her languorous hips and legs. Her apartment is among the most elegant; her adorers are the richest as well as the handsomest of men . . .[2]

And indeed, rumour had it that a few years before she had refused a prince of the blood, beseeching the Comte d'Artois to 'keep his mind on less elevated frivolities, pray . . .'

A veritable aristocracy of loose ladies, beauties baptized, paradoxically, *femmes du monde* or 'upper-class women', formed a group of their own among the rest of the courtesans. They were able to live almost in luxury, usually inhabiting some apartment giving on the garden and on the second floor of the galleries (where the ceilings are lower but the view delightful), and there they would give excellent dinners and amazed their guests by the charm of their manners and the variety of their talents. They played upon the pianoforte, and sang and danced like professionals. Each was the ideal mistress of the house; ideal mistresses too for those fortunate strangers desiring to be initiated into Paris high-life.

Kotzebue, who knew one of them, has explained the ingenious way she performed her ministrations:[3]

> She would arrange with one, two, three or four foreigners or strangers to the capital, for a certain consideration, to be attached to them exclusively; she would visit theatres in their company, or attend them on picnics in the country; she was also an amusing and experienced travelling companion.

But this eighteenth-century Cook's Tour also ran a training establishment in practical morality:

> She will start a kind of college of young men, keeping them out of the clutches of other women, looking after their wardrobes and their shopping and telling them the price of things: in a word, she licks into shape the young bearcubs of England, grooms the red-cheeked youths of Germany and gives a bit of sparkle and flexibility to the amphibious animals of Holland.

All this would be very well if such praiseworthy devotion did not conceal quite often much less disinterested motives. When these fine ladies took in strangers under their charitable roofs, nine times out of ten it was to implant in them a passion for gambling, for trente-et-un and biribi. And whether they were bearcubs, young stallions or walruses, they were sooner or later plucked like a Christmas goose.

At Mme de Saint-Romains', who resided above the *Caveau*

in the Palais Royal, the lure of the cards was added to the attractions of several charming 'nieces'. At Mme Lacour in the Place des Petits-Pères, rouge-et-noire is accompanied by blonde-and-brunette. And Mme Villiers, a most worthy dame, held a salon in the Rue Chabanais, a salon where the blows of fortune are no rarer, alas, than the deceptions inflicted by Venus with her claws in her man.

Such traps probably attracted only one kind of sensation-seeker and not the most interesting type of man, who would have known how to look after himself. But what are we to think of the establishments open to all and sundry, like that shop in the Rue Saint-Honoré where women who claimed to be nuns escaped from their convents without having had time to put on a stitch of clothing related to gaping provincials tales of vows extracted from them by force. Then there were those bathing establishments, which obviously catered to a very particular type of sportsman; there was that shop with the signboard of the *Three Gallant Lads* and which the Goncourts did not hesitate to qualify as a veritable academy of prostitution; and finally, that place in the Palais Royal where two savages from Canada, known as the Algonquin and the Algonquiness, exhibited themselves to Parisians in the costume of the Garden of Eden and who, for a trifling consideration of only three *livres*, would add their own commentaries, down to the final details, to the Declaration of the Rights of Man.

A REFORM PROJECT CONCEIVED BY RESTIF DE LA BRETONNE

In this stink of corruption which rose from the pavements, while the old world gradually crumbled away and another society took its place, there was something which disconcerted even the most liberal-minded men. Some of them proposed remedies whose efficacity unfortunately was by no means certain. We shall content ourselves with quoting the picturesque reform put forward in all seriousness by Restif de la Bretonne.

This 'Emily Post of the gutter' did not recommend that public women should be prohibited, but simply that they should be controlled. His desire was that they should be accommodated in 'convenient but not too ostentatious houses', that they should be protected by the State and that they should be known as Parthénions.[4]

A council of twelve respectable citizens of proved morality – in a small town, for example, the notary and the commander of the National Guard – would look after and keep an eye on each Parthénion. Under the authority of the council, a matron-in-charge and subsidiary governesses would guide our young ladies towards the straight and narrow path of virtue.

The equipment and arrangement of these family-style houses are given long descriptions in which the novelist reveals himself as a poet: here, between the courtyard and the garden, there would be 'various entries masked by trees, bushes and trellises, so that one might without being noticed slip into those regions of the house where offices would be found similar to those at our theatres'. All the pensionnaires would have to be gathered for eight hours every day in two halls, and the most beautiful would occupy the one on corridor No. 1. 'There,' Restif declares,

> they will be fairly quiet, their time occupied with reading or some useful work chosen by themselves; each place will be marked by a different flower which will give its name to the girl sitting there: so that those whose seats are designated by a rose, an amaranth, a lily-of-the-valley, a narcissus and so on will be called Rose, Amaranth, Lily-of-the-valley and so on . . .

There are many other choice passages which reveal in the author a quite adorable ingenuity. There was to be a rule against the use of perfumes; it would be forbidden 'to paint the face with white or red, to use creams to soften the skin, as it has been recognized that all this only gives a factitious bloom and is destructive of natural beauty'. On those days when they are allowed to go out, the young ladies are to be taken to the theatre in 'carefully-sealed closed carriages, and the boxes they sit in shall be hung with screens of white gauze'.

The rest of the girls' time was to be occupied with 'exercises at home' intended to 'elevate the soul'. The directors of the Parthénion never lost sight of the fact that they had to act as parents to their pensionnaires and extend to them all the good offices 'that reason and humanity prescribe' in order to encourage in the dear girls any leanings they might have towards 'living henceforth as honourable maidens'.

This is certainly a touchingly pure programme and must go a long way towards pardoning Restif for other, less innocent, writings.

THE JACOBINS TRY TO PURIFY PARIS

If one abandons dream for reality, it would appear that the problem of morals was not faced very seriously by the public authorities during the first three years following the taking of the Bastille. The Constituent Assembly touched on the subject once only, when it decided, on July 22, 1791, that the only girls who could be arrested were those who caused disorder or committed offences that outraged public decency. This left the field wide open for all the rest, and in an indirect way gave them a kind of legal recognition. It was logical that they should profit from this and endeavour to develop their pleasant industries.

'If things go on like this,' sighs a contemporary,[5]

the shops will soon be occupied only by public women with their three or four twists of tobacco or three or four boxes of powder; on the counter, a mirror and a partition, making a little boudoir, and you have a convent of privacy; a water-jug and a bowl, and you have the convent's appointments . . .

Yet the years went by and as the situation steadily grew worse the Commune and the members from the various sections of Paris began making serious complaints. It is to the

73

honour of the Jacobins that they were the first to act, but their indignation expressed itself in very singular ways. Let us look at the order of the day voted by the section of the Temple in its sitting of April 24, 1793:

> The General Assembly, considering that moral purification is an absolute necessity in a Republic and more particularly so among persons of the female sex, according to observations made by many of the Assembly's members who attest that on various occasions they heard in the streets and at all hours of the day and night, on the part of certain dissolute females, lascivious and very scandalous talk; and desiring to put a stop to the incalculable misfortunes caused by the dissoluteness of public morals and by the lubricity and immodesty of members of the female sex ... hereby nominates commissioners to take the present resolution to the other forty-seven sections and invite them to adhere to it.

The alarm had been sounded: libertinage was declared suspect and the situation it found itself in was made all the worse by being mixed up with politics. Was it not whispered in the clubs that many of these outgoing girls were hand-in-glove with the enemies of the régime? Soon, a number of acts were passed. One afternoon in 1793, suddenly, the gates of the Palais Egalité were closed. Was another St Bartholomew's Eve in preparation, a Massacre of the Nymphs? It was simply Hanriot who collected those ladies known to frequent the place and put them through an interrogation:

'Now are you all good citizenesses?'

'Oh, yes, general.'

'Are you good republican girls?'

'Oh, I should think so!'

'You wouldn't by any chance have hidden in your little dens of iniquity some refractory priest, or an Austrian or a Prussian?'

'Whatever next! We only receive sans-culottes!'[6]

The last statement might have been construed in various ways, but Hanriot saw nothing wrong with it. The citizenesses seemed to be speaking in good faith and the general reprieved the Battalion of Cytherea.

The offensive did not start again until three months later, but this time in a singularly intensified form. It was directed by Chaumette, the Commune's attorney-general, who went about the affair in his own way. According to his lights, immorality was only the last vestige of fourteen centuries of monarchical corruption and slavery. Therefore the Council would 'in the eyes of posterity be judged guilty of criminal negligence if it did not labour without cease to re-establish morality, the fundamental basis of the republican system . . . By cleansing the moral atmosphere, the *Patrie* would be saved!' Placed in this light, the cause was won fron the outset. A clean sweep was ordered.

THE END OF THE CRISIS IN VIRTUE

What whirlwinds of dust it was to raise in the Augean stables! All the women of loose life who traipsed round the public thoroughfares were actually threatened with arrest. Not only did patrols circulate incessantly to prevent smiling and soliciting, but appeals were made for the assistance of virtuous citizens, fathers of families, people of unquestioned respectability, from whose ranks there was formed a sort of voluntary second police force. Old men were invited to become 'ministers of morals' and to prevent 'natural decency from being flouted in their presence'. And this was no mere theoretic mission: these dotards only had to give the sign and the police were alerted and the armed force of law and order was brought into movement.[7] It was probably the first time in the history of the Republic that the right of requisition was given to ordinary private individuals. It is to be hoped that none of them abused their privileges and did not make La Bacchante regret the high prices she charged for according her favours to the older man.

But, after all, the results of this moralizing crusade were fortunately to be somewhat ephemeral. For a few months, the streets and garden walks were more or less cleaned up. Licentious pictures and books disappeared from shop-windows.[8] The young ladies were in penitence behind their jalousies, while their directors of conscience filled in the time once pleasantly occupied in making friendly overtures to strangers by setting their charges to crochet and tatting. But such a fine fit of morality could not last longer than the authors responsible for it. Scarcely had Maximilien fallen than the life of joy took over again, the houses welcomed back their clients, the young ladies began their sweet campaigns once more, and, a few weeks after Thermidor, if an impenitent Jacobin ventured within the Palais Royal, he would merely find that the Commune's laws were now dead letters.

Even a Chaumette or a man with the prestige of Robespierre cannot reform a city with the passing of new laws. Foolish virgins are not transformed into wise virgins, nor Paris into Lacedemonia, quite so easily.

CHAPTER NINE

MARRIAGE AND CHILDREN

Civil marriage and divorce – Consequences of the new régime –
The educational system of Saint Just – Educational reforms
accomplished by the Convention

CIVIL MARRIAGE AND DIVORCE

It must have been very amusing to watch those couples who
were married towards the end of September 1792 according to
the new methods adopted by the Republic.

For centuries weddings had required the blessing of the
Church. But a brand-new law had just replaced the sacrament
of marriage by a civil contract and now one could dispense
with the services of a priest. It was enough to put up a notice
outside the Town Hall worded like this:

> Announcing the marriage of Monsieur . . . and Made-
> moiselle . . . who intend to live together in lawful marriage
> and who today will present themselves at the Municipal
> Offices to reiterate their present promise and to have their
> intentions legalized by the laws of the State.[1]

After this, the couple appeared before the authorities, heard
a little talk and then replied by a double *yes* when asked the
traditional question; then they were man and wife.

Often the duet would become a chorus of twenty or thirty
voices, for the municipal officers liked mass-production methods
and preferred to polish off anything up to a score of marriages
at one fell swoop. It was all one to the crowd awaiting the
newly-weds on the Place de la Grève, and they did not spare

the bridegroom and the blushing bride their rousing cheers and embarrassing jokes.

It is quite likely that the Parisians, most of whom believed in neither God nor the Devil, soon accustomed themselves to the new ways. But what did the good folk of the small towns and villages think of such goings-on?

In the old days a wedding meant that the whole village was given over to rejoicing, the church was decorated, the bells were pealed; the bride wore a beautiful white dress and a wreath of orange blossom, and the festivities were remembered for years afterwards. And now all that jollity was being replaced by vague formalities: some functionary wearing a tricolour sash would mumble a few legal phrases and conclude with: 'You are married,' adding that the ticket for a one-way trip which he had sold them could easily be exchanged for a return ticket if the journey was not a happy one.

And this indeed was the really remarkable innovation: from now on, marriages could be broken as quickly as they were made. In the very room where the vows of fidelity were exchanged there were large notices, surmounted by a Phrygian cap, bearing this suggestive title: 'Laws of Marriage and Divorce.' It could hardly have been stated more plainly that the municipal marriage-store sold both the poison and the antidote.

In order to reach such a point, there had had to be a far-ranging revolution in French customs, because until the end of the *ancien régime* few principles had been less in question than the indissolubility of marriage. Among the resolutions of 1789 only one – presented by the Duke of Orleans – was in favour of divorce. The others did not mention it or rejected the possibility.

Ideas had been modified however during the next three years, and this for two reasons: the anti-religious movement and the ever-increasing cult of personal freedom, resulting naturally in the termination, if desired, of unsatisfactory unions.

In the Legislative Assembly the motion was put forward by Aubert-Dubayet, who succeeded in passing his resolution. A few weeks later, the law of September 20, 1792, settled the question once and for all. From then on, only civil marriage was recognized, but it was given a sufficiently flexible form, allowing it, if need be, a fairly ephemeral duration, in order that the prospect should not scare people unduly.

A pair of amusing engravings which enraptured Anatole France and might have served as illustrations to *Les Dieux ont Soif* (The Gods Athirst) shows the two panels of a diptych entitled 'Republican Marriage' and 'Republican Divorce'. On the first, a municipal officer is welcoming two newly-weds-to-be and is showering them with well-meant advice. The husband, in an English-style dresscoat, holds the hand of his young wife, whose eyes are modestly lowered. She wears neither veil nor wreath; she has a plain fichu round her shoulders, and a little bonnet with strings; she looks like a good little girl going to have her piano lesson. Below the platform, the members of both families are signing the marriage contract at a table. A National Guardsman, holding his rifle like a hallowed taper, surveys the curious onlookers gathered at the back of the hall, and a huge statue of Hymen, bearing flowers and a torch, appears to announce a future of happy fidelity for the new couple.

On the second panel: the same setting, but now the situation has been completely reversed. The municipal officer no longer wears the beatific smile of earlier, happier times. Before him, the hubby and the wife – the latter grown extremely smart and wearing on her head a fashionably elaborate bonnet – are exchanging bitter words and have turned their backs on one another. The two families are still signing papers, but this time for a divorce. As for the statue of Hymen, the torch has gone out and the flower-chain is broken.

How did the disagreement arise? Had the citizeness been flighty? Her spouse a gambler and a drunkard? Or is the excuse simply the usual 'incompatability of temperament', the final resort of those wedded ones who aspire to regain their lost freedom?

Such people must have blessed the lawmaker, for he invented especially for these cases a truly admirable formula: divorce by mutual consent. What could be simpler than agreeing not to agree? No skin off anyone's nose: one loved, and now one loves no longer. The authorities register the fact, and after a few months' delay it's all over: both parties are free.

With such a flexible law, life became no more than a series of passing fancies, a quadrille the one figure of which was 'Swing your partners and get rid of them!' And it should be noted that at this type of game the women are no less eager to change partners than the men. They change their name and their status as easily as they change frocks or hats.

From now on, no one would dream of comparing the institution of marriage with a prison. People enter and leave as they wish, and the operation is so simple that more than one escaped prisoner leaves the door open behind him. One never knows . . . One of the most singular features, indeed, is that many separated couples come together again. Both had longed for forbidden fruit, but once they had been disillusioned by the experience, they dropped anchor in their home port again. Here, too, the law shows itself merciful. Just as easily as it facilitates divorce, it patches up estranged homes.

Chaumette even had a pretty little speech all prepared for those who repented of their divorce. When the couple presented themselves again at the Town Hall, he opened wide his arms and declared:

> Young people whom a tender engagement had already united, the torches of Hymen are lit again for you on the altars of Liberty; marriage is no longer a yoke, a heavy chain; it is no more than what it ought to be – the fulfilling of Nature's grand designs, the payment of a pleasant debt which every citizen owes the *Patrie* . . .[2]

For anyone with half an eye who doesn't believe everything the papers say, this rigmarole covers the fact that France needs children and is determined to get them, wherever they come from. This is the slogan which is seen inscribed on banners in the processions of women that trail through the capital: 'Citizenesses, give children to the *Patrie*! Their happiness is assured!' And articles of daily life such as chamberpots bear devices of a similar nature. 'This is the moment to make a little baby!' is the legend on a bedpan for a woman in labour, exhibited at the Musée Carnavalet. But one cannot help wondering if the potter was not exaggerating a little and if the new generation has really chosen the best time to come into the world.

CONSEQUENCES OF THE NEW RÉGIME

Times of wars and political upheavals are always cruel for children. They suffer terrible hardships. But one must in all justice pay tribute to the concern of the Revolutionaries for the fate of young people, which always occupied their minds. At a period when so many problems demanded their attention, they never lost sight of educational questions; they were constantly concerned with children, not in order to pamper them but to prepare them for the parts they were to play in the future. Interesting reforms emerged from Condorcet's remarkable project and from the efforts subsequently made by the Jacobins. The whole question is to find out whether, in this scheme, the idea of Utopia did not occupy a large place right from the beginning. The Goncourts wrote: 'The eighteenth century had formed man for society. The Revolution formed them for the State.' And it was this formative tendency of the Revolution which only too often spoilt the most generous theories by giving them absurd applications.

Take this mother of a patriot family. Scarcely can her brat mutter 'Mama' before she takes it upon herself to inflict upon the poor creature the questionnaire included by Citizeness Desmarest in her *Elements of Republican Instruction*:

'Who are you?'

'I am a child of the *Patrie*.'

'What are your riches?'

'Liberty and egality.'

'What do you bring to society?'

'A heart that loves my *Patrie* and arms to defend it with!'

In a different tone, but of an equal idiocy, is the novel by Citizen Fréville, entitled *The Life and Death of Little Emilien.* His hero is only eighteen months old but already he speaks the language of the age. The first time he is taken to Versailles, he expresses a wish to play with the Dauphin, but 'a vile slave of the royal troop' prevents him from doing so. Then he asks his mother if the King 'does his duty'. Informed by her on this historical detail, he 'profits by the egality of all men at the water-closet and henceforward calls the monarch Monsieur Capet'.[3]

Childish literature, you may say, pearls of a *Bibliothèque Rose* turned tricolour. But the pronouncements of more serious people are no less ridiculous. For example, the circulars sent by the masters of *pensions* and which instruct parents in the beauties of the teachings to be obtained in those establishments. Even in the primary classes, the study of the Constitution is now given a special course of lectures. So M Donon who succeeds his father in the educational institution in the Rue du Chaume, and respects above all else the sage and sublime operations of the National Assembly, will devote the greater part of his time to explaining its decrees to his pupils, and will inculcate in them a consciousness of the advantages to be gained by conformity to the healthy rationality exhibited in the said decrees.[4] And his confrère, M Rolin (whose name, fortunately, is written with only one *l*), makes the announcement that at his *pension* in the Rue de Sèvres he has engaged a new professor, 'with the aim of instilling in Messieurs his pupils the new Constitution, which should be the prime object of their instruction, the Rights of Man and Common Law.[5]

As one can see, the old *Alma Mater* has been overtaken by politics, but this was only a fair exchange, for the statesmen, for their part, were henceforward to think only of pedagogy.

THE EDUCATIONAL SYSTEM OF SAINT JUST

For the majority of Convention members, this problem seemed a leading one, for they felt that a new régime implied a new kind of education. This idea haunted Robespierre, but it also obsessed to no less an extent Saint Just. Notes by him, discovered about thirty years ago, in the private papers of Maximilien, show us his own ideas on the formation of youth.[6] They may well cause some astonishment, but at least one cannot accuse them of lacking in originality.

First of all, a few general principles:

The child, the citizen, belong to the *Patrie*.

Communal instruction is necessary.

Children belong to their mothers until the age of five, if she clothes and feeds them. After that, to the Republic, until they die.

How will the State carry out its self-appointed task of nursing-father? It will teach its pupils what is good by 'leaving them to nature'. The shades of Rousseau would rejoice at that, and besides, it would cost very little: the pupils would sleep on mats, would be dressed in linen at all seasons and would live solely 'on roots, fruits, vegetables, milk foods, bread and water'.

Let us move on to their moral instruction. Saint Just proclaims that one must neither strike nor caress children, that one must forbid their playing 'games of pride or self-interest' and finally that the little Republicans must be 'rigorously trained to express themselves laconically, as befits the character of the French language'. (They would make up for this brevity later on if they became deputies.)

Education as such would require schools of two kinds, both levels being established out in the country. In the primary schools, children from five to ten years of age would learn to read, write and swim. In the secondary schools, for children between ten and sixteen years of age, education would be mainly in agricultural and military sciences: the pupil would take part in infantry manoeuvres and cavalry exercises and would help farmers at harvest time. The pupils would be divided into companies and battalions and each month their teacher would elect a leader for them from among those who had the best record.

At the age of sixteen the child would be emancipated. He would be forbidden to see his parents before his true majority at twenty-one (how the Republic distrusts family life!) and before then he would be allowed to choose a trade and put off his linen smock, adopting 'the costume of the arts'. But this favour cannot be obtained until after a solemn endurance test has been passed: he will have to 'swim across a river under the eyes of the people on the day celebrating the Festival of Youth'.

It would appear from this that 'the costume of the arts' was to be a simple swimming-slip.

EDUCATIONAL REFORMS ACCOMPLISHED BY THE CONVENTION

Fortunately there were great differences between this fantastic programme and the teaching system adopted by the Convention, a system whose application was to be governed by three successive decrees: the law of December 1793, proclaiming that all primary schools were to be free and attendance at them compulsory; the law of November 1794, removing the compulsory clause and admitting schools not run by the State; the law of October 1795, which proclaimed that a small fee was to be paid for education in State schools and thus marked the taking of a very definite retrograde step. There had been great plans at the start, but financial collapse obliged the Directory to tighten the strings of its purse.

The schools then operating in the majority of regions were very poor. The buildings were inadequate, the classes badly disciplined, the teachers mediocre: this state of things reigned everywhere. An inventory of the Ecole d'Ambert in Puy-de-Dôme, in 1795, includes wretched furniture, rickety tables, empty bookshelves, dilapidated floors.[7] The pupils, particularly the girls, know very little, nor is that surprising, for their masters employ terribly pedestrian methods. Quoted as a dazzling exception is one teacher at Montel-de-Gelat who 'discusses ideas rather than words, and this arouses the curiosity of the children . . .' But surely that is the first principle in the art of teaching?

Truancy flourishes and it is often encouraged by certain parents who look distrustfully upon education not given by priests. The same old story! At Beaumont, the mothers went as far as to burn the schoolbooks belonging to 'republican' classes.

Even more serious is the difficulty experienced in recruiting male and female teachers. One candidate who signs herself Hélène Charvet and is applying for a post to teach spelling drafts the following request: 'I hop that the cittizens comitty will find me suetable. I will do whattever I am arsked.' An old priest who claims to have written a thesis on mathematics turns out to be only just capable of doing a simple addition sum. A former almoner who reads with difficulty and cannot take two from three promises – at the age of sixty-two! – that he will study hard. And as there is no other candidate, the selection board is forced to give him a teaching certificate.

In order to fill in the gaps, an attempt was made to popularize 'double posts'. But Citizen Michaud, member of the selection committee at Riom, expressed a desire that such posts should be kept only for legally wedded persons. 'It is to be desired,' he writes,

that in the small communes where there is only a parsonage, the two sexes should be taught only by couples who are husband and wife, because it is to be feared that two strangers accommodated under the same roof might be given to dissensions and quarrels, or might indulge in improper affairs and passions whose consequences could only be prejudicial to the morality of the pupils; witness the conduct of the majority of country priests with their house-keepers.

Where, then, did the truth lie? The education dished out until now was worthless. The kind being offered now was no better. It was a miracle that young French people did somehow manage to scramble themselves a bit of education.

Such were the painful beginnings of the public schools. There was still much to be done, but a start had been made and we know well the place it was to assume in the moral heritage of the Revolution.

To replace the former colleges, each region was provided with a central school covering three courses of study, and these secondary institutions soon began to flourish. As for higher education, it began to become available in a few special schools in which we may see the origins of the present university faculties.

All these various types of institutions obviously had much that was lacking, but so soon after the grave events that had shaken the country, it indicated in France an astonishing desire for an intellectual renaissance. Biot, the well-known doctor, was right when he wrote that so far there had 'not been a nation nor an epoch that had done so much for the human spirit'.

CHAPTER TEN

THE PARIS CLIMATE DURING THE TERROR

The comparative calm of many Parisians – Ignorance of events – The lack of provisions – The scarcity becomes complete – The good and bad effects of the maximum price order

---

THE COMPARATIVE CALM OF MANY PARISIANS

Such a host of things happened between August 10, 1792, and the IX Thermidor of year II! The throne was brought low, there were the massacres of September, the trial and execution of the King, the insurrection in La Vendée, the fall of the Girondins, the Hébertistes, the Dantonistes and finally of Robespierre himself. Further afield there were Valmy, Jemmapes, the conquest of Belgium and the left bank of the Rhine, then the coalition against France, the invasion, the mass uprising, the prodigious development of military manufactures, the organization of fourteen armies and the successes crowning this great effort: Wattignies, Geisberg, Jemmapes.

In the course of these two years in which 'the sublime existed side by side with the ignoble'[1] and when the country was going through the most terrible upheavals it had ever known, one wonders people's ordinary daily lives could go on with the usual pleasures, occupations and worries. Here all witnesses give an affirmative answer. This twenty-four-month tragedy no more disturbed the daily lives of the majority of French people than a storm interrupts the rise and fall of the tides.

At times difficulties in obtaining supplies were very serious; there were days when, after having waited for hours and hours at the doors of butchers' shops and bakeries, Paris had to go without her dinner. Then the continuous arrests, the guillotine's two thousand eight hundred victims in the capital and nearly fourteen thousand in the provinces, could not fail to move a certain part of the population. But all this did not stop labourers from going to work, shopkeepers from opening their shops, men from courting women and, in short, many people from being perfectly happy.

When Elisabeth Lebas, née Duplay, declared that the spring of year II was 'the most beautiful time of my life', one may attribute her optimistic tone to her devotion to Robespierre. But men of the opposite camp too enjoyed the same blissful delight.

Because he was in love with Mme B . . . in 1793, Jullian, the Royaliste, wrote in his memoirs:

> It may be difficult to imagine that in such dreadful times one could have known pleasure and even happiness; yet such was indeed the case. That period in my life was one of those which left me with the sweetest memories.[2]

And Sébastien Mercier, who adored the Republic but hated the Jacobins, was the first to recognize that during this period the face of Paris had hardly changed at all:

> There are days when the city is very calm, and when we no longer appear to be at war nor in the middle of a revolution. Foreigners reading our newspapers imagine us all covered with blood, in rags and living wretched lives. Judge of their surprise when they reach Paris by the Chaillot road and cross that magnificent avenue in the Champs-Elysées, on either side of which are elegant phaetons and charming and lovely women; and then, as they continue their way, finding their eyes drawn by that magical perspective that opens out right across the Tuileries, and finally riding through that splendid garden, now more luxuriant and better-tended than it ever was in the prosperous days of the monarchy![3]

The fact was that a city of eight hundred thousand souls could not give up its habits so easily. Politics might shake it, there might be a catastrophe, but the next day the cafés opened their doors again and the women came out wearing their finery and everything went on as usual. Scarcely three days after August 10, if we are to believe one lady, 'there were crowds of elegant and happy people in the royal garden; trade was flourishing . . . all faces bore the signs of warm-hearted friendliness'. And while they were still burying the Swiss Guard and the patriots who had got themselves killed in the Tuileries, a small advertisement in the *Moniteur* tells us that 'Mme Broquin is still selling her famous pomade for dyeing red or white hair chestnut or black, on a single application. The price of the pomade begins at nine francs the small jar.'[4]

IGNORANCE OF EVENTS

We must not hold it against the Parisians that they so frequently forgot the gravity of the drama in which they were taking part. Each one's private life had its own demands. When a certain Adélaïde Mareux writes, on August 17, to her brother, that their father Toussaint Mareux, area commissioner, had spent five nights at the Hôtel de Ville where 'he puts himself out ceaselessly', she is mainly worried about whether this class of post carries some monetary remuneration. If not, to hell with rank and title! The family had enough trouble already with the arrival of a cousin from the country and the bans of the elder Javotte girl being published the next day: 'War or no war, people must get married!'

It was after all quite natural for people to be more interested in the price of butter, in their children's health and their sentimental intrigues than in politics. And then so many of them were ill-informed. We have seen how the different quartiers of Paris existed separately one from another, how news was slow in spreading. Quite often people had no inkling of some episode only a few hundred yards away whose violence had wrecked a group of buildings.

89

This state of affairs is particularly apparent during the September massacres. A hundred unfortunates could be assaulted in the courtyard of the Conciergerie without attracting the attention of passers-by in the Rue de la Barillerie or in the Cour du Mail. The same silence shrouded the tragedy at the Carmelite convent. Neither the inhabitants of the Rue du Regard nor the three hundred armed bourgeois who were drilling in the Luxembourg Gardens, nor the customers at the little café set up under the trees of the garden had any idea what was going on. Their ignorance could not have been greater if they had been living at Compiègne or at Orleans.

And when the episode finally came to light, there was of course some concern, but this was far from being general. Especially in the working classes it was considered that the fifteen hundred victims were enemies of the nation and that they well deserved their fate. A young apprentice sempstress, whose adventures we shall be hearing more of soon, writes naïvely:

> Like everyone else, I was shaking with fear lest these royalists be allowed to escape from their prison and come and assassinate me because I had no holy pictures to show them. That was how the massacre of September 2, 1792, came about. While shuddering with horror, one looked upon the action as almost justified; while it was going on, one went about one's own affairs, just like on any ordinary day . . .[5]

After that, it was hardly surprising that Paris very quickly returned to normal: at the Fête de Saint-Cloud which opened on September 8 there were just as many working girls out for a lark, just as many people buying reed-pipe souvenirs, just as many pleasure-seekers watching the parades and country dances as in the days of Fragonard and Gabriel de Saint-Aubin.

Four months later, nevertheless, the populace was to retain a deep impression of the trial and execution of the King. Yet neither the debates in the Assembly nor the interminable seventy-two-hour sitting at which each deputy cast his vote took place in an atmosphere as heavy and anguished as one might imagine. Quite the contrary, according to Mercier, who saw things better than any outside witness could, as he was a member of the Assembly. He writes:

> The back of the hall was converted into boxes, as in a theatre, and in which ladies wearing the most charming attire ate ices and oranges and drank liqueurs. Members would go to pay their respects to one or the other and then return to their seats. The ushers took the part of the women who show you to your box at the Opéra. All the time one could see them opening the doors of reserved sections of the galleries and gallantly ushering in the mistresses of the Duke of Orleans, ladies caparisoned with tricolour ribbons. Although all signs of approval or disapproval were forbidden, nevertheless, from where members of the *Montagne* ultra-revolutionary party were sitting the Amazon of the Jacobin faction would utter long, loud laughs when she was not howling for the death penalty. The topmost galleries, kept open for the common people, were always filled with foreigners and people from all walks of life. They drank wine and brandy, as if they were in some low, smoke-filled tavern. At all the cafés in the neighbourhood bets were being laid on the outcome.

It was not until the royal head had rolled from the guillotine that the capital really grasped the gravity of the act that had just taken place. On that day, 'everyone walked slowly, and we hardly dared look at one another', a spectator was to say later, and the *Révolutions de Paris*, not noted for any tenderness towards Louis XVI, was forced to admit that 'the women in general looked very sad' and that the city took on 'a mournful air'.

But we must not expect too long a period of mourning. In a few weeks, a few days perhaps, all the quartiers had returned to their normal ways of life. In the Champs-Elysées the spring of '93 was particularly beautiful. The police spy Dutard, who was anything but a Jacobin, notes, in the month of May, that 'moderates, aristocrats, landed gentry and very nicely turned-out young ladies were all enjoying the caressing warmth of the springtime zephyrs'. And he added:

> It was a charming sight. This simultaneous concurrence of the return of spring and the emergence of a new order in our politics seemed to make even the old ladies look delighted. Everybody was laughing; I was the only one who did not laugh.[6]

It was, in fact, no time for laughing, because the real Terror was about to begin. It was divided into two periods: one from July to December 1793, the other corresponding to Robespierre's dictatorship, from March to July 1794. It was then that from the Grande Chambre du Palais, transformed into the Revolutionary Tribunal, there went out those lists of the condemned which sent forty to sixty victims to their death every day. In the forty-nine final days, more than fifteen hundred heads fell 'like slates off a roof', to borrow the ingenious metaphor of Fouquier-Tinville.

What was the reaction in Paris to these daily hecatombs? At first, a certain astonishment, and very soon sheer indifference. The people of Paris became so accustomed to seeing pass down the Rue Saint-Honoré those tumbrils proceeding to the former Place Louis-XV, and others, in the Rue Saint-Antoine, rumbling towards the Place du Trône Renversé, that it very soon found such spectacles quite normal and attached no more importance to them than to any ordinary event in the daily life of the city – someone drowning in the Seine or a runaway horse.

It was only when the executions were accompanied by melodramatic circumstances that they affected the sensibilities of the masses: General Custine weeping into his grey walrus moustache and his beautiful daughter wringing her hands;

the Du Barry howling with fright; Camille Desmoulins shaking off his manacles; Danton bellowing in thunderous tones; or, on the final day, Robespierre unable to check an animal yelp when the executioner's assistant tore off the bandage on his fractured jaw.

Such things stirred a public no longer frightened by the sight of blood. But apart from these star performances, there were so many monotonous ones which were given only the most cursory of side-glances. People got used to the horrors. After such a long run, the guillotine was no longer packing them in.

THE LACK OF PROVISIONS

If the face of Paris nevertheless darkened a little it was much less for political or sentimental reasons than through purely material causes. Every day, eight hundred thousand people found it more and more difficult to make ends meet. There was a lack of provisions, food was dear: such was the plague that descended upon the capital as on the rest of the country.

These inconveniences were as old as the Revolution; indeed they preceded it by several months. It will be remembered that in the spring of 1789 food supplies for the great city were already in a precarious position. The bad harvest of the year before, speculative buying, local outbreaks of pillaging in the countryside, all these things combined to prevent supplies from arriving in the normal way; the result was dark, sour bread that was difficult to digest, a really national loaf in the sense that it gave the whole population the skitters.

All the same, it was a rare commodity and people clamoured for it as if for some precious luxury. More than once the bakers had threatened to shut up shop, more than once poor old Bailly, seeing the warehouses of Corbeil and Nogent-sur-Seine completely empty, had wondered how his electors were going to eat the next day.

Many troubles were caused simply by this daily worry, this state of strained nerves of a crowd terrorized by famine.

Fortunately, at first everything was put on a well-organized footing. The provinces came to the help of the capital; once again the highways bore a stream of carts carrying fine big sacks of wheat. Twelve months later, people were still doing all right, thanks to a harvest which this time had been good.

Nothing better proves the restored balance of the economy than the prices in the restaurants in 1790. Apart from houses like Méot frequented by rich society and where, for eight to ten *livres*, one could regale oneself with repasts worthy of Lucullus and served on silver dishes, the customer of moderate means could dine Chez Trianon, Rue de Boucheries Saint-Germain, or at a good restaurant in the Rue des Petits-Pères at a cost of less than thirty *sous*. Even more modest establishments, of which there were many in the city, offered for ten *sous* soup, boiled beef, an entrée and a small glass of wine.

Such was the 'high cost of living' at the time of Federation, and enough to justify the high morale of the Parisians.

There were no great changes the following year. A young man belonging to Besançon, Claude-Ferdinand Faivre, nineteen years old and son of a former parliamentary attorney, arriving from his country home towards the end of July, was astonished at the good food he had, not only in Paris, but at every stage of his journey. There had been a series of blow-outs all the way from Besançon. At the posting-house in Auxonne, they had eaten a carp of twelve pounds, quaffed champagne at Troyes and taken with them a hamper of bottles to wash down, as they went along, cold fowl, pastries, an enormous basket of apricots; and everyone had drunk so well, and laughed and sung so much that when they finally got down at the stagecoach terminus, our young fellow could hardly walk straight.

After eight hours' sleep had more or less restored him to health, he drove to a restaurant. The dining-room was all hung with mirrors. One could choose anything one wanted from a most impressive menu, yet the prices seemed very reasonable, for the young man writes to his father thus:

I was served a potage with vermicelli, enough to fill two ordinary soup-plates, then a big portion of mutton with greens, good bread and the whole for fourteen *sous* a course and two *sous* for the bread. One course was enough for two people . . .[7]

A land of milk and honey, obviously!

THE SCARCITY BECOMES COMPLETE

The same abundance was to last until, the general situation having degenerated very badly, prices shot up of themselves. Then a thousand difficulties made themselves felt almost at the same time: the *assignat*[8] had scarcely been issued before its value dropped thirty per cent; there was the necessity of feeding, as well as the state of things allowed those armies which had departed for the frontiers; there was the insurrection in La Vendée, depriving the rest of the country of a daily average provision of six hundred head of cattle; and finally there was the uneasiness of country districts which, in order not to have to sell their grain at a low price, hid it in the most unlikely places and escaped requisitions. After that, it is hardly astonishing that the provisioning of Paris, difficult enough for the last two years, should have become a grave problem by the beginning of 1793.

Henceforward, each month was to have its crisis: shortage of soap and sugar at the end of February; shortage of bread at the end of May and in June; fresh soap shortage at the end of June; fresh bread shortage at the end of July and in August, when drought stopped the mills. Queues began forming again at the doors of bakeries, and those interminable waits, in which nerves were frayed and bodies chilled, sometimes lasted from midnight until eleven o'clock next morning.

Sometimes, too, when the housewives reached the door it was only to be told that stocks were exhausted and they had to go back home empty-handed. And they had better not cause a disturbance! If they did, buckets of cold water would be thrown over them from the first-floor windows to show

95

them that despite everything service would still be maintained. This is what happened one morning in front of a bakery in the Faubourg Saint-Honoré, a few steps from the Hôtel de Beauveau, if we are to believe a police spy, Grivel.[9]

Despite the fixed prices decreed on September 28, despite the bread-cards that had been issued thirty days earlier, despite the propaganda extolling the virtues of 'civic fasting', despite the vegetable-plots in the Luxembourg and Tuileries gardens, the famine only grew worse. High prices were paid for watered wine, 'a frightful mixture of pernicious drugs – alum, brandy and litharge', a poison all the more treacherous in that it offered 'a suavity that encourages one to drink'. Nor were complaints about meat any less vociferous. The butchers put in their scales the heads and hooves of oxen and told their customers: 'So much for fixed prices! If you don't like it, you can b——y well lump it!'[10] As for groceries, vegetables, eggs or butter, the cooks and mothers of families 'for the most part weak and timid', dared not say no to sellers who charged far more than the official price. But discontent grew, and some dock-workers, sitting with their women in a restaurant in the neighbourhood of La Pitié, did not scruple to grumble, in January 1794: 'These Paris shopkeepers are all scum of the earth . . . They'd better look out! The good old guillotine's always there!'

As the maximum price was so difficult to observe, the Committee of Public Safety could find no other solution than to raise it a little. It had intended, as Barère has said, 'to cure trade, not kill it'. But the new prices that were posted on March 25 found favour neither with shopkeepers nor their customers. The butchers practised their criminal cheating more than ever, and housewives opined that 'paying ten *sous* for ox jawbones makes a dear dish'.[11] The meat-rationing cards put out the next month only went to prove the scantiness of provisions and the smallness of portions. From then on, Paris was to feed herself like a city under seige.

Alas, yet more privations lay in store! As cattle grew scarce there was soon a shortage of fat too. So it was adieu to candles and tapers, to all the gaiety of night life. True, one could have recourse to small oil-lamps. But then, as Citizen Jacquier, national district agent, notes in his report, 'the fine days and the cool of the evenings make people want to extend their walks and conversations; so one does not notice so much the lack of candles'.[12]

They were then in mid-July. But when the month of December arrived, people were likely to be less poetic. Lighting restrictions were followed by fuel restrictions, for heaven alone knows how much a bucket of coals or a sack of logs would cost! The winter of '93–94 was a sad one in which the Parisians caught chilblains in front of their empty fireplaces and pneumonia, at night, as they waited in line for the opening of markets next morning.

THE GOOD AND BAD EFFECTS OF THE MAXIMUM PRICE ORDER

During this so critical period, one item of first importance – flour – was fairly well protected by the maximum price order. Thanks to this, the gap between the two harvests could be bridged without too much difficulty. But in all other items, what frauds were committed! What illicit speculative buyings! On May 17, at the house of one Dubois, a pastrycook in the section des Lombards, there were seized 'two hundred pounds of fresh butter, one hundred pounds of it melted, three thousand eggs and thirty-four hams',[13] all merchandise probably destined for restaurant supplies, as were all prime cuts of meat which certain butchers sold under the counter, in defiance of the price order.

It was even less respected in several suburban communes, notably in Vincennes, where many a gourmet, sending his cook to do the shopping, had to pay six francs a pound for lamb. 'We should be idiots to take our beef and pork to Paris,' said the local butchers, 'when the Parisians come to us and give whatever we ask.'

But let us not lose a sense of perspective. Thanks to various stratagems, some tables remained well-supplied, but the majority of the population was then suffering great hardships. There was still not the great famine which the maximum price order unleashed after Thermidor, but in the less fortunate classes there was already real suffering: very few people ate their fill.

And this is why, twenty years later, someone who escaped the Terror defined it in this way: 'A violent political crisis complicated by no less violent crises in the guts.'

CHAPTER ELEVEN

RURAL FRANCE DURING THE TERROR

The failure of the harvests from 1793 – *Potato production* – *Morale and state of mind in various areas* – *The clash between Catholicism and the Civil Code in the country districts*

THE FAILURE OF THE HARVESTS FROM 1793

As the Revolution continued the rôle played in it by country districts became ever greater. As war had paralysed foreign imports, the material life of the country depended almost entirely on the number of sacks of wheat it could gather in each year from its own fields. Therefore a good or a bad harvest took on the importance of a battle lost or won.

The harvests of 1792 had been excellent, and a German, Charles Laukhard, noted this, not without astonishment, in the month of August, as soon as the frontier was crossed:[1] 'Among other fictions,' he declared,

> émigrés have gulled us with the tale that as a consequence of the anarchy reigning over all the land the French had almost totally stopped cultivating their fields. This was an impudent lie, as was proved by the condition of the countryside in Lorraine as well as in Clermont and in Champagne, a poor, barren region. Here agriculture was manifestly in a flourishing condition, the gardens well tended and the villages exhibiting the diligence and wellbeing of their inhabitants.

The harvests of 1793 promised to be no less fruitful if we

99

are to believe Bédigis, a spy for the Home Secretary, who wrote from Dieppe on July 14:

> Everything seems to be in the best possible state, particularly the various kinds of corn, rye, barley, oats and other grains. Flax suffered a little from lack of rain and fruit trees were affected by the cold. There will not be much cider.[2]

Despite these prognostications, the actual results were meagre, as there was no rain at all. On the other hand, the farmers, put out by the maximum price level, often refused to despatch their corn. So that during the following winter the Parisians suffered a very severe food crisis.

There was the same disappointment with the harvest of 1794, damaged by storms, and with that of 1795, which was simply disastrous, after a summer with no sun at all. These seasonal caprices were unfortunate for the Republic.

POTATO PRODUCTION

How to remedy the lack of grain? It was not so long since Parmentier had published his celebrated *Treatise on the Uses of the Potato*. This was remembered, and agents left for all parts of the country to encourage its production, but their crusade must have been an arduous one, for another report from Bédigis, addressed from Cany on September 5, 1793, tells us that farm workers in the Caux district were still ignorant of the advantages of the precious tuber.

More fortunate was Cathala, the dramatist turned agronomist, when the government gave him the task of exploring the Midi as a potato missionary. Not only did the peasants of the Ariège cultivate this vegetable, but they even extracted from it flour which they mingled with true flour milled from wheat. This was a good piece of news for the Home Secretary. 'I arrived at Peyrat,'[3] the representative writes,

> a village near the Pyrenees. I was welcomed by a farmer and his family. A table loaded with *white truffles*[4] prepared

in various appetizing ways caused me to forget the lack of more tempting delicacies, and bread white as snow, fresh and tasty, though baked a fortnight ago, rejoiced my eyes and stirred my appetite. I tucked into it . . . Sixty pounds of wheat flour mixed with two big panfuls of boiled potatoes produced more than a hundred and sixty pounds of bread. I cried: 'This is the miracle of the loaves without the fishes!'

There was one drawback, Cathala said. Potatoes have to be consumed as quickly as possible. If they could be stored like corn or millet, however, what a splendid source of nourishment they would provide for the people! But the lady of the house had forestalled his objection, and, opening a cupboard drew out a bag full of small potato-rings that had been dried and put away fifteen months ago and thus had been miraculously preserved. All that was needed was to grind them down in order to make superb flour. The miller was not a little put out by this form of competition!

At this, Cathala's enthusiasm knew no bounds. He kissed the august bag of potatoes, bowed before the 'consecrated bread', and, as he found himself in the mood for religious oratory, ended on this note: 'How different, dear God, from the bag of St Francis which was used to feed the pigs!'

MORALE AND STATE OF MIND IN VARIOUS AREAS

The economic map of France during the Terror still has to be drawn. Regions which experienced civil or foreign conflicts, namely the northern frontier, the valley of the Rhône, Brittany and La Vendée, were naturally the ones worst affected, but the problem of supplies arose everywhere and depended nine times out of ten on local production, each district living on its own products.

It would be much more difficult to draw up a map indicating the morale and the state of mind of the various areas. Enormous differences would be found between provinces and even between one village and the next: here politics would dominate everything, there it would be almost totally neglected. This at least is what emerges from the accounts of contemporaries travelling round the country at that time. Of course, one must keep in mind the travellers' own political convictions, which might tend to make some of their testimonies one-sided.

When Brissot fled the capital after the Girondins' debacle, he passed through Gien, on June 9, and saw only strained and anxious faces.[5] In all the thirty-six leagues he had just travelled, and even though he was travelling on a Sunday, only once had he heard the strains of a violin played by a fiddler for a country dance. In the towns, the men, gathered near the post office, were agog for news, for the suppression of almost all the daily papers had cut them off completely from sources of information. Customers at inns hardly dared speak to one another for fear of denunciations, but they tried to read in the eyes of arriving travellers whether things were going well or ill.

There were almost no more coaches on the roads. All that remained were a few small, rickety old conveyances hauled by a single horse and these provided the sole means of communication between one district and the next. The postmasters told Brissot that they sometimes went for three days without seeing a single stagecoach. And how could one travel when 'at each village one had to get out, show one's passport, reply to interrogations, and, at the least suspicion, appear before an examining committee, then cool one's heels in a detention-house until such time as things were leisurely cleared-up'?

This was a region that Jacobin politics did not seem to have enlivened very much. But if we had gone the following month to the Jura district, with two observers, Adant and Saunier, as soon as we arrived at Dôle the picture would be quite different. We would have found there citizens aflame with love of their blessed *Patrie*, all firm *sans-culottistes* worthy of the Faubourg Saint-Antoine itself.

Their People's Society happened to be celebrating, on July 15, the signature of the Bill of Constitution, and the festivities which took place on that occasion enchanted our two observers: 'Illuminations, cannon salutes, civic parades, patriotic songs and bonfires surpassed anything known in Sparta,'[6] they exclaimed in their report. And as far as the cannon goes, it must certainly have been the case.

Elsewhere, enthusiasm was manifested in less costly ways. One charming initiative was that taken on November 19, 1795, by the People's Society at Rodez, when it decided that 'the Watch Committee shall take upon itself the task of shaving off the moustaches of all those who are not worthy of sporting them'. A charitable footnote declared that the operation would be performed 'as a dry shave, and with the bluntest razor possible . . .'[7] Fascists already!

We cannot expect all French communes to exhibit such a wealth of imagination. Even at the height of the Terror, many villages and small towns scarcely seemed to think politics was anything to bother their heads about. In many a country district people were mainly trying to find ways of not dying of hunger, of running their lives somehow or other, often by makeshift methods, of meeting military requisitions, of implementing the thousand and one decrees issued from Paris and which the poor rustic municipalities had so much difficulty in deciphering. They lived from day to day and never looked too far afield; nor could they always understand the march of those events on which the fate of the country hung. In his dry daily commonplace book, an Evreux bourgeois, Nicolas Rogue, whom we have already quoted,[8] mentions neither August 10 nor the massacres of September, nor does he make the slightest allusion to IX Thermidor. On the other hand, he is careful to note that several local thoroughfares have changed their name and that the former Rue des Prêtres (Priest Street) has become the *Rue des Maris*, or Husbands Street.

If we move across to the Manche, we find the inhabitants of the commune des Pieux[9] going on with the election of their mayor, their deputies, their watch committee, planting a Tree of Liberty, later lighting bonfires in honour of the fall of

Toulon. But they are even more interested in the requisitioning of horses, in the official prices charged for butter and eggs, in short, in all the little problems which condition rural life.

Even much nearer Paris, people's mentality hardly changes. We have only to glance through the records of the deliberations of the commune de Vanvres (present-day Vanves) to sense that they were written by an Assembly composed of country folk preoccupied by local affairs. In them there is talk of the price of bread, of smuggled casks of wine, of troubles in the market. Sometimes a band of housewives would invade the meeting-room and demand food. Or else there would be complaints about the schoolmaster who had taken over the keeping of the communal records from the priest, but who had one great fault – he couldn't write.

To bring us back to the realization that we are at the gates of the capital, only a league from the Convention, we find a laundress coming one day and making a curious request. She worked for the Château de Vanvres, whose masters are now in prison. Therefore all their last wash has been left on her hands. As the municipality is now responsible for the château, it should pay the bill! And the good woman unloaded her pile of linen on the council table, where big peasant fingers pawed over it with loud guffaws: the chemises and petticoats of the Princess de Lamballe . . .

THE CLASH BETWEEN CATHOLICISM AND THE CIVIL CODE IN THE COUNTRY DISTRICTS

For the provinces and the country districts the substitution of a civic and patriotic religion for the Roman Catholic cult was probably the most considerable event in the whole revolutionary era. Among the sworn priests the movement found more than one enthusiastic apostle, such as Bias, curé of Boissise-la-Bertrand, in the region of Melun, who wrote on March 2, 1793, to the editors of *La Feuille Villageoise*:[10]

Brethren and friends,

Yesterday I gave the nuptial benediction to Citizen Nicolas

Lefebvre, curé of Nandy, and Citizeness Jeanne-Geneviève Charpin who, the same day, had both gone through a ceremony of marriage with the public officer of the place. Naturally I was invited to the wedding-feast. If we did not dance, we sang, among other things some couplets composed by the curé of Nandy himself and which had been addressed to me.

The honourable officiant reminds the editors that he, too, is a poet. He had already sent some of his own couplets to *La Feuille Villageoise*, which had not printed them, but their author shows no resentment. He simply wants to defend the cause of French Song which, according to him, ought to replace the stupid litanies sung in church:

It is my considered opinion that we must make the People *sing* again! Instead of all that mish-mash of lying complaints and superstitious canticles, instead of the torrents of obscene songs with which we are flooded, particularly since the Revolution, let us choose wise, reasonable and patriotic songs!

There was one air which our curé had a special admiration for, and this preference may well have surprised any disreputable aristocrats and timorous old maids who might have been left in his parish: 'I rejoiced,' he goes on ardently,

when I saw in your number 3, a copy of *La Marseillaise*. Although I know not a note of music, helped by plain-chant I managed to decipher it and have sung it two Sundays running for my citizens under arms, at the foot of the Tree of Liberty. My little parish provided ten volunteers, all armed and equipped and fairly well trained; also the government of the district of Melun saw fit to make honourable mention of this in its report.

And he ends with this admission:

I prefer to sing with my fellow-citizens rather than with my parishioners . . . As soon as I know a good song, I take it to the school; there it is copied out and sung. This is the way to teach people, without tears!

After civic marriages came patriotic baptisms. On June 30, 1793, at Aurou, in the Bouches-du-Rhône, the commissioners sent by the Marseilles section to make federalist propaganda received a numerous deputation begging them to stand godfathers to a babe of the female sex. This ceremony took place with the support of municipal officers wearing the tricolour sash, National Guards and the 'orchestra directed by the worthy pastor of the parish'. The infant was called Paule-Martine-Marseille, and as the crowd gathered outside the church began to dance the deputation was greeted by loud applause: 'Long live the Commissioners! Long live Marseilles!'

Such examples should not lead the reader to assume that the de-Christianization of the provinces and country districts became general in 1793. Without speaking of the peasants of La Vendée and Brittany who rose in revolt to defend their priests, many regions remained faithful to their beliefs, and even in districts where religious observances were officially prohibited, they were not given up altogether.

In the course of his travels in the south-western districts Cathala could not help noticing the obstinate devotion of the people in the Gironde.

> Passing through Souillac, 1 went through a hamlet where all the inhabitants were on their knees at their doors. I asked why: I was told that vespers were being said one league from there.

Even the most diehard Jacobins were to be struck soon by the persistence of religious feeling in certain country districts and realized the dangers that might lie in attacking them too violently: 'Citizens and colleagues,' Robespierre writes from Nice to the members of the Committee of General Safety, 'tyrants have always recruited their armies through extravagances committed against religious worship.' And he writes more precisely, in a letter to his brother at the beginning of 1794:

> Everywhere we have been preceded by the Terror. The émigrés had persuaded people that we were destroying religion . . . The entire population of forty thousand souls in the valley of Oneille took flight. We encountered neither women nor children nor old people.[11]

How could the leaders of opinion not be impressed by such direct eye-witness accounts? In the battle against fanaticism they realized they had gone too far. Danton was one of the first to demand that 'a stop should be made'. Robespierre ordered the Convention to respect the liberty of worship which it had proclaimed: 'Ever since my high-school days,' he added, 'I have been a rather bad Catholic . . . But that does not mean I am not strongly attached to the moral and political ideas which I have just put forward. If God did not exist, he would have to be invented.'[12] And suave Hébert went one better than this:

> I preach the Gospel to the people in the countryside, and tell them to read it. This book of moral precepts seems to me excellent and if one follows its maxims one becomes a perfect Jacobin. It seems to me that Christ was the founder of People's Societies.[13]

Hearing Père Duchesne talk in such a way, what must a *sans-culotte* of Nièvre or Corrèze have thought, after so many months spent in a shameless hounding of the priesthood? His village church is shut up, the chalices and the ciboria from the sacristy had been despatched to swell the Treasury. The curé of the parish had finally thrown his robes into the nettles on the dung-heap or had married his servant. And now there comes along a circular from the Committee of Public Safety proclaiming that 'consciences are not to be commanded', and Robespierre affirms that liberty of worship still exists!

One might as well try to make people believe that pears grow on apple-boughs and that the democratic red cabbage has become a Roman salad!

CHAPTER TWELVE

HOSTESS TO ROBESPIERRE

An ardent bourgeois patriot – Her walks in the Tuileries and Hôtel de Ville – The Robespierre family dine with Mme Jullien – Impressions of the great man – Tender maternal correspondence

AN ARDENT BOURGEOIS PATRIOT

Descriptions of daily life in Paris, during the period from 1792 to 1794 emanate principally from the bourgeois class. The aristocrats wrote little. Many of them are abroad and making frequent changes of residence; others hide in the interior, trying to let themselves be forgotten. The common people, the *sans-culottes*, either do not know how to handle a pen or else are caught up in the thick of events and scarcely have time to uncork their ink-bottles. While on the other hand the old French bourgeoisie preserved its former epistolary habits, so that every day the things they saw and all the great changes they witnessed merely developed an established taste for letter-writing.

One family will prove this: let us now attempt to penetrate the intimate life of that family by looking through the correspondence of Mme Jullien.

HER WALKS IN THE TUILERIES AND HÔTEL DE VILLE

Mme Jullien[1] was the wife of a future deputy of the Drôme at the Convention. The household had two sons: Marc-Antoine-Jules – who will later call himself Jullien de Paris and who, after having served in the armies of the First Empire, was to become, in 1819, one of the founders of the

Constitutionel – and Auguste, still only a young boy. While M Jullien was staying at Romans, in June and July 1792, Marc-Antoine made a trip to England. All the more reason why the letters from their remarkable mother, who had remained behind in the capital, should be particularly abundant.

She was an ardent patriot. She was passionately interested in political life, and as she knew how to see and describe things, not only did she give us a very personal chronicle of contemporary events but also in so doing sketched countless little picturesque tableaux which help us to reconstruct the fevered atmosphere of Paris before August 10.

Mme Jullien's favourite observation-post was the terrace of the Tuileries that lies along the banks of the Seine. Whenever she went walking there towards evening it was very rare for her not to be present at some sensational event.

Thus it was that on May 22, 1792, about six o'clock in the evening, she saw a battalion commander strike a vendor who was selling Jacobin posters. A crowd at once collected, took the vendor's side, mauled the officer, howled him down, trounced him and pursued him as far as the guardhouse, where a detachment of the National Guard tried to give him some protection.

Scarcely had peace been restored than yet another wave began to rise in that rough-tempered sea. This time it was the poet Roucher who had tried to harangue a group. So much the worse for him, because in order to extinguish his flame there was talk of throwing him in the fountain. Fortunately there came along a justice of the peace waving his little white stick,[2] and before this symbol of the law the uproar soon ceased. Those were the days when a white stick, which today can halt only motor-cars, was able to disperse a crowd of demonstrators!

The terrace of the Feuillants offered even more exciting spectacles at the beginning of August, when the Duke of Brunswick's manifesto was thrown defiantly at Paris and when the pulse of the great city beat at one hundred and twenty a minute. Mme Jullien spent long hours then at the Tuileries, 'a delicious spot for the true lovers of Liberty'. She marvelled at the number of people walking about there every day and at the way they respected the silken cordon which barred the forbidden areas of the garden, called ironically 'Coblenz' or 'Austria'.

If she hadn't had little Auguste with her, her great wish would have been to be present at the debates in the Assembly. But however Roman she might feel, she was still a mother. How could one think of exposing a growing lad to that sink of iniquity? 'My little Auguste takes away the great desire I have,' she writes to her husband on August 7. All the same, three days later, she would have witnessed a fine old sitting . . .

Now the inevitable had happened. The King had been dethroned and taken captive. The event quite staggered Mme Jullien.

> I am like that National Guardsman in our quartier whose hat was pierced by a bullet and two of whose comrades were killed at his side: yet all this had no effect on him at all. Only later that evening, thinking over what had happened, did he come all over queer: he turned bilious, and was suddenly stricken with jaundice, as if a painter had taken a brush and daubed his face bright yellow. This is how I feel when I sit down later and think of all the dangers we escaped.[3]

But the Parisian spirit is infinitely accommodating and, six days later, we learn that Mme Jullien had recovered from her nasty shock. She had been to the Hôtel de Ville and saw there Federal representatives from all the eighty-three administrative regions of France, who, to the music of Basque violins, were dancing bourrées and périgourdines with a charming grace:

> They seemed only just to have arrived and were dressed anyhow, all of them looking so strange that one felt they must have come from the farthest outposts of the Empire.

Conclusion:

> Gracious, how gay and pleasant a Frenchman can be! He scatters roses everywhere he goes . . .[4]

THE ROBESPIERRE FAMILY DINE WITH MME JULLIEN

Our republican bourgeois lady already had numerous acquaintances, but among the people who frequented her house there was soon to be a person of the first rank, the deputy whom the Parisians had elected above all others to represent them at the Convention. That man was Robespierre.

The entire Robespierre family – Maximilien, Augustin and Charlotte – came to dine with the Jullien ménage on February 2, 1793, and for the mistress of the house it was an event of such importance that she hastened to impart the news to her son Marc-Antoine, then resident in Toulouse:

> I am going to meet that patriotic family whose head has so many friends and so many enemies. I am most curious to see him close to.

On the great day, Charlotte arrived two hours before her brothers, and her good breeding enchanted her hostess: 'Just the same as we are, simple and open.'[5] With her, she felt she could talk 'as woman to woman', ask endless questions about Maximilien and gather certain bits of information about which we cannot help but feel surprise:

> Her brother had as little to do with August 10 as he had with September 2. He is about as fitted to lead a party as to land on the moon. He is as abstract as a philosopher; he is dry as a business man: but he is gentle as a lamb and moody as Young's *Night Thoughts*.

IMPRESSIONS OF THE GREAT MAN

With her meridional temperament, Mme Jullien was quick to descry the character of the man from the north:

I can see that he does not possess *our* sensibility; but I like to think that he wants to be a benefactor to the human race through the exercise of justice rather than love.

And when Maximilien made his appearance it was enough to look at him to realize that 'never did Nature give such sweet features to so noble a soul'. His brother, on the other hand, was the object of some criticism. Excellent patriot though he was, he seemed 'to have a common mind and a petulant humour which have earned him an unfavourable reputation at La Montagne'.

This first meeting of the two families was to be followed by others. Mme Jullien's housekeeping book tells us for example the menu of a second dinner in honour of Robespierre to which Robert Lindet was also invited.[6] On that day, prices were as follows: milk and cream, 14 *sous*; two loaves, 24 *sous*; vegetables, 6 *sous*; salad, 10 *sous*; oil, 2 *sous*; vinegar, 12 *sous*; pepper, 5 *sous*; cheese, 1 *sou*; cider (probably on Lindet's account, as he was a Norman), 18 *sous*; a fat pullet, 8 *livres* 10 *sous*.

Despite police reports in 1793 which mention the high cost of goods as 'the principal cause of agitations and unrest',[7] the housewives of the twentieth century will probably find these prices extremely reasonable and will be astonished that one *sou*'s worth of cheese should have been enough for six guests.

TENDER MATERNAL CORRESPONDENCE

The friendship of a great man is a gift from the gods. Through favourable paternal relationships, the elder Jullien boy was given important missions in the west and south,[8] but if we are to believe his mother, there could be no one better fitted for such a distinction. All the letters which the excellent lady addresses to Marc-Antoine-Jules brag of his precocious merits in a style inspired by Jean-Jacques Rousseau but in which her maternal sensibility sometimes strikes a most attractive note: 'You are not a youthful person,' she had written the year before,[9]

> because you began thinking of yourself at an early age. Your dear papa always told me – and you know that I take whatever he says to me as Gospel – that his good little Jules, if left to his own devices, would never put a foot wrong, because the quality of his soul and his habit of reflection would make him walk straight along all those paths that lead to perfection. Your dear papa loves you tenderly.

But what has she to say about herself? Not a day passes in which her thoughts are not with her son. She is delighted when she hears the news that he is studying Italian with a certain Signor Bosellini, for she says it is the language of the tender-hearted:

> Your dear papa and I are overjoyed to hear your news; but alas I am just a silly-billy who could only remember enough of it to read Metastasio with your dear little brother and to call you *mio tesoro, mio amico*. Do you know that I could say 'I love you' in almost any language if you asked me to? But only that one phrase, because I'm a slow learner.

We must compliment her on her frankness. If Mme Jullien had been *une femme savante*, one of those redoubtable Molièresque bluestockings, she would probably have left us a mass of pretentious memoirs like those of Mme Roland, and we should have lost those letters full of amusing details about the daily life of a Parisian family.

CHAPTER THIRTEEN

A BOURGEOIS FAMILY DURING THE TERROR

The pleasant existence of a Parisian family in 1793 and 1794 – Citizeness Ziguette – The amusements of a thirteen-year-old during the Revolution – Home life – Visits, musical soirées, country parties

---

THE PLEASANT EXISTENCE OF A PARISIAN FAMILY IN 1793 AND 1794

What a pity that M Louis de Launay has not told us the name of the C—— family introduced to us in his recent study! To be told that it acquired a well-merited reputation in letters and the arts makes us wish to know more about it, all the more so as few documents depict more wittily the daily life of a bourgeois family during the Revolution.[1]

The action takes place in the year II. The star is a young person named Ziguette – less familiarly known as Emilie – who at thirteen is chaperoned by a governess, Mlle G——, who is not much older than her pupil. She learns to play the piano forte on a fine new Erard which had cost a hundred and fifty *livres*, studies painting with David and Chaudet and follows the lectures of La Harpe at the Lycée.

Her family consists of an architect father who, lacking commissions in Paris, has gone to build a theatre in the provinces.[2] A mother fifty years old, a brother who is going into the army in September '93, and a married sister, Mme S——, wife of an advocate. The parents live in the Rue Saint-Marc, but as they possess in Auteuil a little summer residence and a vineyard – there were still vineyards there at that time! – just next to an estate belonging to Hubert Robert, they went to rest there a little during the spring of the year II.

Although horse-requisitioning had made carriages rather scarce, they also made a few excursions round Saint-Prix and in the forest of Montmorency. Then they returned to the Rue Saint-Marc, which they did not care for very much, not so much because of events as because of the extreme heat.

Mme C—— complains of it in a letter to her husband on July 19, 1793:

> Your Emilie (Ziguette), that worldly little miss, forces me to go with her almost every evening to the Boulevard de la Comédie Italienne in order to enjoy what she calls the fresh air: the real reason is that it is the fashionable promenade, with everybody on each other's heels.

Let us keep in mind that on July 19, six days after Marat's assassination, at a time when the country was torn between civil war and foreign strife, when the Federalists were holding Lyons, Bordeaux, Marseilles and Toulon, on the day after the Vendéan victory at Vihiers, on the eve of the surrenders of Mayence and Valenciennes, Parisians still went on patrolling along the boulevards of an evening. In fact, nothing could be more natural; why, then, do so many people insist on seeing the Revolution merely through the narrow window of the guillotine?

Twice or thrice a week, Mme C—— invited to dinner those 'good Republicans' who were charged with the education of Emilie: the Chaudet ménage, Lebrun-Pindare, the dramatist Després and the composer Pradère. The food is still not very ascetic, though the hostess calls it very poor: herb soup, small collar or brisket of lamb or mutton, turnips, potatoes, cheese, sometimes a ham omelette.

We should have known much less about Mlle Ziguette if her young governess had not had the excellent idea of keeping a journal, from January 16 to May 9, 1794, in order to amuse the head of the family, who was away from Paris during that period. She also entertains us, for her confidences are of the highest order, which is our excuse for quoting them somewhat abundantly. At a time when politics overlapped literature and when the style of so many writers was spoilt by rhetoric, it is a great pleasure to discover, from the pen of a young lady, a verve and naturalness worthy of the best eighteenth-century writing.

CITIZENESS ZIGUETTE

The first page of the journal sets the tone:

This is how we spend our days! Citizeness Ziguette leaves at ten o'clock, after having partaken of a fairly spartan breakfast and practised her pianoforte fairly assiduously. She trips away with a great clatter of sabots, hoisting up her blue skirt to expose white under-petticoats much shorter than they should be, and running like a wild Indian, hauling along Thérèse (the cook) by the arm. Thérèse carries her bouillon and bread soup in a tin container. They arrive at Citizen Chaudet's. She draws, is praised by the master. She gabbles what he has said to her as soon as she is back home, about three or four o'clock . . . As she reaches the top step of the stairs I hear her shout: 'Food! I'm starving to death!' Alarmed quite by this ogrish hunger, we make haste to sit down to table where each of us, over a good meal, commends the merits of her sketches. But no appetite equals that of Ziguette. Finally we leave the table. She rests, jumps on the chairs and acts the imp, if we are alone . . . Then there is pianoforte practice until lights are brought in, no longer wax but tallow candles, plain and simple. Then we read Ovid or Horace until about seven o'clock, when we begin to read for instruction or entertainment, such as learning by heart some lines of Racine or from *Anacharsis*.

A studious timetable, as we can see, but one in which pleasant accomplishments hold the larger part, and grace an existence in which, apart from wax candles, there seems to be no lack of anything.

The next day, the same kind of life prevails. Ziguette, who is rather stage-struck, goes to greet her mother while the latter is still in bed drinking her coffee, and recites for her the speeches from Racine learnt the previous evening. She is told that she 'scans the rhythm by nodding her head, drops her voice at the ends of phrases, punctuates badly, does not manage her breathing well and is unable to make the best use of strong sentiments or situations'. And Mme C——, when her daughter has gone off to her painting class, finally gets up about eleven o'clock, pulling a linen *pierrot* over her nightdress, or else puts on, for special occasions, 'a taffeta frockcoat in the fashionable *boue de Paris* (Paris mud) shade. It goes *frou-frou* and gives her a somewhat dandyish air which goes very well with her very Republican bearing.'

Once she had dressed, she might go to pay a few visits, perhaps stopping on the way to call on Citizeness Hubert Robert, who works a tapestry like a latter-day Penelope while her husband paints landscapes in his hide-out at Saint-Lazare.

When January 21 arrives, it appears that the C—— family, however patriotic, did not bother much about remembering the first anniversary of the 'Tyrant's' death. Its members are more concerned with a dinner they have been invited to at Citizeness Houzeaux'. There they went, on the stroke of three, and enjoyed an excellent repast, if we are to judge by the menu: soup, cold beef and gherkin and beetroot salad; skate with browned butter for entrée. Next, a piece of stewed mutton garnished with potatoes. To stay any remaining pangs of hunger, fried soles and a dessert composed of cheeses, apples, pears, plum jam and another kind of jam called *raisiné* which is made from pears, sugar and grape juice. The whole gently bathed in a marvellous Malaga wine and screwed down firmly with cherries in brandy . . . All of which makes us more and more sceptical about the famous famine which was said to rage during the Jacobin period.

After their good dinner the ladies settled themselves round the fire and, naturally, talked about fashions. Just that afternoon as she was walking down the Rue du Bac, Mme C—— noticed in a secondhand dealer's window a ravishing frock which was just the thing for her, because, as one might expect, she hasn't a thing to wear:

'Buy it,' her friend advises her. 'I know the owner of the shop; tell her I sent you.'

Bolstered by this recommendation, as soon as the family leaves it rushes off to the Rue du Bac and purchases the ravishing frock. After a good deal of tedious haggling, they got it for twenty-two *livres*, but only think, dear, of the wear they would get out of it! Later it can be cut up to make a new skirt, a pair of bodices, slippers, gaiters . . . Thus, as they wend their way back to the Rue Saint-Marc, Mme C——, her daughter and the governess build their castles in Spain.

Alas! The next day, they had a rude awakening. The dressmaker they had called in declares that the material is quite worthless: 'Poor dress!' sighs the journal's youthful writer, 'it was the old tale of pie in the sky. Adieu, gaiters, bodices, etc! . . . We shall do well to get one new skirt out of it and bits to patch the old one with. We weep the loss of our hopes!'

The clothing problem is all the more important because the weather is so execrable. Every day it either snows or rains; roof-gutters are turned into rivers that drop vertically on the heads of passers-by. Ladies are seen 'trotting along the streets with their skirts up round their ears and their underskirt worn as a cape or a pelisse, that is, round their shoulders'.

THE AMUSEMENTS OF A THIRTEEN-YEAR-OLD DURING THE REVOLUTION

There was one obvious way of avoiding bad weather, by staying quietly at home. But the C—— family never thinks of doing that. There are all kinds of reasons to force them out of doors: shopping, visits, theatres. One must not imagine that all this type of activity stopped while the gentlemen

The Paris Scene

1 (*top*) A political discussion in the Jardin des Tuileries

2 (*bottom*) The Palais Royal, which became the forum of the Revolution

3 (*top*) The Palais Royal gallery's walk which was the meeting place of the fashionable

4 (*bottom*) A group gossiping outside the Café *Italien*

The Calendar and Fêtes

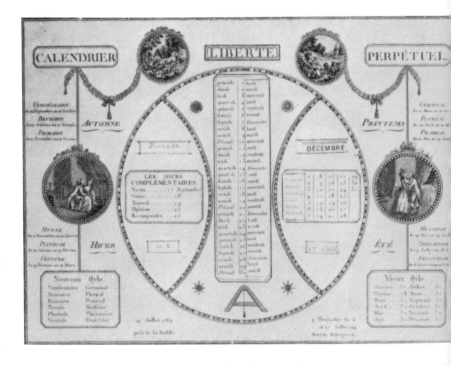

7 The new calendar that was established by the Convention in October 1793 and in force until January 1, 1806. The year consisted of ten months, each month being divided into three decades, and new names were given to the months

8 (*top*) An idolatrous fête in Notre Dame Cathedral where the Jacobins have seated an actress on the altar and are worshipping her as the Goddess of Reason

9 (*bottom*) A fête dedicated to the old

10 The Procession of Reason, which formed part of the Festival of the Supreme Being held on the 20th Prairial (June 8)

11 (*above*) Climbing
the Greasy Pole.
Part of the *Fête de la
République* which
celebrated the
storming of the
Bastille

12 (*left*) Jousts held
on the Seine to
celebrate the *Fête de
la Fédération*, held
on the 29th Messidor
(July 18)

Marriage and Children

13 (*above left*) Republican marriage. A municipal
officer is welcoming the bride and groom while
below the platform members of both families
are signing the marriage contract

14 (*left*) Republican divorce. The couple are seen
exchanging bitter words before the municipal
officer while members of both families are this
time signing the divorce papers

15 (*above*) The dedication of the child
replaced baptism during the revolution

Daily Life in Prison

16 Suspects being rounded up and taken to prison

17 (*below left*) The interior of Saint-Lazare prison drawn by Hubert Robert, one of the prisoners

18 (*below right*) The despair of the aristocratic prisoners reading the lists of those who are to die on the guillotine

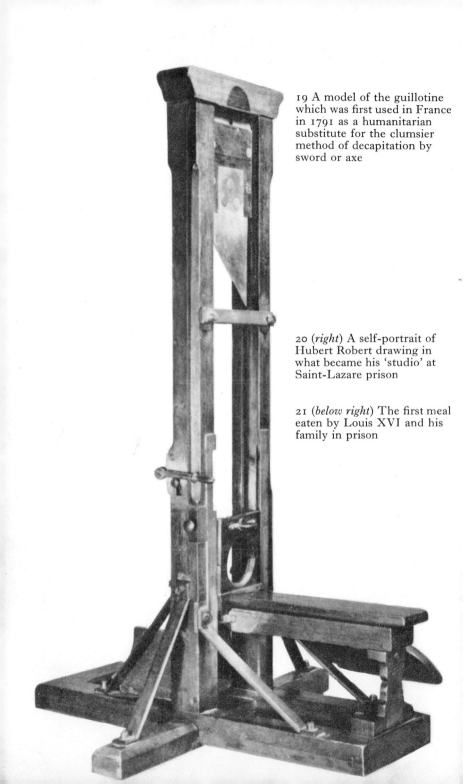

19 A model of the guillotine which was first used in France in 1791 as a humanitarian substitute for the clumsier method of decapitation by sword or axe

20 (*right*) A self-portrait of Hubert Robert drawing in what became his 'studio' at Saint-Lazare prison

21 (*below right*) The first meal eaten by Louis XVI and his family in prison

Revolutionary Events

22 The Tennis Court Oath, June 20, 1789

23 (*opposite top*) The taking of the Bastille, July 14, 1789

24 (*opposite below*) The Prince de Lambese entering the Tuileries, July 12, 1789

25 Patriotic volunteers for the National Guard, 1793

26 & 27 Two armed *sans culottes*. This name was
given to those who abandoned the elegant, old
forms of dress for the more utilitarian dress shown

28 (*top*) Attacking the Tuileries, August 19, 1792

29 (*bottom*) The siege of Lyons

Patriotic Objects

30 & 31 During the first years of the Revolution a
large number of wooden and paper fans were
made and decorated with highly coloured
pictures of contemporary events

32 (*top*) Two watches painted with patriotic figures

33 (*bottom*) Buttons moulded with figures of the National Guard

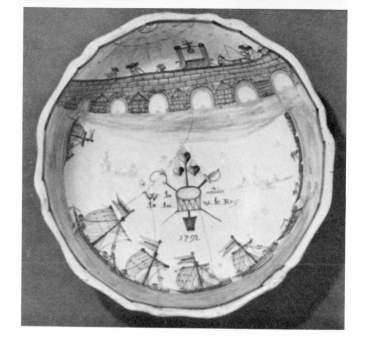

34 & 35 Two plates with patriotic designs. The top one surprisingly includes the words 'Long live the nation, the law and the king' 1792; below 'The Law and the King'

36 Official stamps
used by the
Revolutionary
Government

The Days of Marveilleuses

38 The *Incroyables*

37 (*left*) Promissory notes issued by
the Revolutionary Government, 1790–96

39 Male dress
affected during this
period

40 *La Folie du Jour*,
one of the most
popular dances of the
Directory

declaimed in their clubs and the Barrière du Trône saw processions of tumbrils pass every day.

The interest of the little governess' journal lies precisely in the fact that it shows us how little Parisian life had changed, at least for a certain class. At the Rue Saint-Marc they continued to receive visits, organized little dinner-parties, entertained each other round the fire. One day two of their guests were the painter Gérard, 'pupil of David, and bursting with talent', and the poet Lebrun, who during the dessert gave them a rendering of his *Republican Ode on the Taking of Toulon.*[3]

On another occasion, it was good old Chaudet who came to lunch. He ate a whole pot of jam and paid for it by instilling into Ziguette a few basic artistic principles: if she wants to draw a face, she must begin by sketching the skull underneath. This was David's method. No more entrancing way of making a young lady practise her talent.[4]

Or on another occasion it was the family of friends in Lyons who sent their two little boys, accompanied by their tutor, to have a good time at Mme C——'s house. For this occasion they were disguised as young patriots. They look like perfect little darlings 'with their red woollen caps, their carmagnoles and their big sticks'.[5]

There was visitor after visitor. Sometimes the illustrious Parmentier would come to greet his friends in the Rue Saint-Marc. He took advantage of the occasion to commiserate with them on the fate of the son who is bored to tears in the army and who, despite his patriotic fervour, would very much like to be at home. Then Lebrun-Pindare turns up again and is prevailed upon to give a rendition of his verses *Blue Eyes and Black Eyes.*[6] He was accorded their grateful thanks when they went to see him, one week later, in his new lodgings at the Louvre, but before reaching his door they had to pass certain domestic installations 'the smell of which seizes the nostrils from way away', and which the illustrious lodger 'finds too convenient for others and very inconvenient for himself'.

Apart from these odious appurtenances in the neighbourhood, his lodging is comfortable. But the young governess finds it lacking in imagination: 'I had prepared myself to face,' she admits, 'a fine poetic disorder; I had fully expected it; I was already laughing to myself at the thought of it; I might have been knocked over by a feather when I beheld a very neat, clean, pretty little apartment, all grace and symmetry. I was satisfied, but felt almost put-out.'[7] So much for careless romantic poets!

Another celebrity of the times whom our ladies found excessively interesting was Dominique-Joseph Garat. They braved rain and gusts of wind to go out and hear him at the Lycée giving his lecture on *The Ancient History of the Peoples of the Orient*. The lecturer arrived,

> saluted the whole Assembly, sat on a chair which was just a little too high for him and gave him the air of being perched in space, adjusted his spectacles, gazed about him, pulled an exercise book out of his pocket and gave a very eloquent and much-applauded account on the religion and customs of the Assyrians.[8]

As we may well imagine, Ziguette and Mme C—— were careful to take notes which they sent to M C—— to cheer him up in his provincial exile.

There were, however, less austere entertainments in Paris. On the evening of February 10, why did Ziguette tie her freshly curled hair with a pretty Madras ribbon, why had she put on her white *pierrot* and hung brilliants at her ears? And why had her mother brought out all her regalia? Because the family was going to the *Théâtre de la République* in the Rue de la Loi, formerly Rue Richelieu, to attend the fourth performance of a new tragedy, *Nero and Epicharis*.[9]

We must assume that the impression left by this masterpiece was a profound one, for henceforward the whole family thinks of nothing but the theatre. They were to return there a fortnight later to see *The Two Brothers* and *Michel Cervantès*, while Mme C——'s elder, married daughter went to the *Italiens* and her husband to the *Opéra*.[10] Even the cook-help, Thérèse, became stage-struck: we see her setting out, one evening for the *Louvre*, with a neighbouring domestic who for this occasion had put on a dress of blue satin with box pleats, a shawl as iridescent as a pigeon's crop and a hat that had cost, in its time, fifteen *louis*.[11] Yet another social category which does not seem to be too badly off!

HOME LIFE

But the thing that counted most in the Rue Saint-Marc was family gatherings and intimate celebrations. The one which was being prepared for March 5 had a rather touching character. It was to honour Mme C——'s fiftieth birthday, her half-century which, according to flattering admirers, might well be only her fifteenth and not her fiftieth. For a whole week beforehand, Ziguette had been busy translating an elegy of Tibullus which she was to recite in honour of the occasion.

Finally the great day arrived. The ladies dressed up in all their finery. The heroine of the party wore a lace cap ornamented with a violet ribbon, and, for once in a while, had dabbed on a little rouge. The married daughter, Mme S——, whose black ringlets contrasted agreeably with her pale skin, wore a white dress which made her look like 'mama's younger sister'. As for Citizeness Ziguette, she put on everything she had: the Madras bandanna, a pearl necklace, a linen sheath-dress, a poppy-scarlet belt and her pair of red earrings. She appears to have 'ransacked the Treasury'.[12]

Nevertheless, they grew a little impatient, for the guests were late. The Citizenesses Pradère and Vidal had dolled themselves up so fine that they hadn't been able to resist the temptation to go and show themselves off on the boulevards. But finally everyone had arrived: Lebrun, Cotard, Riguel, Parceval, the Pradère ménage, the Vidals, and they all sat down gaily to table. During the feast, the white wine of Calabria flowed like water, inspiring and uplifting the guests.

Singing did the rest. Bowing to the supplications of Pradère, the two daughters of the house duly performed, one after the other. Ziguette, with her 'stereoscopic voice', as her mother calls it, enjoyed a great success.

The afternoon, if we are to believe Mlle G——, 'was spent in sweet and perfect happiness'. Towards evening, the music began again. Pradère, Riguel and Parceval sang part-songs. Ziguette tinkled on her pianoforte and Citizeness S—— received loud applause when with Parceval she sang the duet from *Oedipus at Colonus*: 'Nay, forsooth, let us stray no farther, belovèd . . .' 'I don't know if it is possible to sing it better,' the governess concluded. 'All I know is that I wept with all my heart.'

Let us leave the gathering to enjoy themselves. After a plentiful supper, it did not break up until well past midnight, and the wine, so copious, mingled with the torrents of music, must have so exhausted some of them that they had to stay and spend the night at the Rue Saint-Marc. The next morning they woke with a slightly thick head and that species of malaise which Hellenists are so fond of calling xylostomy . . . it is better not to translate it into English.

The party was repeated six weeks later at the Pradère establishment. There, too, it was in celebration of the lady of the house's birthday. Ziguette had on a new dress; a concert was improvised; there was an excellent supper; they all ate like troopers and laughed to raise the roof, and none of them went home before well past midnight.

VISITS, MUSICAL SOIRÉES, COUNTRY PARTIES

But Paris must not make us forget the countryside, especially with spring on the way. We cannot close the famous journal without extracting from it an excursion to Auteuil, where the whole family had gone for a wedding feast. They were able to find a cab which took them to the barrier. Ziguette had nothing better to do than to 'stretch her legs in a little meadow, where she had Thérèse chasing after her'. Once they had arrived at the S—— house they sat down to table. They were served with 'a pie weighing three pounds, an enormous pâté, baked cod and potatoes, salad, gingerbread, apples, cheeses, coffee and brandy'.[14]

This menu tells us that the inhabitants of Auteuil were no more dying of hunger than the Parisians. Nor did they bother themselves about tempestuous sittings in the Convention and the imminent attack of Saint Just on the Hébertistes who were to be arrested three days later . . .

Our merrymakers spent a very pleasant day and their one worry was whether Thérèse would be home first, as she had the keys to the kitchen.

The calm displayed by this family is all the more curious in that it consisted of educated persons who knew what was going on. They were living right in the heart of Paris, two steps from the Palais Royal where so many revolts started. When there was fighting in the Tuileries, they must have heard the firing of rifles from their windows.

Money troubles and long separations might also have embittered them. Their son was in the army, the husband in the provinces. They had to haggle over an old frock and pinch and scrape on many things. Not to worry! They take things as they come, remain good-tempered, which is a form of courage.

Many Parisiennes in those days must have been in the same state of mind. When they were not directly affected by politics, they went on living with the same careless freedom, looking after their homes, their children, and enjoying modest pleasures.

It doesn't mean that if the sky is overcast the Seine will stop running under the arches of the Pont Royal!

CHAPTER FOURTEEN

A PARISIAN WORKING GIRL

From a haberdashery in Creil to a drapery in the rue Saint-Honoré – Marie-Victoire is a witness of the Terror – She sees the cartloads of corpses – The mysterious man at the back of the shop – Lucky and unlucky speculation

FROM A HABERDASHERY IN CREIL TO A DRAPERY IN THE
RUE SAINT-HONORÉ

Marie-Victoire Monnard was that charming little girl whose adventures during the Great Panic at Creil we have already related.[1]

The months have gone by since those agitated days, the girl has grown, and, as her parents are finding it difficult to make ends meet with fifteen small children to feed, she decided to try her own wings.

She was attracted by trade rather than by the arduous and tedious work of the fields. She realized her vocation while working for the woman running the grocery-cum-haberdashery store in Creil, who employed her on market days and paid her for five hours' work with a cup of coffee and two *sous*. Although she was very proud of her monetary earnings, in the end she decided that she could do even better in Paris. So one morning she climbed on the roof of the coach to the capital in order to take up employment as apprentice sempstress with Mme Amé in the Rue Traversière-Saint-Honoré.

She was no more than thirteen and shed a few tears on the first nights spent far from her parents. In any case, the existence of working girls, in 1791, was not a very gay one: they had to work hard, sleep in dormitories, did not have enough to eat and the only talk they heard was about revolution. Every Sunday seven or eight pounds of meat were put in a large pot and stewed up, and this had to feed the whole workshop for a week. The apprentices used to go to the Palais Royal market to buy their bread, as it was much more expensive in the bakeries. Their mistress would order huge quantities at a time, considering that it improved with keeping. Never mind if it grew stale and mildewed! One mustn't be too particular.

Fortunately Mme Monnard did not forget her daughter and from time to time sent her a pot of butter or jam to spread on her hunks of bread. M Monnard too was good and kind; as he worked on the stagecoach making the journey between Creil and Paris, he sometimes went to see his daughter. One day, to give her a little pleasure, he even took her to the theatre to see a popular comedy called *Honorine, or the Woman Difficult to Deal with.*

MARIE-VICTOIRE IS A WITNESS OF THE TERROR

The spectacle of the streets, when Mme Amé sent her on errands, was alas much less entertaining. One afternoon in September, coming back from the Faubourg Saint-Honoré, where she had been to take some hats for re-covering, she saw coming towards her six large carts which she took to be cattle-trucks. But the passers-by seemed to be looking at them with fearful expressions on their faces . . . As the carts passed her the young girl got a shock:

> The carts were full of men and women who had just been slaughtered and whose limbs were still fairly flexible because they had not yet had time to grow cold, so that legs and arms and heads nodded and dangled on either side of the carts.

Trickles of fresh blood were falling from the carts, staining the road as far as the Pont-Marie, where the corpses of these unfortunates, exterminated in prison, were set out in rows by half-drunken rogues: 'I can still see those drunken men,' Mlle Monnard goes on, and remember in particular one very skinny one, very pale, with a sharp, pointed nose. This monster went to speak to an acquaintance and said: 'Do you see that rotten old priest on the pile over there?' He left his friend to go and haul the ecclesiastic to his feet; but the body, still warm, could not stand up straight; the drunken man held it up, slapping it across the face and shouting: 'I had trouble enough killing the old brute: and about time, too . . . for he had forged *assignats*[2] in his pockets!'

SHE SEES THE CARTLOADS OF CORPSES

After this scene, which would make any scene in Grand Guignol pale into insignificance, Marie-Victoire must have felt inured to horrors. The following year she was able to watch without too much emotion the batches of candidates for the guillotine being trundled down the Rue Saint-Honoré every day in their tumbrils, just a stone's throw from her mistress' workshop, and we can take her word for it when she writes later:

> People just went on working in the shops when they passed by, often not even bothering to raise their heads to watch or to turn their backs to avoid the grisly sight.

There was only one thing the young ladies of the dress-shop worried about: when they went out, they must never forget to pin in their hats the little tricolour cockade which proved they were ardent patriots. In Mme Amé's establishment, there was always a cockade for the use of the staff, although Madame herself was not a very fervent Republican. The red, white and blue symbol was passed from one hat to another each time a girl had to go out on an errand, and Marie-Victoire wore it more than most, for her mistress, who did not care for the turn political events were taking, frequently sent her to get news. She would go roaming round the quartier, round the Assembly, the Clubs and listening to people talking and bringing back whatever she had heard.

Such services had their due reward. Towards the end of 1793, she was given a week's holiday which she spent with her parents, and the journey to Creil resulted in a striking narrative.

A king entering his golden coach to go to his coronation could hardly have experienced greater pleasure than I did in my father's stagecoach. I was fourteen years old,[3] I was going to see my family and my home town again. I was bubbling over with happiness . . . When I saw the church tower at Creil, my heart beat wildly . . . The two years I had spent in the capital had given me that air of a city dweller which stood me in good stead with my former village companions. I was not at all displeased to hear them say: 'How Victoire has changed! What frills and furbelows she has now! She's a real young lady, she is!' This flattered my vanity, modest as it was, and so I informed them that in Paris I was addressed as Mlle Monnard and not as Victoire.

Her elegance had so much impressed her two sisters Angélique and Agnès that they, too, wanted to find positions as sempstresses in Paris. As for our heroine, she was to change workshops the following year, in order to improve her knowledge of the trade, and after an unfortunate experience with a haberdashery in the Rue Montmartre, she entered the establishment of Mme Rataud, who ran a dress-shop in the Rue des Petits-Champs.

THE MYSTERIOUS MAN AT THE BACK OF THE SHOP

Her new place was even less patriotic than Mme Amé's workshop; sometimes they would have a visit from a mysterious stranger hiding his face in a handkerchief who would pass quickly through the shop and disappear into the back room. One day when they had put in to roast a fine plump chicken that made Victoire's mouth water just to look at, she was suddenly told to eat alone while her mistress and her husband shut themselves up in their kitchen with the mysterious stranger and stayed there with him four hours:

'That wretched chicken lay heavy on my stomach for quite a while,' she admits, 'because I was so mystified about why they had not allowed me to eat my portion of it at their table . . .' Later she was to learn that the 'tall, handsome man' was no other than the Marquis de Ségur, whose servants M and Mme Rataud had once been.

Those times were not very easy for such a couple who remained faithful to the old principles. Anything upset or distressed them. In July 1794, the vogue of holding *Fraternal Suppers* had just been started; each Section would take its turn in giving one: they were held out of doors, in the street. The residents of the neighbouring houses had to lend their tables, line them up with those of other houses, and what was even worse, supply and prepare the victuals.

This was a terrible problem for poor Mme Rataud. 'If I prepare a dish of haricots,' she said, 'the *sans-culottes* will throw it in my face; if I provide roast pheasant the Jacobins will say it is too high-class . . .' In this dilemma she cooked both, and prudently waited to see what her neighbours would put on their own tables before running the risk of displaying one or other of her efforts. The way things went, she saw that she could bring out both. It was a triumph of the policy of 'United we Stand'.

LUCKY AND UNLUCKY SPECULATION

All the working girls had the same ambition: to start up a business on their own. Victoire was no exception to the rule. Deciding that the Ratauds were a little too stingy with their chickens, she hired an attic in the Rue de Cléry, not far from the stagecoach yard where her father stopped.

At that time her sole possessions were a mattress, a bolster, two pairs of sheets and a money-box containing thirteen francs. When she had spent eight of them on a small bedstead, and five to buy a few kitchen utensils, she was set up, and was left with one *sou*.

In order to acquire a little capital, she cut up some coarse thick cloth she had, made it into nicely hemstitched dusters, added her bolster and a nankeen dress to her stock and sold the lot for forty *livres*. This sum allowed her to purchase ten ells of printed cotton which she re-sold the same day, making a profit of eight francs. She had made a start: 'I felt so happy,' she said,

> with this modest beginning in business that I would not have exchanged my position for that of the greatest potentate on earth. The continual fall in value of *assignats* made easier the sale of all kinds of merchandise; one only had to offer them to see them taken off one's hands. I was kept going all day long and also I was making four times as many *assignats* as I laid out, so that if I was not exactly rolling in money I was certainly rolling in paper.

She was in fact rolling on a mattress without a bolster and when her mother came to visit her this rudimentary bed appalled the good country woman. Not even a chair to sit on, and no blankets under the counterpane ... These Parisians! What a way to live! Wishing to save the honour of the family, the good lady announced that she would send bedding; her daughter swore that she would not sell it, and the package she eventually received also contained some provisions of country food.

Unfortunately, Mme Monnard died in childbirth the following year. It was her sixteenth pregnancy, which would seem to indicate that the Creil coachman was no slouch.

The grieving widower now showed even more affection for Victoire ... He had got into the habit of dining with her every other day, bringing her vegetables from his garden or making her other presents. The most beautiful of these was certainly a gold watch that she speaks of with enthusiasm:

> I was so pleased to have it that, in order passers-by might see my treasure, I pretended to look at the time on at least a dozen occasions while returning from the Faubourg

Saint-Denis, where I received it, to the Rue Cléry where I lived.

She had indeed been able to take a new lodging thanks to her early profits and soon, having received a little money from her grandmother, a farmer's wife in Crépy-en-Valois,[4] she felt she was made and decided that the moment had come to embark on more ambitious enterprises.

With her sister Angélique she rented a dress-shop in the Faubourg Saint-Denis, and the two little Monnard girls hopefully awaited their first customers.

One essential thing was still missing in their shop: something to sell. But Victoire was not the sort of girl to let herself be put off by such a small item. She stuffed a few dozen sacks with straw, placed them on the shelves, wrapped in pretty papers ornamented with various names: holland, embroidered caps, etc . . . At a time when shopkeepers complained of having nothing to sell, her establishment must have seemed an enchanted fairyland.

How is that for a young girl who hardly knew how to read and write? A little cheating and trickery were involved, to be sure, but such talents reveal true business sense, a curiously instinctive feeling for what today we would call 'business war', the favourite bluff of modern commerce and finance. Simply for her sacks of straw Victoire Monnard deserves to have her statue erected outside some big shop or outside the Stock Exchange.

Another kind of reward awaited the young lady. Before she found any customers she found a fiancé. Attracted by the fine shop, a young man of nineteen was even more attracted by its mistress and lost no time in declaring his suit. He was called Joseph Huet, and was earning eighteen hundred francs a year at a provision store.

Victoire had great difficulty in deciphering the letter, full of high-flown sentiments and difficult words, which her admirer addressed to her, but she pressed it to her heart and began to compose as best she could an answer, which, as she was to admit later, must have been 'very funny'. She said chiefly that she had no money, that her sacks were filled with straw, but that her own heart was all tenderness and that, if he wished to ask her hand he must write to her father. Monnard gave his consent, even coughed up a small dowry, and the two young people were married at the church of Saint-Laurent, on September 23, 1797. They did not reckon forty years between them.

Let us leave the new ménage to the pleasures of their honeymoon; let us also overlook the difficulties they began to encounter when first one then another child were born, when Huet lost his job and, the dress trade sharing the general commercial crisis, they had to close the shop in the Rue Saint-Denis and take to the pawnbroker's the gold watch that Victoire had been so proud of. Their troubles were not over until 1802, when our young couple went to settle in Nantes, where Joseph had managed to find employment in food distribution.

But this takes us beyond the story of young Mlle Monnard's life as a Parisian working girl. Of that picturesque tale let us remember only the youthful years she spent during the Revolution and in which we see the dear child struggling with such courage to make a living right at the heart of hideous events. Those years emphasize the qualities of heart and mind shown by France's working classes.

CHAPTER FIFTEEN

CALENDAR FEASTS AND FASHIONS

The reform of the calendar and its consequences – Civic festivals replace feast-days – The Festival of the Supreme Being – Patriotic celebrations in the country

THE REFORM OF THE CALENDAR AND ITS CONSEQUENCES
One reform that directly affected daily life was that of the calendar decided by the Convention, in October 1793, a reform that was to be in force for the next twelve years, until January 1, 1806.

A new era,[1] years of ten instead of twelve months, months of three decades instead of four weeks, charming or baroque names dreamed up to replace the saints' names on the calendar – all this was bound to upset the country's ancient habits. But only the broad outlines were retained of the new system as it was devised by Romme, the deputy of Puy-de-Dôme, and curiously complicated by Fabre d'Eglantine when he presented his report to the Assembly.

Could one really give the days of the decade the names of plants, animals or agricultural implements, as the Convention wished, and also use these names to replace those given in baptism? Only a few of the most diehard Jacobins took pride in naming their sons Squitch, Duck or Dandelion and their daughters Cow, Carrot or Rhubarb, but names derived from Greek and Roman history were very much more to the general taste. As for the days, it was finally agreed that they should be designated by their numbers: primidi, duodi, tridi, etc, which put them all on a perfectly egalitarian level. No more Sundays or religious feast-days – this was the most concrete result of the change of calendar; only, to diversify a little the monotony of the year, it was resolved to increase the number of civic festivals named in honour of some great event, a symbolic idea or a Republican virtue.

The Feast of the Regeneration, which took place on the Champ-de-Mars on August 10, 1793, could be taken as a praiseworthy example. But its splendour was to pale before that of another day, created by Robespierre and organized by David, which took place ten months later: the Festival of the Supreme Being.

It has often been described: the sudden appearance of Maximilien in his blue coat with the red facings, the sudden coolness towards him of his colleagues, the apostrophe of the *sans-culotte* who, seeing him throning it on the Mountain of the Champ-de-Mars, cried: 'The little wretch! He's not satisfied with being top dog . . . He wants to be God Almighty as well!' All these were episodes which historians did not neglect. But while the ceremony itself has been minutely documented, one knows much less about what impression it made upon the crowd, the common people of Paris.

CIVIC FESTIVALS REPLACE FEAST-DAYS

As a matter of fact, we have a witness, one whose impartiality cannot be doubted, as she was a girl of thirteen: Emilie C——, in whom you will immediately have recognized our little Ziguette. She watched the festivities from start to finish; it made a lasting impression upon her memory and the very next day she enthusiastically described it all to her father:

> On the 19th (Prairial) all citizens had been invited to adorn their houses with garlands and oak branches for the celebrations in honour of the Supreme Being . . . We used all our artificial flowers. You may well imagine that the night of the 19th to the 20th was an almost sleepless one for me, because of the pleasures awaiting me . . . and because of the uncertainty about the weather. On the 19th, the barometer stood between Rain and Stormy. On the 20th,

which was yesterday, we were all awake before five in the morning; at six, I got up. Our house was decorated already and all we had to do was to doll ourselves up. I made a studied toilet, as did everyone else . . . I wore an overskirt of lawn, a tricolour sash round my waist, and an embroidered fichu of red cotton; on my head, a cambric fichu, arranged like the fillet round the brows of Grecian women, and my hair, dressed in nine small plaits, was upswept on to the crown of my head. Mama wore a cambric dress at whose hem there was a vastly pretty border and on her dear head a wide-brimmed straw hat with violet satin ribbons, Citizeness G—— (the governess) was also in white and had on her head a coloured fichu which I arranged for her.

In our pockets we stuffed some slices of bread and some cooking-chocolate. We set off for Citizeness Chaudet's and at eight o'clock all four of us set off for the *Jardin National*, each of us bearing an oak branch in her hand.

The spectacle awaiting these ladies was worthy of all their expectations: in front of the Château des Tuileries an amphitheatre had been constructed, adorned with bas-reliefs representing Justice, Virtue, Fidelity and The French People Vanquishing their Enemies. The statue of Wisdom which completed the decorative scheme was for the moment camouflaged as a figure representing Atheism. Also on view was a superb chariot drawn by eight oxen with gilded horns and on which was displayed a group of 'instruments illustrating the agricultural and mechanical arts'. There was a statue of Liberty and a small tree covered with tricolour leaves. 'It made us feel,' Ziguette declares, 'as if we had been transported to the days of Ancient Greece.' We are willing to take her word for it, though we are somewhat at a loss to know whether a small tree tricked out in such a fashion would evoke the same response in us.

But the ceremonies were about to begin. From a distance, they saw the 'President' – which the letter does not mention by name, and indeed, what need would there be for that? – set fire to the statue of Atheism. The parade lined up: on one side, the women, on the other, the men; in the centre, a battalion of adolescents. On the stroke of noon, the chariot lumbered into motion, preceded by a procession of members of the Convention. Six men 'in white trousers, short jacket and red caps arranged like Phrygian caps' led the oxen, and the immense juggernaut, as it rumbled slowly past, filled with admiration the little girl who stood in the front row of spectators.

Now they had to reach the Champ-de-Mars. In order to avoid the crush, the best way was to join the nymphs in the procession, which naturally enchanted Ziguette. When she finally arrived in front of the great mountain, her lyricism overflowed:

> You cannot imagine what a sight it was . . . It seemed as if someone had transported a huge cliff from the Pyrenees to the middle of the Champ-de-Mars. On its peak was an obelisk surmounted by a statue representing The People of France holding aloft the statues of Liberty and Egality. It really seemed as though the French are fairies, to have done such beautiful things in so short a time. The Champ-de-Mars seemed to be framed by stepped stands covered with people. The Hymn was played at half-past six. After each stanza the Champ-de-Mars re-echoed with shouts of '*Vive la Republique!*' and there were girls everywhere strewing flowers. My hair was simply full of them. After the ceremony, which finished at seven o'clock, we were just dying of hunger, thirst and fatigue.[2]

Their bread and chocolate must have been polished off long ago...

This almost childlike narration has the merit of showing us that the crowd's welcome for the Supreme Being's solemn glorification was much warmer than had generally been claimed. Did people really believe that a new era was dawning, that Robespierre, to quote Mallet du Pan, was going to 'bridge the abyss of the Revolution'? At any rate, apart from the Convention group, the enthusiasm was practically universal.

Many other accounts support this, notably that of a Parisian working girl who summed up her memories of the Champ-de-Mars thus:

> There is nothing that could be compared with the beauty of that celebration. It seemed to inspire the people and raised it to the full consciousness of its power. The crowds accompanying the processions were prodigious.[3]

THE FESTIVAL OF THE SUPREME BEING

Following the example of the capital, the provinces were not behindhand in organizing patriotic celebrations. Many of these were rather curious because of the violence of the feelings which they aspired to give expression to.

At Limoges, for example, there was a celebration in memory of Marat on October 14, 1793, with all the shops closed and the citizens in their best clothes, 'as if it had been an Easter Day in former times'.[4] The president of the People's Society eulogized the illustrious victim, and the procession set off 'in simple disorder, majestic and imposing'. National Guards, functionaries, men and women were all mixed together and all of them sang the Hymn which had been distributed among them, while a placard on the end of a lance tottered behind the bust of Jean-Paul, bearing the legend:

> *To Marat, friend of the People.*
> *This is how the People honours its friends.*

As a dramatic contrast, a dummy of Gorsas came next, decapitated, bleeding and dragged along the gutter 'by a billy-goat of huge dimensions and stinking so horribly that it was impossible to go anywhere near it'. The journalist's writings were hung on his coat, and a second sign bore this legend about the 'living characature' (*sic*):

> *Infamous Gorsas.*
> *This is how the People treats its enemies.*

The People wanted vengeance in full. It threw the dummy and Gorsas' works on a heap of feudal title-deeds destined to be burnt. The President set fire to them, and the bust of Marat, set on a triumphal chariot, was solemnly hauled to the meeting hall of the People's Society.

It was not just the big towns which enjoyed such distractions. In a small place in the Dordogne, Monpazier, there was organized, on December 30, a celebration at the Temple of Reason which was no other than the former parish church.[5] An envoy from Roux-Fazillac, a representative on a special mission, delivered 'a speech against skirted priests and preached of unity and concord' without seeming to be aware that the two aims of his programme were difficult to reconcile. Then every citizen took the arm of a citizeness and they all went singing to the Tree of Liberty, where proceedings terminated with a 'frugal civic banquet'.

On the same day, at Boulogne-sur-mer, in the presence of Lieutenant-General Vincent, they celebrated the taking of Toulon with a demonstration similar to that at Limoges. Between two rows of fusiliers grouped round the famous Cateau du Nord which personifies a mustachioed giant, came 'the rabble of kings, princes and generals'. A Vendéan priest held a rosary in one hand and a bloody dagger in the other. Behind the king of the marmots, M Pitt and his gentle master Georges Dandin were riding donkeys. The Holy Father was represented by a great magpie afflicted with 'the voracious gluttony of the creature known as the Pope'

A bear covered with medals represented His Serene Highness the Prince of Coburg, standing on a cart pulled by dogs. The noblest members of royal courts and common farmyards in Germany were embodied in hogs and swine, and a barrel surmounted by a lance served as a stadtholder's emblem. After having passed through streets of cheering crowds, this carnival cortege turned into the Place de la Fédération where the kings, princes and their suite were trampled underfoot by the populace.[6]

In 1794 the Parisian festivities made the provinces jealous.

Many towns were determined to emulate the capital, and so it was that the Supreme Being went on tour to Evreux, just like a star tenor with a provincial opera company. Indeed, he favoured the Evroicians, as his visit took place on June 8, or twelve days before the ceremony in Paris.

Nicolas Rogue, the local historian, had the wit to put down in writing for us a description of what we might call this dress rehearsal.[7] He shows us the houses adorned with leafy boughs and garlanded with flowers, the citizens and citizenesses all garbed in white and gathering along the highway from Caen, 'the fathers on the right with their sons, and the women on the left with their daughters, all carrying bouquets of flowers'. It must have been like a Corpus Christi Day but with a different social motive.

Escorted by the inevitable National Guard, by a group of gendarmes and by a regular battalion which happened to be passing through Evreux, the authorities moved to the head of the procession and the people began to sing 'patriotic airs accompanied by martial music'. In the Place de la Révolution, round the Tree of Liberty, a mountain had been erected, a modest preview of the one in the Champ-de-Mars. After the populace had meditated before 'The Temple of the Eternal', and when their voices had grown weary with singing hymns and the young girls had scattered all the flowers in their ribboned baskets, the day ended with a dance, and the two sexes, separated from each other until now by the rigours of protocol, were finally able to come together again.

PATRIOTIC CELEBRATIONS IN THE COUNTRY

The fall of Robespierre in no way interrupted the custom of holding festivals, either in the small towns or the large ones. On October 16, 1794, we see the citizens of Lyons organizing a grand ceremony for the unveiling of the statue of Jean-Jacques Rousseau by Chinard. A solemn occasion at which the mawkish sentimentality of the century seemed to be given a free rein.[8]

According the official account, the procession consisted of six groups:

A group of young boys carrying a banner with this inscription: *He gave us Emile as our model.* A group of young girls: *In us ye may witness the innocent purity of his Sophie.* A group of mothers suckling their infants: *He respected Mothers and made their children happy.* A group of citizens of Lyons who had known and entertained Rousseau: *In Lyons he knew the charms of Friendship.* A group of citizens from Geneva, proud of the homage accorded Jean-Jacques by the Convention: *Aristocrat Geneva had banned him, Geneva liberated has avenged his memory.* Finally a group of old men, artists and citizens, came carrying in great pomp a volume of the *Social Contract* from which they had taken this celebrated sentence: *Man is born free. To renounce one's liberty is to renounce one's dignity as a man, one's human rights, and even one's duties.*

As time went on, more and more Republican festivals took on, as we can see, a moral, philosophical and one might almost say religious character. They became so much a part of life that the Convention, before rising, thought it necessary to give them a definite statute. It created seven national festival days: *Fête de la République*, on the 1st Vendémaire (September 22 or 23, according to the year); *Fête de la Jeunesse*, on the 10th, Germinal (March 30); *Fête des Epoux* on the 10th Floréal (April 29); *Fête de la Reconnaissance* on the 10th Prairial (May 29); *Fête de l'Agriculture* on the 10th Messidor (June 28); *Fête de la Liberté* on the 9th and 10th Thermidor (July 27 and 28); and *Fête de la Vieillesse* on the 10th Fructidor (August 27).

Thus daily life, highlighted by a few grand dates in the calendar, lost some of its monotony; certain days spoke to the spirit of the nation, took on a symbolic value and replaced the traditional festivities which the new calendar had been created to abolish.

CHAPTER SIXTEEN

ÉMIGRÉS IN THEIR OWN LAND

Suspects hidden in the suburbs – The experiences of Pierre Jullian at the Vaugirard barrier – Aristocratic refugees in the country – The de Chastenay family at Rouen – Melancholy walks together

SUSPECTS HIDDEN IN THE SUBURBS

We all remember the passage in his *Memoirs from Beyond the Tomb* in which Chateaubriand describes the distressed state he was in during the period of emigration, in London:

> I sucked pieces of linen which I soaked in water; I chewed grass and paper. When I walked past bakers' shops, my tortures were horrible. One raw winter night I stood for two solid hours in front of a shop selling dried fruit and smoked meats, devouring with my eyes everything before me: I would have eaten not only the eatables but also their boxes and baskets.

This is bad enough, and touches our hearts with pity for the fate of French refugees during those lamentable years. Yet those who found hospitality in London were among the most favoured ones, as many of them drew an allowance of a shilling a day. On the other hand, in German towns like Coblenz, Hamburg, Munich and Bamberg there was no hope of obtaining official assistance, excepting in the case of the most distinguished aristocrats.

In France, when noblemen found themselves without resources – and this soon became their general condition, as they were unable to collect their rents – they had to beg in the streets or enter the unlikeliest occupations. At the corner of the Place d'Erlanger, the Comte de Vieuville shined shoes and ran errands for bourgeois clients; the Marquis de La Londe was cashier in a café; the Marquis de Montbazet was a lamplighter, the Chevalier d'Anselme an actor, Mlle de Saint-Marceau a salesgirl in a shop, while the Comtesse de Virieu darned stockings on the pavement, like some ordinary streetvendor on the Pont-Neuf.

There were many other strange metamorphoses. Wigmakers, dancing teachers, café waiters, scrubbers of floors, doormen – no matter what the occupation, it could be filled by these members of a once-brilliant high society, once so avid for pleasure, and whose last act in the social comedy had turned tragic with hunger.

The strain must have been terrible, but it may well be that for some of its victims the punishment was well merited. The perverted loyalism of those who had encouraged emigration, of those who had departed en masse, after 1789, in the wake of the Comte d'Artois, the Prince de Condé and the Vaudreuil and the Lambesc families could have only fatal consequences.

A desire to save the monarchy by declaring war on France and calling on foreigners to come to her aid inevitably cut the nation in two, exasperated class struggles and gave the Revolution a violent character which it did not have at the beginning: the consequences were that formidable reprisals were made, first on the aristocracy and then on royalty.

Whether emigration was a grave fault committed against the *Patrie* is a question of feeling, and we know how this kind of idea, in the eighteenth century, could differ from our own sentiments today; but it was a plain fact that emigration spelt a kind of suicide for the nobility.

The first victims of this madness were those aristocrats who had remained at home, people of good will who, unwilling to quit their ancestral hearths and thinking that the troubles would die down, had tried willy-nilly to adapt themselves to the new régime. When the provocations at Coblenz and later the invasions of French territory unleashed popular frenzy, it was these aristocrats who suffered for the rest. Scapegoats of the emigration, they soon found themselves treated as enemies. Irked by a thousand vexations, menaced in their private lives and with their property confiscated, they had only one solution: to hide away as best they could, seeking concealment wherever it offered, changing their names and often their facial appearance. Fewer existences could have been more terrible than those led by these unhappy wretches. The letters and memoirs from those times bear witness to this.

In the Parisian region alone, many noblemen had not waited for the police edict of April 16, 1794, forbidding them residence in Paris; they had very soon realized that Paris life was not for them and had taken refuge in villages on the outskirts of the capital. After the spring of 1793, the *Club des Cinquante*, where a few royalists still used to come fairly regularly to read their newspapers and play billiards, was deserted as if at the wave of a wand. The gentlemen had decided their health would benefit from a little country air. They hid themselves away at Suresnes, Saint-Cloud, Meudon, and only very rarely, when business required it, did they make an excursion *intra muros*.

But this kind of trip could turn out badly, for once they had entered the mousetrap they ran the risk of remaining there. One of these temporary country-dwellers, Pierre Jullian, whom we met earlier at Montpellier while he was reading law and attending balls, very nearly was caught in this way in September 1793.

THE EXPERIENCES OF PIERRE JULLIAN AT THE VAUGIRARD BARRIER

Having come on foot from his retreat at Meudon, he presented himself at the Vaugirard barrier with false papers and wearing the most picturesque of disguises: 'I had long been accustomed', he writes, 'to wearing on these trips only a working man's trousers and jacket. I would dirty my face and in this way I could pass myself off as one of the workers at the glass factory, whose manager had given me a passport to this effect.'

The Vaugirard barrier was not his usual route, so he had to be interrogated by the guard, show his papers and have all details taken down. Fortunately for him, the commander of the post seemed to have got out of bed on the right side; he was even obliging enough to tell him: 'On your way back, if you get into difficulties, you only need ask for me. I am Citizen Champagnat.' Naturally, Jullian was careful not to forget the patriot's name, and felt full of confidence when, towards the end of the day, having finished his business, he returned to the same gate to obtain his *exeat*. One may imagine his dismay on being told that Citizen Champagnat was not there.

> Some said he was on the Revolutionary Committee; others that he was at the Section's General Assembly; for Champagnat belonged to everything. He was looked for everywhere, but without success . . . I was desperate, and did all I could to soften the hearts of the soldiers on guard, saying that my wife and children would think I had been killed, that they were expecting me for dinner, that it was unjust to keep me a prisoner like this, and couldn't they see that I was only a poor working man who had nothing to do with aristocrats . . . All in vain: my *sans-culottes* comrades were obdurate and would not listen to my pleas.

Now poor Jullian knew well that if he were prevented from leaving his ruse would be discovered – disguise, false passport and everything. Arrest would be certain, followed by an appearance, with the least possible delay, before the Revolutionary Tribunal.

He was in a dreadful sweat, when, after such fruitless searchings, his liberator was located at last, explaining the reason for his absence: this confidential agent of the Revolutionary Committee was a wigmaker and barber by profession, and as his recent rise in position had not altered the democratic simplicity of his character, had simply been spending the past hour shaving some of his men, in the nearby guard-house.

One word from him and the 'workman' was able to proceed along the road to Meudon. But he had had a narrow escape. Never had a cut-throat razor seemed to him so like the blade of the guillotine.[1]

ARISTOCRATIC REFUGEES IN THE COUNTRY

Such alarms were frequent in the lives of aristocrats who had not wanted to move too far away from Paris. Some of them went so far as to think that the safest hiding-places would be in the city itself. But with what a tedious wealth of precautions they had to surround themselves in order to escape denunciation and the vengeance of individuals!

Many of the old Parisian buildings still have hideaways in attics, tiny cubby-holes cleverly disguised and in which many a wretch spent day after day during the period of inspections by the police. Not so long ago there was demolished, in the Rue Vaugirard, a house in which certain cupboards, with their very special construction and their walls covered with graffiti, seemed really to have been former revolutionary hiding-places. But here romance and historical fact run the risk of being confused, and we must exercise prudence.

Less exposed to danger and generally less unfortunate were those former noblemen whose instinct of self-preservation had driven them into the provinces, often fairly far from their homes, and who employed all kinds of subterfuges to have themselves accepted by the local authorities.

THE DE CHASTENAY FAMILY AT ROUEN

The *Memoirs* of Mme de Chastenay[2] depict in a rather moving way the existence these émigrés in the interior might have known when their concern for their own safety had made them fly their château homes. These memoirs concern the life of a family belonging to good provincial nobility and coming originally from the Côte-d'Or. The father had served as an officer in the regiment of the Bauffrement Dragoons. His wife was a perpetual invalid who hardly ever left her bed. They had two children: one of them a young man, Henri, and his sister, who was addressed as Madame, as she had already been received as a canoness in the noble chapter of Epinal. When the Revolution began to take a tragic turn, the Chastenays left Paris and sought asylum at Rouen, where, suffering great hardships and living in a more than austere retreat, they were able to ride out the storm.

MELANCHOLY WALKS TOGETHER

Certainly for a young girl, even if she be a canoness, such a life could not be anything but austere. Her mother hardly ever went out. M de Chastenay spent the greater part of his time in useless proceedings, or in reading in his cell. When she looked upon her linen *pierrot* and her hair 'cut quite flat', the poor girl must have sighed for her pretty dresses and the splendour of festivities at Versailles. She found consolation in music, in composing songs and walking with her brother in the fine garden at Saint-Ouen. She writes:

> One must have lived through that incredible epoch in order to even begin to realize what we felt. We had no illusions: as my brother and I roamed, one evening, through those delightful glades, we told ourselves that within the next six months we should have all been annihilated by the fires of the Revolution. Yet the flowers still had power to charm us. I never saw a spring as beautiful as that of 1794; it was as if Nature desired to console the world for the crimes committed by society. The walks round Rouen revealed to us some enchanted spots of greenery. I remember the road from Les Cottes, all shady with huge pear-trees loaded with blossom. Happiness lay there, it seemed to me then. How happy I should have been if suddenly some benevolent genius had been able to circumscribe our universe in that place, with the promise of peace.[3]

Alas, the benevolent genius appeared only in the guise of a decent fellow, Pierre Sergent, who worked for an uncle of the young lady and who had bravely taken it upon himself to look after the Chastenays. When things got too bad – for in Rouen just as in Paris there were queues at the baker's and a few pounds of rice would have seemed like infinite wealth – their good friend would arrive with a big loaf of bread hidden under his cloak, and sometimes a choice joint of meat.

Festive days, when that happened. Then they would send word to a few friends, Mme d'Aubusson, M Berry, M Leyris. After dinner, which was served about three or four o'clock, they read novels aloud, gave each other the latest news, played chess or backgammon. A pleasant provincial life, in fact, darkened only by the more or less sinister rumours which were spread every morning and by the constant threat that their house would be searched by the police. When such a search was announced in the neighbourhood, they went on the defensive: the big loaf of bread was carefully cut up and each member of the family carefully hid his own portion. The same for the packets of candles and the stock of potatoes, which were shared out among friends.

Financial difficulties too became all the more acute, for naturally the Chastenays were receiving no revenue. They made ends meet, as so many others did, by selling the remnants of their former luxurious life: silverware sold at a rate of exchange of fifty *livres* the mark – in paper, alas! – and the cellar, full of excellent wine, which had probably gone to some restaurant near the Palais Royal.

Finally, there was a delicate question to be settled every three months. Legally our Burgundians should have lived on the Côte-d'Or, and so every quarter they had to supply a certificate of residence signed by nine witnesses of Châtillon-sur-Seine. We can well imagine what a tedious procedure this was, and what devotion it required from those people who bravely served as witnesses at the risk of their lives. 'It needed a great deal of courage,' sighs Mme de Chastenay, 'to act as witnesses for people in our situation. It could cost a witness his life.'

These constant worries were enough to upset the most serene philosophies. But when one is twenty-three and one has read Gesner, how could one not allow oneself to be recaptured very soon by the charms of the countryside?

As soon as there was a burst of sunlight, especially when the fruit trees decked themselves with red and white blossoms in the orchards of Saint-Aignan, we find the little canoness forgetting all her troubles. And that tragic spring of 1794, that spring which even the poets themselves did not dream of celebrating in verse, could still bring happiness to the heart of a sweet French girl.

CHAPTER SEVENTEEN

DAILY LIFE IN PRISON

Improved arrangements in revolutionary prisons – The poet Roucher at Saint-Lazare – The Comédie Française at Les Madelonettes – Les Recollets

---

IMPROVED ARRANGEMENTS IN REVOLUTIONARY PRISONS
The prisons from 1793 to 1794 had a certain reputation; is it merited? We generally find them depicted in the blackest of colours, but considered individually and forgetting for the moment the tumbrils of Fouquier-Tinville, there was nothing particularly hard in the life prisoners led. In fact, the régime applied to detainees was often almost liberal.

The majority of the former convents of Paris had been transformed into detainment centres. Port-Libre, formerly Port-Royal, Les Carmes, l'Abbaye, Les Ecossais du Luxembourg, Les Benedictins anglais, Les Anglaises de la Rue de Lourcine, Sainte-Pélagie, Saint-Lazare and so on, all were completely lacking in comfort because they had been adapted too hurriedly, but communal life in them gave the prisoners a certain sense of freedom and they enjoyed privileges which residents in our modern prisons would certainly envy.

We shall not concern ourselves with establishments of a very special kind, like Dr Belhomme's rest-home in the Rue de Charonne where crafty aristocrats, cosily ensconced away from the Terror, had themselves locked up and cocked a snook at authority, sure of being protected by their host's influence and of being able, as long as they had money, to give elegant suppers, organize concerts, receive pretty actresses like Lange or Mézeray and, in short, to indulge in every form of licence but that of jumping over the wall. Rather let us visit a real prison, entering for example the black porch in the Faubourg Saint-Martin.

As Saint-Lazare was lacking in beds, its involuntary pensioners were allowed to bring their own. Many of them took advantage of this rule to have complete sets of furniture brought: cupboard, chest of drawers, library and if necessary a pianoforte. The rooms were generally occupied by two or three persons, but they were large, airy and commanded a view which stretched as far as the slopes of Mont-Valérien. No bars on the windows, no bolts outside the doors, and, especially during the first months, no fixed curfew. How could one fail to enjoy a feeling of being in one's own home where one could wander about as one pleased day and night, keeping one's room open or closed, lounging and day-dreaming as much as one liked?

Letters were delivered unopened and were sent in the same way. It was also permissible for detainees to be sent parcels. Nothing more convenient for gourmets who thus could have their purchases delivered from outside and then cook their meals on the small portable stoves which were installed in the corridors.

Once one had seen to one's domestic chores, one became a person in high society again: one went to visit neighbours and pay one's respects to persons of quality following the rules of an etiquette which was as scrupulously observed at Saint-Lazare as at Versailles. For lovers of sport, there was (appropriately enough) prisoner's base and other ball games organized in one of the yards which had recently been gravelled. Others occupied their time with all kinds of work, played music, painted and sketched. In a fairly big room which became his studio Hubert Robert painted charming little landscapes on plates with the prison stamp on the bottom. Waiting for André Chénier to come and share his exile, the poet Roucher composed verses and admired the rosebush which his daughter had sent him. What a pleasure it must have been for the author of the *Months* to feel he had a little of the springtime with him!

As an even greater favour, he had been allowed to have his little boy stay with him, a young suspect of four whom the female contingent of course came to adore. All the fine ladies caged there showered him with toys, cakes, solemn invitations to dinner; they gave him a canary, some doves and a tame rabbit, all of which soon transformed his father's cell into a menagerie.

As long as things went quietly along, that is, until the time of what was claimed to be a conspiracy hatched in the prisons, this was the régime at Saint-Lazare. After one and a half centuries, if such a state of things existed in the Santé its political prisoners would certainly welcome the change.

Among the various revolutionary prisons there may have been differences: a greater or lesser degree of salubrity, food more or less bad, but the general atmosphere remained the same.

At Les Madelonettes the former ministers Saint-Priest and de Latour du Pin received every day visits of protocol from the former lieutenant of police and members of parliament who, despite their captivity, were always dressed up to the nines, with their wigs well powdered.

THE COMÉDIE FRANÇAISE AT LES MADELONETTES

In the big building of rather sinister aspect once ruled over by Ursuline nuns, the actors from the Comédie Française had been confined – kings of tragedy, noble fathers, *jeunes premiers*, all of them a trifle astonished to be playing their unrehearsed rôles:

'I can understand them imprisoning *you* lot,' Dazincourt declared to his colleagues, 'for you played emperors, marquises and kings and wore red heels. But to think they also imprisoned me, who always played footmen and valets, poor, humble *sans-culottes*!' And to cheer him up, La Rochelle got up to all sorts of antics, Champville played Rabelaisian tricks; comedy took over . . .

At Port-Libre there was the same atmosphere: performances were organized at which Larive was the great star. He declaimed lines from *William Tell*, verses by Marie-Joseph Chénier, and Mère Angélique must have turned in her grave.

LES RECOLLETS

One could find similar scenes in almost all the houses of detention in Paris by glancing through the *Almanachs des Prisons*, the *Mémoires sur les Prisons* or the *Mémoires d'un Détenu* by Riouffe. And it must be added that in the provinces things were no different. Without moving far from Paris, let us follow to Les Recollets at Versailles the Royalist Jullian, the man at the Vaugirard barrier who, after having thrown the police off the scent for a while, was finally arrested.[1]

As soon as he arrived there, he had the feeling that he was 'free'. There was a fairly big yard, two storeys with corridors where everyone wandered about as he wished, a good room, a large refectory – what more could one want? His days were spent as he pleased. Every morning he devoted two hours to writing his journal, then went to find M de L——, former equerry to Mesdames, the daughters of Louis XV, or received the worthy gentleman's visit in his own room, where they might have a game of chess.

The two friends' one regret is that the fine set of ivory and ebony chessmen which Jullian had bought had been mutilated. Before he would allow it to enter the prison, the gatekeeper at Les Recollets, a fanatical patriot, had insisted that the crowns should be broken on the heads of the kings and queens.

Evenings were generally spent in Mme de F——'s room, where they played whist and reversi, and where the Sainte-M—— young ladies inspired more than a passing interest in Jullian and in the Marquis de C——. The little circle was soon extended to include a new recruit, M de R——, the most entertaining of men. Jullian tells us:

> He possessed all the arts of mimicry and was particularly skilful at rendering with perfect tonalities the sound of the

hunting-horn, by applying a dinner-plate to his cheek; often during the King's hunting expeditions he had thus managed to deflect the hounds and deceive the huntsmen.

After this, how can we go on thinking that the prisoners of the Terror spent only tragic hours? Certainly it is never pleasant to have to forfeit one's liberty, but when there are others sharing the same fate, privation is less keenly felt. At Les Recollets as at the Luxembourg, at Port-Libre as at Saint-Lazare, people soon adapted themselves.

Alas, there was one shadow – the fear of having to make the acquaintance of the public prosecutor. When one lived under this perpetual threat, how could one enjoy to the full one's games of whist and imitations of hunting-horns?

CHAPTER EIGHTEEN

IN TIME OF WAR

Excuses for violence – The constitution of the new army – The National Guard at the frontiers – The volunteers of 1792 – Conscription in 1793 – Those who deserted

---

EXCUSES FOR VIOLENCE

One would not be paying the men of the revolutionary period their full due if one forgot that from 1792, and especially from March to December 1793, France was at war with half Europe.

The outstanding feature of the epoch was a wartime mentality, one which was complicated by the fact that a part of the nation – the most brilliant, the richest part, which had been dominant until now – was fighting in the ranks of the enemy. It was a tragic situation, one which gives the true tone to the drama of '93 and differentiates it from the other great testing times in our history like those, for example, of 1870 and 1914.

Poised between exterior and interior dangers, the First Republic was above all a wartime régime. The most magnificent successes can be explained by this, and the worst violences excused by it. If the battle rapidly became one of the utmost savagery, if the most humanitarian and happy people in the world let themselves be drawn into violence we must look for the reason less in pure politics than in the dangers of invasion which the people felt themselves threatened with.

Such a peril was bound to shake the nerves of the country. As soon as it was felt, all eyes, whether in town or countryside, were turned upon the army, for the peace of every fireside was going to depend henceforth on its successes or reverses.

This was a fresh aspect of daily life in a France where war was going to play the leading rôle. But let us not attempt to describe it without first recalling the broad outlines of how the Republic's legions were formed, that youthful army arisen from the ranks of the people and which rose to defend it.

During the first years of the Revolution, a speedy process of disintegration had been effected in the regiments of the former monarchy, diminishing considerably their military value. While simple soldiers and non-commissioned officers threw in their lot with the patriots, a number of higher-ranking officers proclaimed their sympathy with the aristocrats and handed in their resignations in order to enrol in the opposite camp. In 1791 particularly, after the King's abortive flight, the crisis in the high command took on serious proportions. Now just at that moment it began to look as if war would break out. There was no time to be lost. The army must be reinforced, its effective force increased, its general staff re-grouped. This was a mighty task.

Two years earlier, Dubois-Crancé had indeed proposed that universal military conscription should be brought in, but the Constituent Assembly had preferred a system of long-term recruitments, the periods of engagement to last for eight years. As this system produced no result, Alexandre de Lameth had given warning that, should war break out, we should find ourselves in a most awkward position. Events proved him right in 1791, and as it was necessary to move fast it was decided, as a last resort, to call upon the National Guard.

THE CONSTITUTION OF THE NEW ARMY

This famous bourgeois militia was improvisation personified; it had been born during the crisis of July 1789. The statute accorded to it the next year established that only active *citizens* could take a part in its affairs, that is, those who paid a contribution equal to the value of three days' work. It was desired that a National Guardsman should dispose of the necessary cash to fit himself out at his own expense and pay out of his own pocket for the fine royal-blue coat with the white lining and scarlet facings which dazzled the citizenesses who watched processions and parades.

Disguised as heroes, proud of their yellow epaulettes and the grand words 'Constitution and Liberty' embroidered on the facings of their tunics, our guards were divided into companies and battalions. They elected their officers and each battalion received a flag on which could be read, on one side: *For the People of France*, and on the other: *For Liberty or Death*.

After the flight from Varennes, the Constituent Assembly ordered mobilization (they called it 'putting the country on an active footing') of all National Guardsmen in the frontier provinces. Moreover, in order to swell the ranks, it ordered the levying of one hundred thousand volunteers from among the National Guardsmen of other regions.

It was hoped to form thus one hundred and sixty-nine new battalions, but the task was an enormous one, and as the National Guard, a civilian institution, depended entirely on the elected bodies, it fell to the municipal councils and district administrators to recruit, organize, equip and embody the volunteers. One can well imagine the feverish activity which went on from one end of France to the other for several weeks. Large cities and small hamlets were rivals in good will. From Sunday, June 26, 1791, that was four days after Varennes and even earlier in certain regions, registers were opened at town halls in order to record 'the names, surnames, age, profession and residence of those wishing to enrol in the defence of the *Patrie*'.

THE NATIONAL GUARD AT THE FRONTIERS

In Lorraine, near the frontier, this sudden levying of manpower was accompanied by intense emotionalism. The villages sounded the alarm bell, the National Guards assembled, bearing arms, and

at all points of the compass brigades of gendarmerie and detachments of troops of the line blocked the roads.

Able-bodied men left in the village barricaded their houses, as if they expected the sudden Austrian invasion which the royalist gazettes had been announcing for months past. Entire families, among which the memory of the Thirty Years War was still fresh, were fully expecting to see the arrival of the odious Swedes, and fled in terror to hide themselves in the woods.[1]

In the regions of the west, on the contrary, where the danger seemed less imminent, the recruiting campaigns proceeded with an almost festive air. The mayor of the little town of Craon, for example, took advantage of the fact that the district's patronal feast fell on June 25 to go down to the meadow where his townsfolk were dancing, beat the drum, read the mobilization order and exhorted the lads of Mayenne to respond to the appeal of the Assembly. The future general Pouget, witnessing the scene, described it in his *Souvenirs*:[2] 'There I was,' he informs us . . .

All the young ones shouted: 'If M Pouget will sign up, we shall do so too!' At once I took up the pen and signed my name, and all my youthful fellow-citizens did the same.

Such examples must have been frequent, for all classes of society vied with each other in appearing among the volunteers. The lists even included a few noblemen and priests. But the most numerous were the bourgeois – lawyers, merchants, men of independent means. There were also artisans and workmen. Contrary to what happens today, only the farmers refused their services, for they were held back by love of their land. Yet a few young peasants decided to join up; their parents had just bought church property and they wanted to prove their zeal.

Patriotism aside, the new troops were assured they would enjoy very appreciable advantages: one-year engagements, fairly high pay, easy discipline, regular holidays and rapid promotion: each man would be sent to a company formed of volunteers from his own region. Really, everything had been done to encourage enlistment, and these clever manoeuvres soon bore fruit: scarcely two months after Varennes, the one hundred thousand recruits had been found.

It remained to turn them into soldiers. This was the task of 'commissioners' nominated by the administrative districts, and most of them were former officers. There were great difficulties in equipping our future veterans of the Napoleonic wars, for many of them, contrary to what was stipulated by law, were *passive* citizens who lacked the means to pay for the least bit of equipment.

If the proverb has it that 'one lends only to the rich', that is probably because one is forced to *give* to the poor. In order to buy boots, tunics and rifles, collections were made, there were requisitions and when the new battalions were more or less armed and clothed, when they had received their lovely new flags, many of these blessed, after high mass, by a Constitutional bishop, they were finally able to proceed towards the frontier.

Need we say that their progress from town to town was marked by enthusiastic receptions and innumerable wine parties? After having played the part of an outfitter's shop, France was transformed, during all this period, into one vast banqueting hall.

THE VOLUNTEERS OF 1792

War was not to be declared until April 20, 1792. We know that during the first months one defeat followed another. Nevertheless, despite the routing of the armies of Dillon and Biron and the disintegration of our lines in the north, the Assembly, afraid of provoking a reaction it could not control, had refrained from making an appeal to the country. It was only because of growing anarchy, the court's double game, the shifty intrigues of La Fayette that the Assembly overcame its reluctance and decided to adopt, in the sitting on July 11, the following proclamation:

Numerous troops are advancing towards our frontiers; all

those who hate Liberty are taking up arms against our Constitution. Citizens, the *Patrie* is in danger.

CONSCRIPTION IN 1793

This time it was no longer a question of militarizing the National Guard, but of calling to the colours every kind of volunteer. It was a difficult task indeed, and it required considerable and dramatically effective propaganda.

On Sunday, July 22, the warning cannon on the Pont-Neuf was heard, with the one at the Arsenal booming in reply, hour after hour. The call to arms was sounded in all the quartiers. Municipal officers, preceded by horsemen, standard-bearers and military bands, visited every section of the city, stopping at all the crossroads to read proclamations. On the important squares, surrounded by a ring of flags, tents had been erected where planks laid across drumheads served as tables where men signed up.[3] In Paris alone, in three days, there were more than four thousand volunteers. After August 10, the movement spread further and it may be said that all over the country the results were splendid. It was this army of volunteers which stopped the Prussians at Valmy and beat the Austrians at Jemmapes.

However, great as this effort was, it was not enough. The drawback of short-term military engagements is that once a victory was gained the victors had only one aim: to go back home. This is what happened at the end of 1792: thousands and thousands of soldiers demanded leave and created a manpower crisis which became all the more threatening when the execution of Louis XVI made the European powers decide to form a coalition against France.

The levy of 300,000 men which had been decreed in February 1793 was intended to counter this threat; but this time the operation, especially in the western regions, met with fierce resistance. During the summer of that year it was necessary to have recourse to a more radical measure: mass mobilization. Assisted by the active support of Convention members on various missions to the interior, this general mobilization – the first the country had ever known – was carried out in perfect order and 500,000 new soldiers were soon being trained as fresh cannon-fodder.

It was thus that the famous Republican armies were formed, in several successive waves, and these armies were to be the wonder of the world. In a France which until then had only had regular armies, such a great mass of quickly conscripted citizens truly presented a new problem of formidable dimensions. From then on, there was not one family which did not have one or several of its members with the colours, not one in which news from the front was not impatiently awaited. In the shops of the Marais as well as in the farmhouses of Beauce the same questions worried everyone: How are things going? What is happening? And everywhere people's spirits became more tense and serious. Everyone was mad about the war, because everyone found himself more or less directly mixed up in it.

THOSE WHO DESERTED

There were, it is true, in the big cities, and particularly in Paris, a number of fine young gentlemen for whom general mobilization was nothing to worry about. The art of avoiding military service is one which has been perfected over the centuries, and the laws of the Republic, severe though they were, offered countless loopholes for young men with their wits about them.

One could gain exemption if one was in public office, or obtain a special dispensation to work in armaments or in the construction of military wagons and other means of transport, and these escape routes were always available for the 'rich and healthy'.[4] Others suddenly discovered that they had a passion for the land and for the tedium of agricultural work; yet others took refuge in something they had never dreamed of contracting, marriage: for bucolic labours and lip-service to Hymen had the advantage of procuring for one numerous exemptions.

As soon as one had got oneself well and truly exempted one was perfectly at liberty to take one's hand from the plough – or from one's wife's shoulder – and dash back to the capital where one could help the war effort by sauntering along the boulevards carrying, just for appearances' sake, rustic walking-sticks and wearing the very latest in large cravats, the badge of the fops and dandies known as *muscadins* or *miriflores*, who were always scandalizing prim bourgeois and virtuous coppers' narks.

But let us not attach too much importance to a minority which hardly deserves our sympathy. The daily life of this gilded youth was just too peculiar for the eyes of honest citizens. It is much more elevating to follow, day by day, in all their various peregrinations, the gallant and glorious careers of the soldiers of the Republic.

CHAPTER NINETEEN

LETTERS FROM SOLDIERS

The notebooks of Sergeant Friscasse – Xavier Vernère: his childhood, his engagements, his romance at Lunéville – Gabriel Noël's love letters – The letters of Etienne Gaury – The letters of a young drummer-boy to his mother

THE NOTEBOOKS OF SERGEANT FRISCASSE

In this glorious domain there exist two kinds of documents: letters written by soldiers and the memoirs which certain of them have left us.

They are not all of interest; in most of them one realizes that the sword, alas, was mightier than the pen. Nevertheless there is nearly always something of interest to be found in these campaign notes scribbled somewhere in a tent on the eve of an attack or of some tough assignment, and which at least have the merit of showing us military life through the wrong end of the telescope.

Let us cast an eye over the notebooks of Sergeant Friscasse, for example, pompously entitled: *An anthology of the campaigns I have fought in the Service of my Country, the One and Indivisible Republic.*[1] The author is the son of a gardener living near Chaumont who had already enlisted in the army. When the son was nineteen, he followed his father's example and signed up as a volunteer on August 24, 1792, in the first regiment of the Haute-Marne.

There were arms drills and rather confusing marches and countermarches between Chaumont and Saint-Dizier: the first pages of the journal are concerned with little else. Nevertheless we learn that a soldier's daily pay is fifteen francs and three *décimes*,[2] in paper money, naturally, and that a corporal commands twenty-three francs and eight *décimes*, on which lavish pay he has to find his own food. But as the price of foodstuffs was still fairly reasonable, it is possible to make ends meet.

On September 12, 1793, in the forest of Mormal, our hero received the baptism of fire. His battalion bumped into the troops of the Prince of Coburg who had just taken Le Quesnoy. But the result of this first encounter was not very encouraging. They had to fall back on Landrecies, and a week later on Mauberge, for the Austrians had succeeded in crossing the Sambre.

With the defence of Mauberge the story takes a more colourful turn: 'On October 5,' notes Friscasse,

> on the left-hand redoubt, between Tilleul wood and our advance posts, a French sentry and a Dutch sentry were within sixty feet of one another, which enabled them to carry on a conversation. Four soldiers from my own post went forward; the Dutch who were in the Tilleul wood had their curiosity aroused and came to join in the conversation...

It is the old story of siege wars. Ever since the days of Homer, soldiers of opposing camps have been drawn together by common humanity.

The Dutch asked the French how they were getting on and scoffed at them for having nothing to eat.

'We Republicans do not lack for anything.'

'Go on! You're eating your horses. Your *assignats* are worthless. We've got you in a tight spot. We'll soon have you dancing the carmagnole for the last time!'

But as the argument grew more heated, one of our soldiers thought he recognized the voice of one of the men on the other side:

'Let me get a good look at the old swine! Why, it's my brother that was!'

The other jested: 'If I *was* your brother, I must still be . . .'

'You bloody fool!' the Frenchman shouted back. 'When I

left for the front you promised me you would look after our old woman, and you left her without support and broken-hearted. You deserve to die! You're not human! You barbarian!'

And then a shot rang out from our lines. The pseudo-Dutchman fell with a shattered thigh-bone.

This family drama had its counterpart in another tale taken from the same diary. One evening, an Austrian cavalryman from the Coburg regiment, under Friscasse's very nose, charged a Frenchman of the 12th Dragoons:

> After both had shot their pistols at one another they drew close to attack with their sabres. Surprise, surprise! They found they were brothers; they had not seen one another for fifteen years. At once they dropped their sabres, dismounted and flung themselves upon each other's necks, speechless with emotion. A moment later they were vowing never to part again and to serve under the same colours. The dragoon went to ask General Jourdan not to class his brother as a deserter and not to hold him prisoner, and the general agreed to reinstate the man in the regiment.

Such diversions did not prevent the troops defending Mauberge from being bored stiff, and they suffered cruel hardships. The enemy had taken all the corn, covering the roofs of their temporary hutments with the straw and feeding their horses on the grain, so that the surrounding countryside was quite bare of food resources. In the town, there was a dearth of provisions and water was foul, for the river bordering the camp had been diverted and it was necessary to draw water from ditches along the entrenchments 'where the men went to do their business'. More than one volunteer suffered from a 'flux of blood', what we would call today raging typhoid fever.

Fortunately the victory at Wattignies relieved Mauberge. Four months later, Friscasse was promoted sergeant, while his battalion took up its winter quarters successively at Colleret,

Damousies and Jeumont, always fairly close to the enemy, which allowed them to exchange a few rifle-shots, or, as the old sweats called them, 'Republican greetings'.

Our hero's sojourn in that northern sector has given us valuable details about the life of the region. It was fertile land whose soil produced good wheat and all kinds of vegetables. Wine was scarce and dear, and beer was the usual drink. Cattle there were in plenty, giving an abundance of milk and cheese and spending most of the year out in the fields, in vast, well-shaded meadows.

> One hardly notices the villages unless one actually enters them; everything is enclosed, with thick woods all round and encircling every house. Most of the houses are roofed with straw. In this region, both the sexes are friendly and humane.

When the victory at Fleurus allowed the generals to prosecute a more lively campaign, we find Sergeant Friscasse again in Belgium. During the next few years his campaigns were to take him to the Rhineland, then to southern Germany, to the edge of Lake Constance, later to Switzerland and Italy. The author of the journal always describes the countries he is passing through – the sights, what there was to eat, the costumes and customs of the inhabitants. Descriptions which, we must admit, are not without a certain tincture of naïvety.

Thus we learn that the people around Aix-la-Chapelle take jam with their morning coffee, and drink beer and 'chenik'; that the people of the Black Forest, having a plentiful supply of timber, use it to construct chalets; that the men's trousers are pleated, that the women do up their hair in plaits under straw hats with four horns; that they have very wide décolletages, and heads as 'big as a three-month-old calf', that they wear three skirts one on top of the other, are 'laced and bundled up like bundles of faggots' and possess 'very large bosoms' inside their bright red bodices. Friscasse completes his documentation by revealing that the natives eat bacon and choucroute or sauerkraut and that 'their language is German'.

One might have guessed it.

XAVIER VERNÈRE: HIS CHILDHOOD, HIS ENGAGEMENTS, HIS ROMANCE AT LUNÉVILLE

Xavier Vernère[3] belonged to a social class rather different from that of Fricasse but his childhood and youth were no happier.

It would be impossible to imagine a start to life more terrible than his. A child whose parents were ruined and then separated, he saw his father, a hot-head, join the Trappist order. His mother begrudged the boy the crusts of black bread she gave him, and he had an abominable sister who gave him away to a shrew of a woman. He ran away several times, was caught and escaped again, trudging the roads in the company of an itinerant hawker. Then he passed through a painful schooling at a college where he was tormented by one of the masters. He returned to his home in the Jura, where he was the butt of everyone. Beside his experiences, *David Copperfield* and *Poil de Carotte* grow pale by comparison.

In 1789, young Vernère, aged fourteen, walked right across France on foot and was taken in, at Rochefort, by one of his uncles who tried to get him an apprentice pilot's certificate. But his troubles were by no means at an end! The proximity of marshes surrounding the town soon brought on a fever which prevented him from sailing for India with the other cadets of his school.

As the navy did not want him, why not try the army? Another of his uncles, who was a sergeant-major in the Anjou regiment, was garrisoned at Tours. At the beginning of 1790, Xavier went to join him there, worked under his direction and that of an almoner, was vastly pleased by life in military circles, followed the regiment to Saint-Malo and, about twenty months later, was delighted to be able to join up himself. His uncle had just been promoted to second lieutenant, and our recruit was to serve under him.

By an amusing paradox, this lad of sixteen already had the 'old sweat's' attitude. When there were arguments between regulars and volunteers – or between *culs blancs* (white arses) and *bleuets* (cornflowers) as they were known – he was always on the side of the former. He had nothing but contempt for those battalions of Jacobins 'which often get together wherever there is rowdiness or licence', for those *Brothers and Friends* who, after having taken the military to their bosoms, allow themselves to give them explanations of successes or losses, to censure or commend the generals and to propose, with a burlesque dignity, addresses of congratulation to those who had distinguished themselves.

But war had been declared. The former Anjou regiment, now become the 36th Infantry Division, received orders to join the army in the north. It passed through Dol, Fougères, Mayenne, Alençon, Evreux, Vernon and Mantes, and on July 15, 1792, was camped in the plain of Saint-Denis. To feel themselves so close to Paris but to be forbidden to enter the city – what heart-break for young soldiers!

Accompanied by a few comrades, Vernère first of all permitted himself a slight consolation: he clambered up the Butte de Montmartre, from where the whole city could be seen. Then the little group allowed itself to be tempted by the offer of a Parisian who saw them through the barrier. Then began a wonderful walk that filled our provincials with delight: the boulevards, the Chinese Baths, the Place Louis-XV, the Pont Louis-XVI, the Legislative Assembly, with some fresh curiosity to be noted at every step they took, and finally the Palais Royal, where they lingered quite a while to eye 'those Nymphs who, as night falls, come out to spread their silken snares for free-thinking gentlemen'.

But they had to get back to Saint-Denis. When the friends returned to their quarters, with aching feet but memories stuffed with sights that would last them a lifetime, they were relieved to hear that there had been no second call. Paris brought them luck that night.

The regiment soon departed, but in a different direction. Instead of proceeding towards the north, it was sent to join the army of the Rhine, and it tramped there by stages through Nancy and Lunéville. It was here that a little romance took place which Vernère describes in a very telling way: 'The daughter of my host,' he writes,

a charming young woman, and infinitely kind, appeared to be so much taken with the little soldier lodging under her roof that on one of those fine summer nights whose silence and calm sometimes make the soul thrill with such sweet sensations, she was not averse to passing a large part of it alone with him, sitting on a garden seat, where the hours floated by, it seemed, with an astonishing rapidity as they abandoned themselves to the delicious pleasures of an innocent and agreeable conversation. We did not separate until after midnight, lavishing kisses upon each other.

This was a fine beginning, but let us not be too quick to assume the worst, for the author hastens to add:

I was unaware of all the happiness I might have enjoyed during that charming tête-à-tête . . .

There could hardly be a better explanation of why certain volunteers were nicknamed 'cornflowers'.

The next morning, at cockcrow – which however was scarcely required by the circumstances – Xavier was already buckling on his pack, never thinking he would see the young person again. But she had risen as early as he, for she wished to bid him a proper adieu. The tender young lover tried to restrain himself; he knew that duty called, but Venus proved stronger than Mars. They crossed the yard together, concealed themselves in a doorway and the embraces began all over again.

We could not leave each other alone. The steps of a staircase nearby offered us a place where we might dispose ourselves; the silence all around us, the darkness we found ourselves in and which was only just beginning to lighten

. . . our fevered caresses increasing with an amazing ardour, all conspired to make us feel an agitation that perhaps would have led to the discovery of enjoyments we could only guess at. We were perhaps about to emerge from the ignorance of love's pleasures that still held our bodies in thrall, had it not been for the inopportune arrival of a captain of the regiment who had come to look for his horse, which had been stabled at the house.

Never could the appearance of an officer have been more catastrophic. I imagine that later Alfred de Vigny was to find his admirable title, *Servitude et grandeur militaires*, in similar circumstances. The captain addressed Vernère in no uncertain terms: 'What are you waiting for, you great goose? We've been given orders to start at once!' There was nothing for it but to obey, and with his tail between his legs our despondent lover went off to rejoin his regiment. He had gone over a league, but still kept turning round every dozen yards to gaze at the roofs of the Château Stanislas and the towers of the church of Saint-Jacques.

The next stages in the march were lugubrious ones. At Haguenau, carts carrying the wounded passed them on the road, their planks dripping with blood; this taught the young soldier that war is not all gentle dalliance. Soon the lines were reached, though they did not take any great part in the attack at Custine. After passing the winter in the region of Rudesheim and Bingen, they retreated on Wissemburg, and to his great delight Vernère found himself promoted quartermaster-sergeant. 'No Marshal of France,' he confesses,

> ever received his bâton with greater pride than I felt when I put the silver galoons on my sleeve. Ideas above my station fired my mind and I fatuously calculated that, at seventeen and a half, I had a rank which raised me well above nine-tenths of the entire army.

But there were more serious satisfactions in store for Vernère, for he was to end up in the leather breeches of a Colonel of the Empire. But let us linger no longer over his notebooks. As he rose in rank, he tended to write merely simple accounts of military operations, and we must look elsewhere for picturesque details on the daily life of our brave boys.

GABRIEL NOËL'S LOVE LETTERS

More than one sketch of this kind is supplied in the letters of Gabriel Noël,[4] a young volunteer who campaigned with the second Meurthe battalion. Born at Nancy in 1770 in a family of well-to-do farmers, he had been brought up by his godmother, Mme Durival, a friend of the Marquise de Boufflers, and who gave him an excellent education. He had a great fondness for her, a tender feeling which M Durival – if he existed – might have been justified in taking some umbrage at. Let us glance through the pretty love letters which Noël addresses to the dear lady from the small garrison of Sierck where he was learning to be a soldier in January 1792. If Cherubino himself had been mobilized he could not have written more charming letters to the Countess Almaviva:

> I feel, when I receive your letters, a contentment such as I cannot express in words. On a first reading, I devour them, if I may use such an expression, with avidity. Then I read them again several times and each time with greater satisfaction, for being so famished prevents me from enjoying the first perusal to the full. If someone comes in and interrupts me during this banquet, I pay no heed to him, like a ravenous beast with its jaws fixed in its prey.

Noël would hardly be of his time if he was not able to compose a pretty madrigal, albeit in prose, like the above. But he would be even less typical of his time if he were not sensible to the charms of Nature. Already in February he is noticing 'with vast delight the first signs of spring: green gooseberry bushes, elders beginning to put forth shoots, and tiny leaves on the rosebushes'.

To complete his portrait, let us remember that he loves

study, that he is working at German grammar, reading the Abbé Vertot's *History of Roman Revolutions* and that these innocent distractions help him to bear the boredom of his little garrison town. What a dull hole was the wretched town of Sierck! The entire battalion cheered when they learnt that they were going to be stationed somewhere else.

But perhaps they cheered too soon, for the village in German Lorraine where they found themselves a few days later seemed to have even less to offer: 'We have two beds among five men,' Noël writes from his fresh quarters:

Fate has decided that I should be in the one containing three persons. Our beds are made of straw with a sheet spread over it. On top of the sheet, by way of covering, is a feather bed. What makes it even less inviting is that every detachment in France seems to have used our sheets . . .

Then we enter a chapter which will cause no astonishment to those old sweats who were in the Great War:

There are bugs also, but let's skip that. I am a soldier and a citizen; in this dual quality, I am permitted no squeamish thoughts. So I shall go to bed fully clothed except for my coat; in this way I shall be ready all the quicker when I have to go out on patrol.

Nothing new under the sun, indeed. The letters addressed to Mme Durival, tell us that wartime godmothers existed before 1914, and prove no less clearly that the soldiers of the Revolution already knew those little beasts which twentieth-century troopers became so familiar with, and called affectionately by the diminutive of Antoine.

Disdaining to allow themselves to be affected by such painful contingencies, Noël and his bedfellows nevertheless were able to keep their spirits up and their ingenuity helped them to get along with a populace which did not understand one word of French. Witness the following anecdote:

We very much wanted to have some milk . . . But how to

ask for it? I am not yet sufficiently advanced in my German studies; so I left it to the others. But all the gestures and signs they could think up failed to make the people realize that milk was wanted, and they just laughed at our antics. When my comrades were weary of their dumbshow and I saw they were resigned to going without, I took my German grammar, hoping to find the word in the vocabulary: but it was not there. But I did manage to find the word for cow. Then I looked for a receptacle and, using my four fingers to imitate a cow's udder, I 'milked' them as best I could with my right hand, indicating that there was liquid falling into the bowl, which I had placed underneath. The Germans, watching us closely, suddenly burst out laughing, as we did ourselves; they had understood, and said *Ja, ja*. Tomorrow we shall have milk.

The declaration of war on April 20 put an end to this sedentary life and Noël prided himself on being able to carry the good news to the peoples beyond the Rhine, for, of course,

it is only kings who do harm to nations. The spirit of Liberty will spread throughout the world. But it behoves those citizens who are already free to come to the aid of the rest. Thus the French shall prove themselves superior to the Romans who only wanted liberty for themselves.

The young man's enthusiasm was to be dampened a little during the abominable summer of 1792, which made marching so hard. And they never attacked! 'To be always on the defensive,' he wrote, 'is to accept a life of inaction. We should attack and make the tyrants tremble and liberate those peoples they have enslaved.' His impatience changed to despair when he learnt that the Prussians were entering Lorraine and seizing Longwy.

But at least he had the consolation of hearing (from fairly far-off) the cannonading of Valmy. It was for him a memorable occasion, which he was often to evoke later.

Once his campaigning was over and he had gone back home in 1797, he married for love and had many children and felt entitled to recall that date, declaring proudly, while his family sat round the fire in the evenings: 'The day I was at Valmy . . .'

THE LETTERS OF ETIENNE GAURY

And while we have our hands in the soldier's mailbag, let us look at a few more eye-witness accounts.

If we are to believe Etienne Gaury,[5] the second Battalion of Charente-Inférieure to which he belonged as a volunteer and which was quartered at Fort-Vauban, formerly Fort-Louis, did not have too wretched a time of it during the first months of 1793:

> When it is fine, the battalion sometimes marches along the banks of the Rhine. The walks there are spacious and charming. We have our military band, which plays well. We can see whole enemy posts coming out of the guard-rooms to watch us. They could very easily shoot their cannon at us, but up till now they have not done so, which only goes to prove that they are not nearly as bad as we are, for whenever we see a goodly number of them we never miss.

There were only two drawbacks, according to our volunteer: the high cost of living and the stupidity of the inhabitants in that region. The latter are 'brutish and coarse', and they are particularly criticized because they have remained extremely devout: on the roads, 'one cannot go a hundred yards without finding crosses, crucifixes, shrines and other superstitious monuments'.

As for the food problem, it would be fairly simple to solve if one were satisfied with pork, potatoes and vegetables, for the country produced these things in abundance, but bread and wine were far too dear, and it is well known that a French soldier can hardly get along without both these commodities. Just try making Gaury, a product of Charente, drink beer! He missed the good vintages of his native region and was miserable at having to pay fifteen *sous* a bottle for the wretched local red biddy.

This theme recurs in an infinite number of letters signed by other names. From the camp at Landau, on June 25, 1794, young André Desbruères[6] writes to his mother living in Châteauroux:

> You tell me that you had the cards read and they told you I had a pretty mistress; I tell you the truth when I say that since leaving Besançon (his former garrison) I've had nothing but trouble, but not with the girls. The trouble has been finding cheap wine, and now we have neither wine nor brandy and most of the time we have no bread . . .

The shortage of supplies that the volunteers of Year II complained of was to grow still worse for the Year III volunteers, who were taken advantage of by the wartime commissariat, that is, by the State, as much as by doubtful middle-men and by munitioners' private enterprises. There were many brave heroes then who were forced to punch an extra hole or two in their leather belts.

The longer the war lasted, the more the troops complained of lack of food. Those operating in the south seemed no better off than those in the east and north. Proof of this comes in a letter which two young men, brothers, Jean and Michel Auvray, stationed at l'Aiguille fort, near Toulon, wrote to their elder brother Gabriel Auvray, himself a captain at Mauberge, on February 4, 1795:[7]

> We can tell you this much, everything's damn dear down this way. The wine which we paid five *sous* a bottle for five months ago now costs twenty *sous* a bottle. A regulation loaf runs at three *livres*. Cloth is also so expensive, we cannot touch it. To make a pair of trousers and a waistcoat of nankeen or Siamese calico you have to put down seventy-five *livres* . . .

Such missives generally end with the classic appeal to the

family's generosity. But apart from the fact that no one is rolling in money these days, the people at home are also suffering many privations, the post is still in its infancy and the modest *assignats* which a doting mother or a liberal father might slip into an envelope might easily fall into the wrong hands. Soldiers in all regiments complained time without number about these – errors of distribution.

THE LETTERS OF A YOUNG DRUMMER-BOY TO HIS MOTHER
Correspondence between civilians and the military was none the less active, for it was the sole link one had with departed loved ones. Ah! with what swelling heart one awaited them, those little soiled notes from the army and which had come such a long way! With what haste they were opened, and with what haste they were answered, as if to prove to absent ones that one's thoughts were ever with them!

It must be kept in mind that many families had all their sons at the front. We need look no further than the example of good old Jean Auvray, a Parisian gardener, whose two young sons we have already met (the young volunteers at Toulon); but he had two others also with the colours. The letter he wrote to the elder on July 9, 1794, shows how calm the old man remained, with all his troubles:[8]

To Captain of Artillery Gabriel Nicolas Auvray, garrisoned at Saint-Quentin, Département de Laisnes.[9]

I write to you to let you know our news and to tell you that we are all in good health. I received letters from your brothers Jean and Michel who are at Lyons; they are both very well. I had news from them about two days ago; they tell me that they wrote to you at the hospital but they don't know if you received it. It seems to me they were very upset to hear you were wounded and so they wrote me a letter which touched me very deeply with the sincerity of their feelings.

I wrote to them not to worry, that your wound was not

dangerous and that you were garrisoned at Saint-Quentin and that you were going on well.

What disturbs me is that I have had no news from your brother François; if you can tell me anything you would be doing me a great favour and also if you would give me precise news about the army. If you can find some way of coming to spend a few days with us, it would give us great pleasure, because I have many things I want to tell you. Come for a few days if you can. No more for the present.

Your father,

Auvray.

Letters from parents to their sons or from soldiers to their parents, letters either naïve or well-turned, the scribbles of poor uniformed devils or the rhetoric of orators in uniform, souvenirs gleaned from day to day, protestations of affection or prosaic lamentations on the price of wine or butter – how curious and varied it is, this series of military epistles!

One could make an infinite number of telling quotations, but space is limited. One last letter perhaps may be allowed: one which a boy of twelve, little François Daigueplats,[10] volunteer drummer-boy with the army of the Rhine, addressed to his mother, living at Saint-Claud in Charente:

My dear Mama,

I received your letter with the *assignat* which you had the kindness to send me. It fills me with all the sense of obligation that a son should feel for his mother; I shall never be able to repay you for all the things you have done or shall do for me in the future.

Be assured of my friendship and my warm heart and my good will.

I want you to believe in a son who loves you more than himself and who will never forget you, lest he be thought the most ingrate of men; such could never be the thought of a true Republican; you do not deserve being rewarded with ingratitude. It would be too bad for you.

Adieu, my dear mama; I kiss you with all my heart and my little sister too; tell her that if I can come home I shall look forward to seeing her.

My godfather left for home on the 17th; you'll know how long it will take him. We have just been read the Constitution; both my father and I signed it.[11]

We kiss you with all our heart and soul. I say, mama darling, won't it be wonderful when we see the blossoming of our dear Republic, despite its enemies?

Childish prattle through which we can see glimpses of maturity already, a mixture of big words repeated without being fully understood, and sentiments that bring a tear to the eye: but the valiant lad's epistle has a real charm.

I do not know how another little drummer-boy, Joseph Barra, of about the same age, was able to write to his mama, but I doubt whether she ever received a prettier or more tender letter . . .

CHAPTER TWENTY

DAILY LIFE ON THE ROADS

Convention representatives on missions: Barras and Fréron at Marseilles and Toulon – Goupilleau goes to the Midi – His second tour – Patriotic drinking

CONVENTION REPRESENTATIVES ON MISSIONS: BARRAS AND FRÉRON AT MARSEILLES AND TOULON

The daily life of sedentary people interests us certainly, but that of the travellers who kept moving about the country during the Revolution is no less worthy of description. Among these road-users, we naturally think first of all of those most official of tourists, Convention representatives sent on missions to various parts of France.

Exploring ceaselessly every region of the land, taking their plumed hats and seven-league boots from the Pas-de-Calais to the Bouches-du-Rhône, and from the Atlantic to the Jura, they knew better than anyone the cities, towns and villages; they ate all kinds of food, slept in every kind of inn, and despite the speed with which they moved, managed to glean, as they travelled the roads, direct observations of things and people which sometimes have real charm. These globe-trotters of politics were therefore also, in many cases, observers of provincial life whose evidence cannot be ignored.

About half of the Convention members were sent on missions, either to the army or to the various administrative districts of France. But here we shall not study their military or administrative rôle. We merely want to observe them as travellers.

Among those whose activities roused the greatest criticism were Barras and Fréron, who were sent to Marseilles and

Toulon. Denounced in the Convention and in the Clubs, Fréron undertook to justify his conduct, and the letter which he sent from Marseilles on December 12, 1793, to Moïse Bayle, deputy of the Bouches-du-Rhône and member of the Committee of General Safety, gives some precise details about his everyday preoccupations:[1]

It is said that denunciations are raining down upon us in Paris, and on me in particular. There is talk of our insolent luxury, of our farmer-general style of dining. Malicious tongues wag about everything . . . All we have is a meal at four in the afternoon. We have neither too much nor too little . . . We almost never invite anyone to share with us. Sometimes we cannot refuse to give a bowl of soup to *sansculottes* if they come and ask for it. Every ten days we have four workmen dine with us, turn and turn about. They work in the armaments factories.

Regarding our luxurious ways, all this boils down to is that we wear a blue coat and a red waistcoat, the accepted costume for representatives, with our hair dressed plain. Sometimes I do not go out for several days, but sit in my dressing-gown, busy writing and working on my reports; and if I go out, it is always at half-past seven in the evening, to enjoy a little fresh air . . . And I always come back before ten o'clock.

As for women, I have no time to see any, though I like them very much. But I love my country a hundred times better, and my country has all my time. We are living at the inn, but we prefer to dine alone, because otherwise it would cost us twice as much, and not be so well served . . . Those who saw me in the mountains of the Esterel dining off raw onions had a good laugh at the name of 'dandy' which Hébert so gratuitously laid upon me.

Further on, Fréron speaks of the energetic steps he has taken or is about to take, and which do not give us any very high opinion of the morality of the Marseillais. But are not the *nervis* of as ancient an origin as the little streets of the Vieux-Port?

There were no police in Marseilles; we established a force. One could enter without a passport. We have already discovered four gaming-houses where people address each other as *monsieur* and *madame* and where the louis cost sixty *livres* in paper money. We are going to raid the gamblers tomorrow morning. Marseilles is going to be paved and cleaned up, for it is of a horrible filthiness. Moreover, this will give employment for many idle hands. All the public women who infect our volunteers and entice them from the army shall within two days be placed under arrest. The order has been signed and a place readied to receive them. Diseased girls will receive treatment and healthy ones will work at sewing uniforms or shirts for the brave defenders of the *Patrie*. We shall bring Marseilles into line.

GOUPILLEAU GOES TO THE MIDI

We remain in the Midi with Philippe-Charles-Aimé-Goupilleau, known as Goupilleau de Montaigu, to distinguish him from his cousin Goupilleau de Fontenay. This deputy from La Vendée made several trips south in 1793, 1794 and 1795.

When the Convention, by a decree passed October 8, 1793, had ordered an extraordinary requisitioning of horses, it had divided France into twenty parts, each of which was placed under the supervision of a representative. Goupilleau was given the ninth division, including Vaucluse, les Bouches-du-Rhône, Var and Les Alpes Maritimes. On the 10th he left Paris to go on an exploratory tour of his fief. Let us follow him in the fine carriage taking him towards the south.[2]

Unlike certain others, Goupilleau did not in fact depart on horseback, at full gallop, followed by a postilion guide. He did not even content himself with a two-wheeled conveyance pulled by a pair of horses. He hired a carriage with four wheels, which required three strong horses to pull it, an equipage which comprised a trunk or (as it was called) a *cow*, an enormous hamper covered with leather and attached to the roof. Horses and postilion were changed at every posting-house. For each post – about eight kilometres – the fare was twenty-five *sous* for a horse and ten *sous* for a postilion. So the journey from Paris to Marseilles cost four hundred and fifty francs. Add to this the cost of crossing rivers and streams by ferry-boat, for which twenty-five *sous* to two francs was asked. Add yet again the charges for inn meals, and one is forced to realize that transporting a parliamentary representative from Paris to the Canebière cannot be done on the cheap.

But our man has to travel comfortably. Well bolstered with cushions, he can gaze at the countryside, observe the local customs and fill his travel notebook with personal notes.

The first of these are devoted to the form of female head-gear, a subject which would seem only distantly connected with the requisitioning of horses. Between Nevers and Roanne, all the women were wearing straw hats. The same observation is made between Roanne and Lyons, but now the straw is black and the brims are wider. This inexhaustible source of interest was returned to at Marseilles, where women would have dark skins were it not for their protective head-dresses, and, a little later, at Nice, where imprudent beauties, grilled like toast, are coiffed only with a light gauze scarf.

But we return to Lyons, and Goupilleau makes no secret of the fact that the place has no attraction for him:

> It is an immense city, but most of the streets are narrow, badly paved and always muddy; the *quais* and the houses are neither as pleasant nor as well constructed as at Nantes. Nevertheless (and here he shows a prudence that does him honour as a tourist), one would have to stay longer in order to judge.

After Vienne, where he arrived on October 15, Goupilleau really began to make contact with the south. He felt as if he were travelling in the month of August, it was so warm. Making for Valence, he crossed the Isère by ferry: 'A rapid, though shallow river.' Along the road he saw mulberry and almond trees, and very large swine, black as wild boars. On the 17th, at Mondragon, mulberries again, but now also figs and olives; that evening, a halt at Avignon.

Let us not praise too highly the ancient capital of Comtat. Obviously the food was good there; they served excellent wines. But its innkeepers were rogues:

> They lavish caresses on you when you arrive and skin you alive when you depart. They are Italians, in the wider acceptation of the word.

After this meridional parting shot, Goupilleau climbed back into his berlin and on the 19th arrived at Arles, at seven in the morning, along a highway constructed on a high, narrow embankment. He was not in a very good humour, for the gnats kept him awake all night, forcing him to close the carriage windows. Probably the odious little beasts kept up their concert at the inn that night, for our traveller set off again with a splitting headache.

At Aix, however, he relaxed. A speech in dialect addressed to him by the president of the People's Society managed to cheer him up. And then, the sea was close by. On the 21st he was in Marseilles:

> The approaches are delightful, and she promises well; the streets are broad and clean (what *was* Fréron talking about?), the houses well constructed. It is a city as beautiful as Nantes, but of a different character. The streets here are wider and better arranged; the main thoroughfare (la Canebière) is the most lovely of streets. The theatre is not as good as the one at Nantes (our Vendéan definitely seems to think that Nantes is the very last word in provincial grandeur . . .) but it is very fine. The port is nothing but a large pool surrounded by dilapidated buildings. Only one frigate, also dilapidated. The *quais* round about are admirable, all paved with bricks set on end. The one defect is that they are too narrow; the buildings on them almost touch the houses.

If Goupilleau finds the complexion of the Marseilles people

too dark, their language seems to him 'very gay'. He is not so keen on the prices charged at the inns, whose keepers are every bit as 'Italian' as those in Avignon. The mistress of the Hôtel de Beauveau, Mme Simon, practically holds him up to ransom, so high are her charges, and he swears never to set foot there again. In his room, so expensive, a delightful invention allowed him to enjoy sound sleep.

At Marseilles it is the custom to drape round the bed a curtain of muslin, tightly closed and called a 'mosquito-net'.

Having been relieved of the burden of several bundles of *assignats*, the honorable Convention representative now proceeded towards the interior of Provence. There he found a great deal of dust, trees green as in springtime, but still those damned mosquitoes.

On the 23rd he passed through Roquevaire, Auriol, Saint-Zacharie. Everywhere the grape harvest was in full swing and the vines seemed loaded with juicy bunches. Finally on the 26th, he entered Grasse, the capital of the Var since Toulon fell to the English. Scarcely had he booked in at the inn than a delegation came to invite him to dine 'with the entire administrative corps'. A touching demonstration of loyalty in which the guest of honour noted 'great friendliness and unity and a gaiety typical of Provence'.

Continuing his tour, we find him next day passing through Antibes. This was a very Jacobin town where, after having passed through the Gate of the Convention, one proceeded down the Street of the 10th of August and others named after July 14, May 31, Brutus and *Ça ira*: 'There is a patriotic fervour everywhere.'

Another few leagues and we are in the region of Nice, 'a rich and charming country', where the representative stayed with his colleague Augustin Robespierre who was on a mission to the army in the Alps. Both of them went to spend the evening at the Club, and learnt on their return of the victory at Wattignies. Goupilleau went to bed enveloped in an aura of victory, and also in 'a good mosquito-net, which is essential at Nice'.

Already autumn was far advanced and the end of October was marked by a few stormy days which also had the stamp of the Midi. As the traveller's windows gave on the sea, he had a magnificent view. Then as soon as it cleared up he went out to explore the city, was amused to hear 'a dialect very close to Italian', deplored the narrowness of the streets but on the other hand admired without reserve the Place de la République, later to be called Place Masséna: 'It is surrounded by porticoes, like the Palais Royal, but in a prettier taste . . .' Surely admirers of old Paris have a right to protest at this?

There were few remarkable incidents during the return journey. The exuberance of the Provençals had begun to weary Goupilleau a little, for after all he was a man from the west: 'The inhabitants of these southern districts,' he sighs, 'are very honest, decent folk, but terribly fatiguing. One cannot walk a step without being surrounded by their chatter.' At one point he felt he would be suffocated by the embraces of the people of Antibes. At another, the inn at Tourves contained a troup of actors who forced him to drink and sing. Elsewhere the National Guard hauled him off to the Club, though all he wanted was to sleep, and forced him to make a speech.

And then there was the mistral! With the first days of November the weather really began to deteriorate: 'Don't believe them when they say it is never cold in Provence,' he writes. 'I've never felt such an icy blast as that which has been blowing here ever since I left Nice.'

The chilliness of the Rhône valley however did not prevent the deputy from stopping at Arles and staying there a whole month in order to attend at last to the real object of his mission: the requisitioning of horses. We find him there until December 6, dividing his time between the inspection of stables, official or private correspondence and a few trips to Tarascon or Beaucaire.

The Arlesians tried hard to amuse him with their local

festivities, but they were none of them to his taste. On November 8, he writes:

> After dinner, I was taken to see some bulls that were being tormented and made to fight one another for the entertainment of the people before they were slaughtered. I considered this custom as a relic of Roman barbarism.

Hardly worth the trouble taking to the bullring a man so devoid of sensitivity to the beauties of bullfighting?

In the course of his long trip, Goupilleau rarely mentions his family. He did receive, it is true, at Nice, letters from his wife and his brother, telling him that his son, young Samuel, had the smallpox, but the news did not appear to distress him unduly. Was he not 'plagued by gnats' himself?

Nevertheless, as he approaches the capital the consciousness of being the head of a family gradually reasserts itself in him. Through his friend Courvoisier in Marseilles he had purchased oil, soused tunny, olives and anchovies. These are the souvenirs of his trip which he tells his wife about in a letter of October 29:

> My dear, good citizeness,
>
> I am bringing with me some of the products of Provence: anchovies, tunny and above all olives which I look forward to eating with you. They are, you know, the symbol of peace. Not, I hope, that I shall have to make peace with you; but they will help to maintain it and make it as durable as the feelings of attachment I have for you.

Dignity and tenderness. The language of a sensitive husband who still had the Pax Romana at heart.

HIS SECOND TOUR

Despite all the sympathy we feel for Goupilleau, it would be rather tedious to follow him on his second trip to the south, which began on August 11, 1794. This time, anyhow, there is no travel diary to consult. Nothing but private letters, some to Claude Marin, former censor royal, others to Rovère, the

Vaucluse deputy, a person whom we shall meet again in the next chapter.[3]

The memorable thing about this double correspondence is less the detail of the journey undertaken by the representative, less his lyricism at the sight of certain natural beauties like the Fontaine de Vaucluse than the jovial tone and good humour of a Goupilleau who seems to have been transformed by Thermidor.

However ardently he protests his patriotic zeal, however often he tells everyone that he is not on a pleasure trip, the number of excellent dinners he treats himself to makes us think differently. The abolition of the Maximum Price Control has sent the prices up. Never mind! Delegates from the Convention are above such sordid things. They live off the land, as it were, just like old campaigners.

PATRIOTIC DRINKING

We see how well treated Goupilleau was at Bonnieux, while his friend Rovère was away, in the enthusiastic account he sends him:

> I was expected at your house and I did the honours of the place to six or seven patriots who accompanied me there. Your majordomo took his duties very seriously. We ate like ogres and drank like Templars to the health of the Republic first, and then to your own, to that of your wife, your brother and Fréron. I counted up to thirty toasts!

In the Gard administrative district, the reception given him at Sommieres was no less lacking in cordiality, according to what he wrote to his friend Marin:

> At the top of the mountain, as soon as the blue-clad sentry saw us, he began to blow on a long trumpet, and at this signal, in less than five minutes, the whole commune had gathered to greet us. I shall spare you an account of all the harangues we had to reply to, of all the compliments in prose, and, indeed, in verse, which we were treated to; but

I simply must tell you about a banquet of forty guests which we attended, a feast presided over by candour, patriotism and the gaiety of some very charming citizenesses. We sang ourselves hoarse, and we drank so much we simply couldn't get drunk. I drank long and deep, and loudly hailed the Republic, thinking of you all the time, and wishing you could have been with me.

He struck the same note, that of chinking glasses, at Sète on October 5. He wrote to Rovère:

We found time, in a day and a half, to do all the good we were able and in addition to drink, eat and laugh to our hearts' content; I even went for a sail out to sea.

And to the former censor Marin he sent a similar report: 'Nothing but feasts, nothing but dice . . .' Boileau, who loved good living, must have been turning in his grave with envy.

On his gastronomic tour Goupilleau, who was a man of principle, never failed to bring back some specialities of Languedoc for his friends, and he wrote to Marin, by way of conclusion:

I leave you, my dear Dean, to go and eat my supper, for since I started travelling I have been taking supper, not dinner, and finding myself very well with it. I want to cultivate this habit until I return to Paris, where I look forward to drinking with you the excellent wine I am bringing as your present. You well know that we have at least a thousand and one healths to drink, beginning with that of the Republic, which is the greatest and highest thing we can drink to, so much so that after drinking its health we must break our glasses . . .

This refrain of a health to be drunk to the Republic is on the whole an excellent scheme which many a citizen would like to take part in. Unfortunately we are now at a period when a half-bottle of ordinary wine already is costing patriots twelve hundred and fifty *livres*, and not everybody has the good fortune to be a representative on a mission from the Convention.

CHAPTER TWENTY-ONE

THE HONEST FAMILY OF A DISHONEST DEPUTY

Rovère-la-Glacière in private life – His taste for family life and speculation – His overwhelming love for little Adolphe – His heir has teething trouble – His first breeches – Rovère dreams of another son – The Jacobin renegade's hopes come to nothing

ROVÈRE-LA-GLACIÈRE IN PRIVATE LIFE

The 'sinister' Rovère, the 'hideous' Rovère – this is how Albert Mathiez, in his *Réaction thermidorienne* refers to the former Marquis de Fontvielle, one of the most justly decried persons of the revolutionary period.[1]

This former nobleman of Comtat-Venaissin, after having served with the King's Musketeers, had thrown himself with violent abandon into his country's rising against the Pope. In 1791, Jourdan the head-chopper was one of his faithful agents, and he bears the major responsibility for the massacre of the aristocrats which took place at the Glacière in Lyons. When his compatriots elected him to represent them at the Convention, he took the surname of Rovère-la-Glacière in memory of the unfortunates he had 'chilled off'.

We find this deplorable creature again after Thermidor, but he has a new look. A divorce freed him from his first wife, Elizabeth de Chaix de Claret, and he married, a second time, a very fashionable *Mérveilleuse*:[2] Angélique Belmont, Marquise d'Agoult, bosom friend of Mme Tallien, one of the habituées of the *Chaumière* in the Allée des Veuves.

If we are to credit her description, the lady did not lack

charms: twenty-seven, blonde hair, regular face, pretty nose, laughing mouth. Like Rovère, she was divorced, but as the Marquis d'Agoult had emigrated she had had his property made over to her, including the château at Belmont in Dauphiné, with its land and its forests, a house in Grenoble, the whole worth nearly a million. Such was the far from negligible dowry the blonde Angélique brought her second husband, who possessed several properties in Vaucluse.

Let us not try too hard to discover how he came by them. His position as deputy doubtless allowed him to have knowledge of the sales of national properties at advantageous prices. Did not many of his colleagues in the Convention and later in the Conseil des Anciens operate in the same way? La Paige, in the Vosges,[3] Balmain in Savoie,[4] and André Dumont in the Somme, who snapped up for 50,000 *livres* the Château de Plony, valued at 650,000.

Nor should we delve too deeply into the political vagaries and variations of the former Jacobin, who, after the fall of Robespierre, became a fanatical reactionary, instigator of the most terrible measures of reprisal, creator of the famous military commission whose rigours often were to surpass those of the former revolutionary Tribunal. Altogether a highly contemptible creature, with his finger in every political pie and drinking all the deepest dregs, provided they tasted of blood.

HIS TASTE FOR FAMILY LIFE AND SPECULATION

Rovère's public life has nothing to do with our subject; but on the other hand his private life deserves to be described here, for the one forms the most weird contrast with the other. The traitor and abominable rogue who was the representative for Vaucluse had reserves of affection and generously shared them between his wife, his little boy and his brother Siméon-Stylite, constitutional ex-prelate, living at Avignon, and with whom he kept up an assiduous correspondence.

The land deals in which both brothers were involved naturally have a big place in their letters. Rovère had bought two properties, new ones, situated at Sorgues and Bonnieux. They belonged, before he got them, to his compatriot the Marquis de Sade, that 'divine marquis' whom we scarcely expected to meet on these pages. Could it be that the appointments left by the author of *Juliette* – beds of nails, whipping-posts, complicated torture-racks and the like – provided inadequate ease for the new owner? However it was, before going to live at Bonnieux our parliamentary representative intended to send furniture from Grenoble, sending them by boat down the Isère and the Rhône.

For the moment, he was chiefly worried about getting the land in order again, and he charged Siméon-Stylite, promoted to the functions of steward or agent, to have the mulberries seen to, as well as the vines, the almond trees, the quinces. If he cannot find a youth to look after the vegetable garden, he was advised to ask his neighbour the Abbé Testanière to come and put in the leek plants, the kind that grow at Cavaillon . . . It does seem somehow fantastic: a constitutional priest requisitioned by a former prince of the Church to plant leeks in the former kitchen-garden of the Marquis de Sade, on land acquired by regicide and underhand speculative dealings on the part of a nobleman turned revolutionary turned reactionary . . .

HIS OVERWHELMING LOVE FOR LITTLE ADOLPHE

But Rovère's letters would be nothing if they did not contain anything but agricultural advice or if they showed us merely the affectionate relations between two brothers who were constantly expressing their devotion to one another, often in the form of large gifts of chocolate. What gives the letters their true savour is the deputy's interest in and enthusiasm for a member of his family about whom he is always writing: his heir, little Adolphe.

In this respect uncle Siméon-Stylite cannot complain of lack of news. He is deluged with it. Thus on August 3, 1796, 'Adolphe took his first steps alone', an event that amused both parents vastly. They took a naïve pride in their offspring, a pride only slightly tempered by small reservations:

> Little Adolphe will be very pleased to meet playmates of his own age. You will be delighted with him when you have your first meeting with him; he has fourteen teeth, and knows how to use them . . . Though he has not an exactly handsome face, it is an interesting one, and he has an intelligence well beyond his age.[5]

HIS HEIR HAS TEETHING TROUBLE

The next month there was fresh news. He 'was beginning to ride, on a hobby-horse'. But Adolphe, who until then had been in the pink of health, had caught a little cold. Nothing to be alarmed about; he will soon recover, for on November 30 they wrote: 'Our little man is just as charming as ever, and getting to be a big boy.'

A week later he had sixteen teeth. 'The last two gave him some trouble, but this did not interfere at all with his tremendous appetite.'

The dawn of 1797 finds him still, of course, as wonderful as ever. He 'is beginning to say a few words', sends kisses to his uncle, though he had not yet set eyes on him. But he wants to have kisses by return:

> Little Adolphe complains that you have nothing to say to him . . . He complains about your silence.[6]

And if he does not complain very vociferously it is probably because his vocabulary is still not very extensive.

HIS FIRST BREECHES

But then we are treated to a really sensational item of news:

> The little one has begun to wear breeches; he looks like a child of three; you will be enchanted with him when you make his acquaintance.[7]

The next day:

> Little Adolphe is feeling completely at ease in his first pair of breeches; he is doing his morning drill. He will be a good soldier!

Never too soon to learn . . .

Obviously, paternal sentiments have unfrozen the heart of Rovère-la-Glacière. All his letters in the month of March overflow with the same lyrical note:

> Little Adolphe is charming. He is extremely advanced for his age; you will be delighted to see him in his little breeches, which he manages wonderfully well.

There was not even the smallest note without some detail about this adored infant.

> Our big boy laughed happily when we told him that he would be going to eat peaches, pears and so on in the garden at Bonnieux.[8]

The uncle, who cannot have forgotten his episcopal eloquence, must have treated them to a rapturous sermon on the sacred duties of parenthood, for the reply sent to him on March 21 draws moral conclusions about the subject that are indeed worthy of Rovère's lofty soul:

> Nature wishes it so: new trees grow in the forests where old ones stood; in the meadows spring fresh flowers, and in the hedges twitter the young fledglings. It is a great cause for satisfaction to think that, when we cease to be, we transmit to our own offspring those things we received from our fathers.

ROVÈRE DREAMS OF ANOTHER SON

But despite all the satisfaction the parents feel in their offspring, despite the twentieth tooth which has just come through, despite his oratorical talents and the great desire he has to go soon and kiss his uncle and fish for shrimps in the lake at

Bonnieux, the member of the Conseil des Anciens' paternal ambitions are still not completely satisfied.

The father was a speculator in more than one field. It was all right for God to have an only-begotten son, but Rovère, feeling less certain of the future than the Eternal Father, preferred to spread his investments. Moreover, he was deeply in love with his wife, and a ménage like his could not restrict itself to a single child, however incomparable he be.

Therefore, towards the end of '98, he hints to Siméon, after fresh dithyrambs about little Adolphe:

> We are labouring night and day to give him a little brother.[9]

But this labour of love took longer than was expected. Not until three months later did the couple's combined efforts appear to be crowned with success:

> We have given him a little companion, for it's as much of a torture to have only one than to have a score.[10]

After five days of reflection the victory proclamation became more specific:

> I believe that in six or seven months he will have a brother. It will be a great relief for us all.

But they had crowed too soon . . . The cock-of-the-walk's second masterpiece, little Jules, was not born until May or June 1798. And at that period, with the veering of the political weathercock, disaster had descended on the whole family.

THE JACOBIN RENEGADE'S HOPES COME TO NOTHING
The 'Triumvirate' of the Directory, Barras, Rewbell and Larevellière-Lépeaux, having received information through the spy Verat about the royalist activities of Rovère and of his connections with the secret police of Dossonville, took advantage of the 18 Fructidor to get rid of him and pack him off to Guiana . . . Coming from La Glacière at Lyons to Sinnamary

might seem to be a somewhat sudden transition. After 'blowing hot and cold' in this way, the life of our hero took a turn for the worse and he gave up his soul on September 11, 1798.

The incomparable little Adolphe survived him only by two years. His younger brother's career lasted a little longer, but it was not a happy or fortunate one. He disappears from sight, completely *déclassé*,[11] about 1850.

Thus all the Jacobin renegade's hopes came to nothing, one by one. Which only goes to prove that morality, even in the most troubled eras, sometimes has the final word.

CHAPTER TWENTY-TWO

MME HUMMEL'S ACCOUNT BOOK

Daily expenses – They hold their own until Thermidor – The account books close

DAILY EXPENSES

We have had intimate glimpses of the private lives of a number of Parisian bourgeois ladies. Now we have to look at the life of a provincial bourgeoisie, and none could be more representative than Mme Hummel, wife of a great Nantes merchant, a woman devoted to order and economy, and to whom an eminent professor of the University of Bordeaux has devoted some excellent pages.[1]

The documents at his disposal are unlike any we have studied so far in this work. There are no letters, no personal diary, but only an account book in which the expenses of daily life are set down with the utmost scrupulousness. They come under two headings: food purchases and miscellaneous payments, the latter including tailors' and toymakers' bills and even the rent receipts.

Such reading matter might be somewhat tedious if the good lady's accounts did not concern the period of the Revolution. But given a time like that, what a precious document it is, and what a wealth of insights it gives us! There was never a closer connection between political and èconomic upheavals. Never did the price of goods and the fluctuations of money values have a more direct influence on the march of events. So let us take a close and careful look at Mme Hummel's clerking.

Her husband was about forty, and, like herself, of Alsatian origin, and Protestant. He came from two generations of merchant drapers whose trade he continued. On March 4, 1793, he married at Nantes Louise Schweighauser, daughter of an armaments manufacturer richer than himself; the ménage belonged to that 'Huguenot bourgeoisie, cultivated and intellectual', which for several years had played a considerable rôle in the region.

Hummel was a member of the 'Reading Circle' and affiliated to the Lodge of the 'Coeurs unis' (United Hearts), and his wife was no less drawn to intellectual pleasures. During the winter of 1794–1795, they subscribed to the *Courrier de l'Egalité*; priding themselves on a bold, eclectic taste, they purchased the works of Molière, Regnard, Mme de Genlis and Piron.

These expenses did not make them neglect charitable donations; apart from regular alms-giving which amounted to about ten *livres* a month, Mme Hummel was associated with the most various charitable causes. She gave thirty-five *livres* for the widows of patriots massacred by Vendéans at Machecoul; and seventeen *livres* for the prisoners at Sainte-Claire who were almost all rebels or suspects: here we can recognize her impartiality.

It is to be noted that her love of her neighbour does not make her forget that of her own person. Charity begins at home in August 1793, when she settles an account at Sarradin's, the scent-shop in the Rue de la Fosse, for eighteen *livres*: and in December of the same year she purchases from him eau de Cologne to the value of two *livres* two *sous*, together with ten *livres*' worth of Waters of Heliotrope and two flagons of toilet vinegar called by the rather exciting name, for such a friction, of 'the Four Robbers'.

This was the month in which Carrier imposed his 'stern measures'. The Vendéan disaster at Savenay ended with frightful repressions. But that was no reason why a newly married young lady – even though Huguenot – should give up the volatile pleasures of eau de Cologne and other scented decoctions.

The family was to be increased, in 1794 and 1795, by the birth of two daughters, Caroline and Rose. As the parents are 'progressive', they have the eldest 'innoculated' a few months after her birth; but Jenner's discovery still creates so much terror among the good ladies of Nantes that Caroline's nurse, Prouveau, refused to stay in the house during the critical period. They had to rent a room in town for her, and paid twenty *livres* for it.

Let us hope that the other Hummel servants were less nervous than that silly old woman. They also had a chambermaid named Garreau who received ten *livres* a month, Jeanne Brain, the cook, whose wage was twelve *livres*, and the steward-cum-coachman, Hédouin, whose salary was thirty *livres* a month.

Was this a very large establishment for the time? Certainly not. The eighteenth century kept its old habits, and these have nothing in common with ours today. Four servants for two masters and two children in those days was considered a most modest standard. Mme Hummel well knew this because on her 'days' she was obliged to borrow her parents' or parents-in-law's servants. Her account book mentions, for example, 'thirty *sous* as tip for papa's coachman'.

The same writings tell us that all these faithful servants were frequently given presents. In June 1793, Garreau was offered an Indian muslin kerchief; its cost: nine *livres*. Jeanne Brain received twenty-five *livres* on the occasion of her marriage. They paid nine *livres* for a cab in order to attend Hédouin's marriage. And in the spring of 1795, Mme Hummel bought three identical dolls for Caroline, Marie-Rose and the steward's daughter.

THEY HOLD THEIR OWN UNTIL THERMIDOR

We shall not attempt to penetrate any further into the family's private life. The psychological elements furnished by an account book are naturally somewhat scanty. What is important to find out is the extent of the repercussions from events in the world outside on the peaceful existence led by the people of Nantes.

These repercussions were at first very mild. In July 1793 we find that one *livre* and ten *sous* were paid out for the banquet offered to the soldiers of Canclaux and Bonvoust who had repulsed, the month before, the royal Catholic army's attack. The purchase of a tricolour cockade cost ten *sous* in the month of November. During Germinal in Year II (March-April 1794) the trifling sum of three *livres* was contributed for equipping one soldier. The following month, two hundred *livres* were doled out as a forced loan. But on the 11th Thermidor (July 29), the day when the fall of the 'new Cromwell' became known at Nantes, Mme Hummel merely noted in her accounts the acquisition of thirty *sous*' worth of plums.

THE ACCOUNT BOOKS CLOSE

The great event for the town was the blockade by the English fleet. This made the import of foreign goods almost impossible. Fortunately the household possessed considerable stocks of tea, coffee and sugar. But other victuals, for example the Dutch cheese to which the Hummels were so partial (they consumed twenty pounds of it a month) were scarce from the beginning of 1793.

At least during the early period of this year scarcity of meat, fowl, vegetables and local products was less severe. Stabilized by the dictates of the Committee of Public Safety, the prices could even be said to have risen only the merest fraction. Merchandise became more scarce, but prices remained constant.

It was not until after Thermidor, when the reactionaries had abolished the Maximum Price Control and brought back free enterprise that anarchy really broke out. Then money suddenly began to lose its value, the markets were emptied of goods and the poor housewives had to make what looked like astronomical computations in their account books.

It would not have been so bad if the crisis had been limited to foodstuffs, but Mme Hummel's account book shows us that it extended to almost every other commodity. There was only one thing which did not cost our Nantes couple more: their rent. They were still paying six hundred and fifty *livres* a year, half at Christmas and the other half at midsummer, a simply ridiculously low figure.

But for everything else – clothes, linen, furniture, household goods – there was a continual rise in prices. Without being at all spendthrifts, the Hummels nevertheless made a number of purchases during 1793. There was not much need for new clothes, as the young couple were well provided for in that department, but there were small outlays on ribbons, scent and so on: the account book mentions all that.

But in the course of 1794, these expenditures grew rarer and very soon disappeared altogether. They could not dream of buying any luxury article, as the majority of shops had exhausted their stocks (a draper knows this better than anyone) and as the fall in the value of *assignats* made replacements impossible.

Each year that went by emphasized the disastrous nature of the crisis. In order to make one louis of twenty-four *livres*, on the 27th Frimaire, Year II, 5,300 paper *livres* were required. On the 3rd Ventose, it took 7,000, and on certain days the value fell 700 points in a few hours.

How on earth could the best possible of cashiers see her way clear in such confusion? What was the use of giving oneself so much trouble for such illusory ends? Would not one be discouraged from the start, on realizing, looking over the accounts for Brumaire, that the family had eaten 1,400 francs' worth of bread and paid 17,000 *livres* for a barrel of potatoes? And indeed in the face of these horrifying figures Mme Hummel's heart failed her; she gave up her accounts. As her historiographer says: 'It was the capitulation of thrift and order in the face of the disorder reigning in public finance.'

As long as it was only the Revolution she had to deal with, our bourgeoisie remained at the helm. Neither the bombardment of Nantes by the Vendéans, nor the persecutions of

Carrier, nor the decrees of Prairial, nor the tyranny of the Maximum Price Control could demoralize her. But when in the end one could no longer rely upon figures and make one's own accounts every day, she decided that her rôle was finished. The great social class, brave and hard-working, which had grown rich since Colbert, no longer knew its own country that had been delivered up to sharpers, speculators and madmen.

She cowered in her corner, waiting for the squall to pass. One day the sky would brighten again and money would recover its value. And that would bring Mme Hummel's victory and the end of her tribulations. She would open her great ledger, take up her goose-quill pen and start again by noting:

Pullet: 4 *livres*.
Salad: 3 *sous*.

CHAPTER TWENTY-THREE

THE TEMPER OF THERMIDOR

The workers are hostile to the Maximum – The Maximum is abolished – Ensuing crises – Julie de Beaumarchais' letter – The misery of the middle class and revolts – Intervention of the army

---

THE WORKERS ARE HOSTILE TO THE MAXIMUM

The 9th Thermidor not only marks a deep rift in the political development of the Revolution but also a radical change in the material life of the country.

We have just seen how the overthrow of the Maximum caused Mme Hummel's accounts to fall into confusion. But in order to understand the event we shall have to explain its causes. Let us go back to a few days before the fall of Robespierre.

Thermidor has been defined as a conspiracy of fear. The expression is valid for those deputies whose lives were threatened by the guillotine. But for the lower classes in Paris this explanation will not do. If the popularity of their idol had remained intact, how could his fall not have provoked a tremendous reaction? Can one imagine the great bell of Notre-Dame remaining silent all night, the great mass of common people in the sections not rising as one man? Surely the faubourgs of Saint-Antoine and Saint-Marceau in particular, those natural forcing-houses of revolt, would never have hesitated a second in taking up arms?

None of the uncertainties of opinion that occurred then[1] could be justified without the quite recent fall from favour of the Incorruptible; the real reason for this was the publication, five days earlier, of a table stating the daily wages to be earned by workers, and which was repudiated by the workers themselves.[2] After having imposed for the last twelve months or so a maximum price for essential goods, it was now desired to fix a similar maximum for manual labour, without taking into proper account the now very high cost of living. This was an imprudent act which very soon cost Robespierre his head.

When he and his friends were conducted to the guillotine, the crowd booed them unmercifully, but as the tumbrils passed by, there was one shout which dominated all others: 'Down with the Maximum!'

THE MAXIMUM IS ABOLISHED

Benefiting from experience, the victors of Thermidor hastened to announce that they were going to study a means of 'making a day's working wage proportionate to the cost of living'. But we can only assume that this was a difficult thing to arrange, because five long months passed before the promise was kept.

Finally, the Convention thought of a stroke of genius: it abolished the Maximum which, although unpopular, and made life at least fairly possible by limiting a rise in prices, it also quite simply restored the principle of free enterprise.

The idea would have been an excellent one if the period had been a normal one, but the country was then in a state of famine and in the midst of war. Free enterprise by definition meant opening the door to profiteers, putting goods up to the highest bidders, selling them for the best offers. It also meant an almost fatal inflation, the definitive collapse of a monetary system that was already ailing. The lower classes, which had so loudly cursed the Maximum, holding it responsible for the scarcity of goods, were naturally the first to suffer from a measure whose folly was to unleash the direst catastrophes.

ENSUING CRISES

Almost immediately, in Paris, two distinct cities were created: one crammed with every luxury, the other lacking even the barest necessities.

Certainly, a foreigner arriving in Paris and seeing the re-opened salons, the clusters of *Merveilleuses* on the terraces of the Palais Royal and the pyramids of cakes in the pastrycooks' windows could only with difficulty realize that behind this opulent décor a large part of the population existed only on a hunk of bread or a handful of rice every day. Yet this was the cruel truth: the new régime had increased the number of empty bellies.

It was the eternal tale of crises, and no other epoch was better suited for comparison with our own. So many *assignats* had been printed that their purchasing power had become almost *nil*. To make three *livres* in silver, after the summer of 1795, required one hundred *livres* in paper money, and that was only the beginning. How did prices compare with the old ones? One curious table gives us the costs of main commodities towards the middle of 1795, compared with prices as they were in 1790:[3]

	In 1790		In 1795
	Livres	*Sols*	*Livres*
One bushel of flour	2		225
One bushel of barley		10	50
One bushel of oats		18	50
One bushel of haricots	4		120
One bushel of peas or lentils	4		130
½ barrel of Orleans wine	80		2400
2 steres of wood	20		500
One bushel of coal		7	10
One litre of olive oil	1	16	62
One pound of sugar		18	62
One pound of coffee		18	54
One pound of Marseilles soap		18	41
One pound of candles		18	41
One bunch of turnips, carrots		2	4
One good cabbage		8	8
One pair of shoes	5		200
One pair of sabots		8	15
One pair of stockings	3		100

	In 1790		In 1795
	Livres	*Sols*	*Livres*
One decent hat	14		500
One ell of cloth	4		180
One ell of Elbeuf cloth	18		300
25 eggs	1	4	25
One pound of butter		18	30
Totals	164	11	5148

JULIE DE BEAUMARCHAIS' LETTER

After a few months we see these figures tripling, quadrupling, decupling. A letter from Julie de Beaumarchais, written in 1795, completes this sad documentation by making it even sadder:[4]

When you gave me those four thousand francs (in *assignats*), my dear friend, my heart was stirred. I thought you must be mad to give me such a fortune; I swiftly slid them into my pocket and changed the conversation to other channels, to make you forget your action. When I got home I rushed to buy wood, provisions and so on before everything went up again in price. My old servant Dupont ran all over the place buying up stocks for me; then the scales fell from my eyes when I saw what 4,275 francs had bought me, not including food for the month:

2 steres of wood	1,460 fr.
Nine pounds of candles	900 –
Sugar, 4 pounds	400 –
3 litrons of corn	120 –
7 litres of oil	700 –
12 lamp wicks	60 –
1 bushel and a half potatoes	300 –
Month's laundry	215 –
1 pound of face-powder	70 –
2 ounces of pomade	50 –
	4,275 fr.

Remains food for the month, butter and eggs at 100 francs, as you know, meat at 25 or 30 francs and the rest in proportion . . . No bread for two days. We now get it only every three days. Additional expense. I haven't bought more than 4 pounds of bread during the last three days, at 45 francs. Total: 5,022 francs.

When I think that this royal expenditure, as you call it, forced me to spend from 18 to 20,000 francs without food and without any kind of little luxury, I wish the government to hell; it is true that those 20,000 francs represent six to seven *louis* and that my 4,000 francs (pension) gave me one hundred and sixty, a big difference . . . 10,000 flung away during the past fortnight has given me such a fright and made me feel so sorry for myself that I no longer know how to count my money in that way; in three days the price of wood rose from 4,200 to 6,500 francs, and all other costs in proportion. So that, as I informed you, two steres of wood cost me, after being delivered and stored, 7,100 francs. At present I must count every week 700 to 800 francs for some boiled beef and broth and other meats for making a stew, without thinking of butter, eggs and a thousand other details: laundry charges also are going up so fast every day that 8,000 *livres* a month are not enough to pay my bills.

Eight thousand *livres* for laundry for one month! After one's francs have gone through the wringer, that beats the lot!

THE MISERY OF THE MIDDLE CLASS AND REVOLTS

The Government, recognizing the collapse of its monetary system, had published a 'proportional scale' which forced the taxpayer to pay in kind half of his land-tax and farm rents and gave functionaries salaries calculated according to the official price of bread.[5] Without receiving these same guarantees, the workers had received such raises in wages that they could no longer be considered as the worst off citizens.

But what became of the old people and people with small

private incomes who were unable to do manual work? Some of them, after selling their watch and having made a few *sous* on their clothes and furniture, set up shop at home, selling sugar, coffee, candles and flour. A new kind of speculation! Others thought it better to go and drown themselves in the Seine. Large numbers of them were caught in the fishing-nets at Saint-Cloud.

It is not surprising that so much misery caused more than one revolt. The days of Germinal and Prairial were probably caused by this. They were, in fact, hunger-protests.

INTERVENTION OF THE ARMY

While a detachment of *muscadins*, armed with whips and knotty walking-sticks, was sufficient to disperse the first uprising, the second was much more serious. Seeing Féraud's head stuck on the end of a pike, and behind it fifty thousand men, the Convention finally took fright. It repealed the famous decree forbidding the armies to approach the capital. The next day, twenty thousand soldiers entered Paris and the suburban riots were quelled.

But by this illegal gesture the Assembly pronounced its own death sentence. After first having relied upon the bourgeoisie and then on the people, it seemed as if the Revolution, adopting Mirabeau's saying, was no longer to have confidence in anything but the power of the bayonet.

It was at once a denial of principle and a kind of suicide. Five months before the 13th Vendémiaire, four and a half years before Bonaparte's coup d'état, we can say that the Republic had in fact already come to an end. It was not doctrinal conflicts, not political jealousies, not threats of dictatorship so much as the exigencies of daily life that had killed it.

CHAPTER TWENTY-FOUR

BESIDE THE SEA-SIDE

*A Parisienne takes the sea baths at Dieppe in 1795 – Fanny,
the former woman friend of André Chénier – Her disagreeable
stay on the Norman coast*

A PARISIENNE TAKES THE SEA BATHS AT DIEPPE IN 1795
We shall probably have proof one day that it was not Franklin
who invented the lightning-conductor, nor Parmentier who
made the potato popular in France. For the moment, it is
sufficient to know that the discovery of sea bathing at Dieppe,
generally attributed to the Duchesse de Berry, came long
before the niece of Louis XVIII made a trip there. Thirty
years earlier the Parisiennes during the Revolution were already
beating a path to the stony Normandy beach. They went there
to spend the season, as the taking of sea baths was recommended
for persons in delicate health and especially for children.

This was the reason which brought to Dieppe, in 1795, a
very delightful young widow, Mme Laurent-Le-Coulteux de
la Noraye. Her personality is all the more interesting to us
when we realize that she was the former woman friend of
André Chénier, Françoise Pourat, the companion of his walks
at Louveciennes, she whom he immortalized under the name
of Fanny and who inspired his famous ode:

> May crowns itself with fewer roses,
> The autumn with fewer vines;
> In harvest fewer cornfields flow
> With gold than on my lips, my lyre,
> Songs come to bud and blossom,
> Fanny, 'neath thy smiling gaze . . .

FANNY, THE FORMER WOMAN FRIEND OF ANDRÉ CHÉNIER

At the time we meet her, Fanny was twenty-nine. Her husband, a rich banker, died leaving her two children; she herself was suffering from tuberculosis. Where, now, on that pallid face, was the image of 'the beautiful adored one with the calm and gentle gaze'? Perhaps only one man, her cousin by marriage, Lecoulteux de Canteleu, could have seen it shining there still. She seemed to nourish for him something more than affection; he was her last support, her only reason for living.

He was moreover a most worthy gentleman. He was himself a banker, and possessed large interests in the Anzin mines, and after the Brumaire coup d'état he became one of the founders of the Banque de France.

He it was to whom the young widow wrote after she arrived at Dieppe, where she had gone less for her own sake – for her health would have been better, it would seem, in some less rigorous climate – than for the sake of Nelly, her daughter, whose health, she hoped, would benefit from sea bathing. But their first contacts with the pearl of the Caux region was scarcely encouraging, if we may judge from the letter of August 20, 1791:[1]

> Crippled with fatigue, broken-hearted at the great distance I had placed between us, seeking our dear correspondent in darkness in order to find out where to get down, knocking at all the doors, turning in nasty little narrow streets, taking with us at every revolution of the wheels a piece of someone's house, to the great horror of the proprietor shouting after us as if he had been flayed alive, finally I arrived at M Le Grielle's door; he came running out into the street carrying a lighted candle, and his servant told me where I was to lodge and handed me your letter. My first thought was to re-read it on getting down at the Hôtel de Londres.

HER DISAGREEABLE STAY ON THE NORMAN COAST

While the innkeeper was praising in English the reputation of his establishment, his brilliant clientele and its meticulous cleanliness, the traveller had time to see that her room was furnished chiefly with spiders' webs, curtains in ribbons, rickety tables, chairs.

Fanny, worn out, just flung herself on the bed, but as it smelt of 'a hen-run' she was unable to get a wink of sleep. The next day, she paid a morning visit to M Le Grielle who assured her that her room at the Hôtel de Londres was the very best in Dieppe. Her correspondent added that the little town was in the throes of famine, that it was impossible to buy anything and that his servant had been scouring the countryside for days trying to find a fresh egg. A nice start to a visit!

Never mind! All adversities will be met with a good heart, provided they can enjoy the sea bathing: 'I wanted to begin yesterday evening,' the young woman declares,

> but the wind was too strong. This morning, at eight o'clock, I set out on our expedition, but it was not successful. The sea was too far out, we were obliged to walk for miles over the pebbly beach, and there was a high, cold wind blowing. When we finally reached the water's edge, the waves seemed so big and violent and seemed so set on coming in again and cutting us off that we were overcome by terror and we ran back through chilly pools of sea-water.

Fanny deplored the lack of amenities at French sea-bathing establishments, compared with those in England. Oh, if only there wasn't a war on, that's where she would take her children. But until peace returned she was to have to stay a long time in that 'odious town'.

She could not even escape boredom by visiting the surrounding areas. As soon as she began to walk she would feel depressed and we can well believe that the air of Dieppe was not good for her.

A few days later, however, the gusts of wind had died down, and they started off for the beach once more: 'I let my children bathe this morning,' she writes.

The weather was warm and the sea very calm. Despite this, they put up all kinds of foolish resistances. Though she had been so brave the day before, Nelly uttered piercing shrieks. Unfortunately, I was feeling so ill, I could not bathe with them. My own courage might have awakened theirs. And I stood there at the water's edge, observing with disappointment that the bathe was doing her more harm than good. This evening, I shall endeavour to bathe, thus setting them a good example, I hope.

From Paris, her cousin, who must have been dismayed by the tone of her letters, was prodigal with his encouragement and medical advice. But in this department his recommendations do not seem to be very happy ones. In the case of coughs, he advised the use of ipecacuanha and frog bouillons, but the first of these only made Fanny all the more ill: 'The ipecacuanha which you had the goodness to recommend me,' she writes,

has done me much harm. If it were a stomach cough, it would be all right for me, but *it is not that.* Tomorrow I shall take some turnip bouillon, and I shall try to get some frogs. You see, my dear one, I obey your orders faithfully and am looking after myself. I long to see you again. Adieu.

After the wretched ipecacuanha, Lecoulteux had another idea. As Dieppe is so unpleasant, why not go to Boulogne? But this time, the beautiful exile revolts:

No, my dear friend, I shall not go to Boulogne. I've had enough of travelling and of being far away from you. Moreover, as you can well see, when one has spent a winter like the last, one realizes that, after all, one does not die of boredom . . .

Obviously local amusements are very few. The only distractions are the curious errors of pronunciation of a certain Mme de Cavellier who spends all her time declaring she is dying of hunger, that the town is completely ruined, that there is absolutely no social life there at all. But when Fanny wearied of this human donkey, she consoled herself with some real ones:

> They are going to find two donkeys for me; the serving-girl and I shall carry the two children behind us and we shall go and see if we can see anything, for we feel as if we are buried at the bottom of a well and I can't get out of it by the strength of my legs alone. I hope that Nelly will benefit from such exercise. (August 26.)

Should the sick lady's change of humour be ascribed to this new sport? Does the apartment at the Hôtel de Londres now contain less spiders' webs or else have M Le Grielle and Mme de Cavellier become a little less tiresome with their endless chatter? Whatever happened, Fanny seems in her last letters to have become reconciled to Dieppe. She even finishes by declaring, probably with the desperation of sickness:

> It is only here that one can live in peace; the certainty that one will see no one is delicious.

Yet she will soon see the capital again, and with joy, because a loved one waits for her there. But their reunion was short-lived.

Victim of an implacable disease, poor Fanny was to succumb a few months later. She was barely thirty, two years younger than her poet friend André Chénier when he mounted the steps to the guillotine.

CHAPTER TWENTY-FIVE

MEMOIRS OF A DERANGED YOUNG MAN

The theories of a young soldier on marriage and love –
Experiments with magnetism and love – A lady with a warm
heart – Project for a serious establishment – Before and after
marriage: the extravagances of a philosophical mind

THE THEORIES OF A YOUNG SOLDIER ON MARRIAGE AND LOVE

'I am only twenty-seven and a half. But my youth is over. Never shall I know a nice woman! I shall never have tasted one of life's most blissful happinesses!'

Who made this confession? Not René, not Obermann, but one of their much less illustrious contemporaries: Augustin Aumont, a teacher in the Ecole Centrale de Paris.[1]

Born in 1770, he belonged to a family in easy circumstances, owners of a house in the Rue de Condé, another at Auteuil and enjoying an income of six thousand *livres*. He studied medicine but then in 1793 he was enrolled in the army in Italy. His sentimental experiences were to begin under the colours.

The young soldier lodged with some Provençal people, whose daughter was called Angélique. As she had beautiful eyes, 'golden hair' and mended his linen, they soon began to address each other in affectionate terms, and the young girl was already talking of marriage.

Other suitors might have tried to gain time, the best way of gaining what they really want. But Augustin was no diplomat.

He held very personal theories about love and virtue and women, and he did not dream of concealing these notions.

Seducing a girl without marrying her did not mean that one had deceived her, according to him. Quite the opposite:

> In this way the truth is respected and one has the right to tell her that if she defends her virtue she is a victim of prejudice. Ninety-nine per cent of men have prejudices, and there is no reason for it . . . One is not guilty unless one does harm to someone, and a girl who grants something to her lover is not harming anyone.

'But if I take a husband afterwards,' Angélique must have thought, 'I shall have done him some harm by . . .'

'Not at all!' Augustin would counter this. 'One cannot be held responsible for former infidelities by a man whom one did not know at the time. A woman's past is her own business . . . And she has no obligations in the future either; as soon as a couple are no longer in love, they get a divorce. Virtue does not consist in not fulfilling Nature's vow!'

And he ended his lecture on morals thus:

> A woman is honest as long as she has only one lover at a time, because then she is deceiving no one. She only begins deceiving when she takes a second lover without telling the first!

This strange young man was quite sincere. The proof of this was that his first care, in writing to his mother, was to tell her the whole of the fine speech he had made to Angélique. What on earth must Mme Aumont have thought of it?

EXPERIMENTS WITH MAGNETISM AND LOVE

A few years later, we find Augustin again in civilian life and teaching in Paris. He is living with his parents, leading a pleasant existence and having connections with various notable people in the arts and sciences. His journal mentions dinners with Gérard, Geoffroy Saint-Hilaire, with the engineers on the eve of their departure for Egypt to make bridges and roads for Napoleon's campaign, with Bertholet who had just come back from that country, with Cuvier, Lacroix, Humboldt and a certain M Delglas, who was concerned with magnetism.

Now these were the kind of experiments with which the young man felt himself in sympathy! On October 12, 1798, he noted in his journal that before his very eyes they had 'magnetized' Cuvier, Lacroix and Duméril without obtaining any results, but that three other subjects, Mme Bell, MM Séligny and Humboldt had gone to sleep and that the first two had even had nervous attacks. On the 17th, another operator, Dr Bouvier, again performed on Mme Bell and provoked a similar crisis. Finally, on the 27th, there was a third seance after which Mme Bell declared that she was in need of rest.

Who was this woman who lent herself so willingly to these experiments? Sophie Bell, daughter of a friend of Mme Aumont, and who had always been considered a member of that family. Separated from a husband who had given her a child now with a wet-nurse, she lived with her sister and brother-in-law, the Silvains. She was well-educated, a musician, sang, danced, composed and was the author of a score entitled *The Palace of Augustus* and her artistic gifts were supported by other talents which a charming gentleman, her friend Pelé, fully and justly appreciated.

The liberty she enjoyed allowed her to make frequent expeditions with Augustin who for his part found her very agreeable. He only regrets he is not more ambitious and deplores his backwardness in his journal:[2]

> No one has any idea what I feel, or people would be astonished, as I am myself, at my extraordinary and ridiculous timidity. No one has any idea what I suffer. Here I am thinking always about women and without a mistress! Mme Gérard offers me the most frightful temptations; but I think she is happy with her husband and I do not wish to disturb her ménage. Mme Bell, on the other hand, can do as she pleases; she is witty, pleasant, *not bad*. And from what I

hear she is not all that *difficult*. But she loves Pelé, indeed adores him; when she leaves him, she will still only regard *me* as a respected friend. And anyhow, is their love-affair likely to come to an end?

The affair was slow in getting started between Augustin and Mme Bell. By the time October had arrived, they were still doing their magnetism stunts at Mme Bell's dinners, which were held in her house, a few steps away from his door. There is nothing outstanding in the journal, excepting one simple phrase:

> It seems to me that I am about to enjoy with her such adventures as could not be committed to the pages of this journal.[3]

Only three days later the prognostication was proved correct. There were further magnetic experiments at the Silvains'. The master of the house, in order to walk back Dr Bouvier, left his sister-in-law alone with Augustin, in an unlighted room. What followed is not hard to guess.

> She was laid rather uncomfortably across an armchair. I approached her and attempted to lift her. I took her by the arms, the hands. She pressed my hand fervently in hers. Oh! that was a real magnetic shock for me! Adieu, all my resolutions! Instead of running away, I went closer, our mouths met and remained glued to one another. Never did I experience such a lively emotion . . .[4]

Nor such remorse, alas! For scarcely had the imprudent swain snatched a kiss than he regretted it. The plan of campaign he had mapped out was so much more ingenious!

> I had resolved not to declare myself until I was sure that she had forgotten Pelé. Before that happened, I wanted to have a long conversation with her about inconstancy, the men she had made unhappy, the bad reputation she had (very tactful subjects!) . . . But I was not responsible for my

actions. I was too moved by the spectacle of the sufferings she had just experienced, by her odd position, by my nearness to her. Ah! Aumont! how little control you seem to have over yourself!

A LADY WITH A WARM HEART

Despite all his self-reproaches, the self-surprised Don Juan was both moved and flattered when he next saw Sophie – the very next day – about to render an aria from *Oedipus at Colonus* before a large audience. He seated himself in a corner, devoured her with his eyes and murmured to himself: 'That woman there, who has upon her the admiring gaze of every spectator, that woman is – my mistress!'

His rapture increased still further when she slipped him a little love-letter though its style was somewhat frigid. Sophie told him in it that she felt for him something more than friendship, but that her emotions were not engaged. She was still in love with Pelé; but in order to thrash things out she suggested a rendezvous at her house the next day, at two in the afternoon.

Augustin would not have missed it for the world, but as he climbed the stairs he made a thousand good resolutions: 'Let me exercise prudence, reason, strength of will, character!'

But all in vain, for the young lady was curiously nervous. She claimed to have certain grave objections to Pelé, and they talked only about him. It was a singular interview, at which the misbehaviours of the absent gentleman finally enraged not only their fair victim but also his eventual successor:

'Pelé!' he cried. 'You have not behaved well towards this young lady. Did her goodness of heart, her violent sentiments deserve to be treated with such severity? Ah! Pelé! Didst thou verily treat her thus? Thou of the loving heart! Thou, O thou my friend!'[5]

Such quantities of affectionate fervour could not long go unrewarded. Two days later, in his bachelor apartment in the Rue de Condé, Sophie finally capitulated: 'What intoxication of the senses! We left at ten the morning after, not without some embarrassment on meeting the servants . . .'

And there followed one delicious evening after the other:

> After dinner, I close the doors and windows, etc. Sophie arrives . . . Next morning Sophie slopes off and goes downstairs to my sister's where we breakfast. Then we go to one of her female cousins, where she supposedly passed the night after returning from the ball!

For Augustin, one of the great joys of this affair is that it has not estranged Pelé. He went, like a faithful friend, to tell him all, the morning after the decisive night, and Pelé received his confidences in a friendly way, 'albeit with some astonishment'. Sophie's former lover even was kind enough to offer the new one 'some items of advice'. We should rather like to know what these were.

Perhaps he was secretly exulting over the probable consequences of the affair. He knew Sophie better than anyone and was well aware that her romances were usually rather short-lived. He must have had a good laugh a few weeks later when he learnt that the musician Lamparelle had already supplanted Augustin and that M Aubert, a young doctor from Geneva, had also entered into relationships with her. The lovely lady was to go from one to the other without the least difficulty and even made use of all three of them, so as not to offend anyone. She was truly a woman of her time, coquette, carefree, easy-going: the frivolity of a *Merveilleuse* and the morals of a mattress.

But meanwhile what had become of the Alceste of the Rue de Condé? He was the most jealous and miserable of men, but nevertheless his feelings for Sophie remained disconcertingly indulgent. On January 30, she told him that Aubert had come to see her that morning and had been so importunate she had been quite unable to resist him:

> As she was telling me about her follies, she sat herself on my knees, bent over me and tried to diminish the pain her

confessions caused me by covering me with her caresses, whose empire over me she knows so well. I listened to her confidences. I should even have been vexed if she had not told me all. But I alone know what I suffer . . . And yet this mistress is the best of women. Her conduct with me could hardly have been better.[6]

The poor boy is easily pleased! But if he found himself disappointed, he had only himself to blame:

It's nobody's fault. Why am I not a nicer person? I shall always be a mediocrity and I shall soon be even worse – a nobody. I am not a genius. I haven't the wit to make myself loved!

PROJECT FOR A SERIOUS ESTABLISHMENT

It would seem however that one event, which occurred in April of the same year, should have restored his self-confidence a little. With his sister acting as a go-between, some friends discreetly inform him that they would be glad to have him as their son-in-law.[7] They have been long acquainted: M and Mme Dussert have more money than the Aumont family; and the young daughter is very nice. In short, every advantage.

The reader will be thinking that our misanthrope, who despaired of ever being loved for his own sake, would jump at such a fine catch. But he little knows our hero! The latter held the Dusserts in high esteem, having written in his journal the year before that they were 'a charming family', that their daughter Lucile was 'very sweet, very good, very sensitive', that he hoped she would find a good husband, yet adding this corrective note: 'Nevertheless, it would give me great sorrow to see her marrying someone . . .' In short, despite so many favourable indications, the advances made to him elicited at first only a polite reply. He wanted to be quite sure that Mme Dussert knew what she was about, and he himself wished to have 'a mind calm enough to examine my feelings objectively'.

Three days went by, then the Dusserts came to dine with

the Aumonts. Augustin observed Lucile with more attentive eyes:

> She is really nice, she is interesting. Two or three of the glances I intercepted had such an effect upon me that I felt sure I was not far from falling in love with her.[8]

Striking the iron while it was hot, the future mother-in-law next day sent him a kind of diary she had kept detailing her daughter's education: the chef-d'oeuvre was accompanied, as it were, by guarantees of origin and ownership. And the next day it was M Dussert who called his young friend in order to settle money matters.

The parents were certainly in a hurry, but our Augustin was not . . . How perplexed he felt! On May 22, he wrote again: 'That Sophie . . . I can't get her out of my mind!' True, we read further on: 'Lucile was quite pretty, this evening, and I can see that if I let myself fall in love with her she would cure me of the torments that madwoman makes me suffer!'

Finally, towards the end of June, the mistress appears to have been disposed of and the young man considers himself otherwise engaged.

The end of the holidays saw several pleasant meetings with the Dusserts; at their country home, particularly on September 18 and 19, at a party organized in honour of Lucile and her sisters and in the course of which we see Augustin playing the triple rôle of MC, pyrotechnist and poet. There could be no better way of finding out how ordinary people under the Directory amused themselves at home.[9]

The four young ladies took up their positions on a kind of mobile platform decorated with white draperies and oaken garlands. The little copse towards which they were drawn was ornamented with a poetic inscription from Augustin's lyric pen:

> Charming souvenirs or cruel turns of fate
> Depend on you these summer days:
> You make them dear unto our memories,
> You who are your parents' honour and delight.

The author modestly admitted that these were the first verses he had ever composed. One can only marvel at his frankness.

After luncheon, there was a fresh seance in the copse, where the young ladies, costumed as priestesses, chanted occasional verses. The family was led to another corner of the garden towards nightfall. There they found a stone altar on which these words, *To Friendship!* were outlined in luminous paint. Phosphorescent paint was also used for the inscription carried by the young ladies and which proclaimed, as was fitting, the qualities of Mme Dussert:

> Who in Friendship shows more ready will?
> The answer comes: She!

The scene turned highly emotional. Augustin, standing behind the altar and holding a hot iron and a lump of phosphorus, lighted a big lantern and set off a Bengal Light which illuminated the group of priestesses. As the phosphorescent letters died away, others, in black, formed these words:

> His presence increases our happiness.

A charming sentiment but a little vague, for it might apply to any of the gentlemen, including Augustin . . . This marked the end of the party. The young ladies climbed back on their festive chariot, and were hauled back to the house by torchlight.

BEFORE AND AFTER MARRIAGE: THE EXTRAVAGANCES OF A
PHILOSOPHICAL MIND

After an evening of such celebration, the autumn had to bring some final decision. This came on November 1, but naturally our fantastic hero had to go about it as no one else would have done. He thought it was more romantic to slip into Lucile's handbag a long and complicated letter, in which he explained his reasons for delay and which ended with the words: 'Do you love me?'

A few days later, the reply was brought, by Mme Dussert

in person, and from then on all that had to be done was to arrange the wedding.

In order not to lose his touch, Augustin was soon to indulge in further eccentricities during the two-month engagement. He who had taken such ages to make up his mind now wanted to proceed with all possible swiftness. Looking upon marriage simply as a formal ceremony, he considered it superfluous to wait for the blessings of mayor and curé before enjoying the fruits of his legitimate joys:

> Scruples on this account are mere prejudices . . . We have given our word and that is enough . . . Laws are not made for honest people . . .

As may well be imagined, such theories appalled the poor mother-in-law, who no longer knew which way to turn. And for his part Augustin was suffering deeply at being misunderstood:

> What! Shall I never be able to accomplish any of my philosophical projects? They want to make me deny my own principles of conduct in an important matter which will affect me only once in my life!

The young people were finally spliced on January 8, 1800. They were given good measure, because after the civil ceremony they were given a blessing next day at the Chapelle de Suède by M Gamba, a Lutheran minister, and yet another at the Dedacary Temple which had taken the place of Saint-Sulpice.

Then the wedding party broke up, as the husband did not want any wedding procession. At the end of the afternoon, they all went to the concert given by the doctor, Charles, he whom, to Lamartinians will always be the husband of Elvire; then they returned to the Aumonts', who gave the customary dinner.

But there were further surprises in store for the family. When it was time for the couple to retire to the bedchamber, lo and behold, Augustin said good night to Lucile and let her mother accompany her back home.

The same thing happened the next day. The lucky man was to lunch and dine with his blushing bride, but after dinner he returned to sleep alone at the Rue de Condé.

So for forty-eight hours the man who had appeared to be in such haste doused the ardour of poor Lucile who could only rage and bite her pillow and scream that she was being made a fool of.

But if only she had been able to read some of the pages of his intimate journal, the mystery would have been cleared up! 'It was my desire,' Augustin wrote,

> that we should not go through any of the motions of marriage inspired by the heart or by custom. I wanted to give her time to become even more dependent on me, more attached to me. I endeavoured to divide our emotions, whatever their nature, and not expend them all in a single night.

It was not until the third night that, the emotions having been sufficiently 'divided', our philosopher went to get a cab for his wife and brought her back discreetly to his apartment, had a fine supper served and let her have the revenge she so justly deserved.

We must congratulate good Mme Dussert on having found a son-in-law, and as she still had three unmarried daughters, let us hope that she had less trouble when she came to marry them off.

CHAPTER TWENTY-SIX

IN THE DAYS OF THE
MERVEILLEUSES

Psychology of the Merveilleuses – *Lightness of clothes and morals – The pleasures of the newly-rich – The dance craze – The country imitates Paris – The love market of the* Petites Affiches – *The moral decadence of French society is only skin deep*

PSYCHOLOGY OF THE 'MERVEILLEUSES'

The *Journal de Paris* of the 23rd Messidor in Year II reported a new malady which afflicted young people in particular and was called the *Sexa*, an abbreviation of the phrase *qu'est-ce que c'est que ça?*[1] Its symptoms were relaxation of the optical nerve and the constant use of spectacles; it generally caused also 'a cooling of that natural warmth which is difficult to treat unless the patient wears a very tight-fitting buttoned suit and a sextuple cravat behind which the chin disappears and threatens to mount to the nose'. Finally, and most serious of all, it brings about semi-paralysis of speech.

The unfortunates who suffer from this affliction are careful to avoid all consonants, inflections and accentuations of speech and are forced as it were to 'fillet' their native language. When their lips rub against each other, there emerges

> a confused buzzing which is a fair approximation of the sounds *pz-pz* used to attract the attention of pussy-cats. The conversations of these sick people are quite incomprehensible. The only words one can distinguish in their endless series of vowels are: *ma paole supème!* (*ma parole*

suprême), *d'incoyable* (*d'incroyable*), *d'hoible* (*d'horrible*) and other disfigured words.

It is a pity that there is no portrait of a *Merveilleuse* accompanying this character of the *Incroyable*. If there were, we should find united two of the most brilliant ornaments of Paris after Thermidor. Fortunately, other witnesses, from Mercier and his confessions to the drawings of Carle Vernet, are able to fill in the gap and give us pictures, in a natural setting, of those amusing marionnettes who paraded on fine days at the Petit Coblenz and Frascati.

Take a somewhat round-shouldered man or one who endeavours to appear so, do his hair in an urchin-crop with long, shaggy locks falling over his ears but raised up at the back by means of a comb; make him wear a square-cut frock-coat with wide godets or a coloured coat with long skirts; imprison his neck in a cravat such as has just been described; encase his nether extremities in shapeless breeches which make him look like a hen; place in his hand a rustic, knotted stick nicknamed *executive power*, on his head a two-cornered hat or a low-crowned hat with broad brim, golden rings in his ears and you have the perfect type of the Directory *Jeune premier*, such as might have been encountered every day at the Glacier Velloni or in the Passage du Perron, admirer of Garat and Elleviou, the *bête noire* of Augereau's soldiery but the great favourite with all the ladies.

He is very ridiculous and full of faults, for he spends his time gambling and pursuing prostitutes when he is not quarrelling with people whose opinions he disagrees with.

If a Republican, for example, were to ask him, on seeing him wear a black collar, the rallying-sign of the royalists: 'For whom are you in mourning?' 'For you!' the charming young man's reply would come, and drawing his pistol would kill the questioner pointblank.

LIGHTNESS OF CLOTHES AND MORALS

The *Merveilleuse* was not nearly so combative. As all she

desired was to attract, she suffered tortures that would try the patience of a saint. She changed her wig three times a day; she wore buskins so thin-soled that every step was torment on the pavements of Paris; finally, she wore Grecian tunics, probably quite practical for the ancient Greeks, but which exposed French ladies to endless inflammations of the lungs. All this because they lived in the period of David, when there was a universal taste for classical nudities and because it was considered amusing to enter into the skin of the ancients by showing as much as possible of one's own.

So every beauty transformed herself into a sort of living Paros, unveiling every possible inch of her person, as much for Christian charity as for love of antiquity.

All the new fashions launched at this time, whether called *Ceres* robes, *Galatea* gowns, *Minerva* tunics, *Diana*, *Omphale* dresses, were inspired by the same idea – everything must be transparent. One may well say that X-rays were discovered at the end of the eighteenth century.

The finer a lawn, the more diaphanous a spangled tulle, the greater the pleasure a woman felt walking down the Champs-Elysées with the step of a goddess, holding over her right arm the folds of the revealing material. She would place divinely in evidence what a moralist who loved metaphors called 'the reservoirs of Maternity' and she displayed to advantage too another treasure which Venus Callipygian was not alone in possessing.

In order to figure as a true *Merveilleuse*, one had to know how to hide nothing, all the time appearing to be fully clad. This was the secret of the art of drapery which the fair sex cultivated from their tenderest years. In a dialogue composed by Mme de Genlis, a tailor tells his neighbour that his little girl, a child of ten, playing with her sister the night before, had pulled her skirt and petticoats over her head. Her father had asked sternly: 'What are you doing that for?' But the little one replied: 'Why, papa, I'm draping myself!'

The audacity of this fashion was judged severely even by

contemporaries. Old dowagers were never tired of repeating that in *their* young days panniered dresses, whale-bone bodices and even complicated hairdo's, that took so long to arrange – and disarrange – were means of defence. It was as safe as being in an armed fortress. Whereas at present, there was nothing to prevent a girl from giving way to the lightest passing caprice: 'It doesn't show, afterwards.'

One of the luxuries of the *Merveilleuses* was the vast number of wigs they had, for no one showed her own hair. This was hidden by a collection of switches of false hair, generally of the brightest blonde, and fashion decreed that one must change one's wig as often as one's pocket handkerchief. Any self-respecting woman had to possess at least ten wigs, one for each day of the decade, but a really elegant lady, a Citizeness Lanxade or a Citizeness Lange, would certainly have at least double that number and it is said that Mme Tallien had as many as thirty.

This allowed pleasant variations of colour and form, and one had no qualms about changing one's hairstyle several times a day. Let us take a look at the amiable Ophise described for us by the *Nouveau Paris*:

> In the morning, she is all transparent, our nymph, in her dress of diaphanous lawn. Her wig has the conical form of a beehive. She goes to lunch in the country, that is, at Passy. At three o'clock, she glitters with a thousand attractive charms: her billowing shawl with its bright red colour almost makes one take her for a butterfly with ruby wings. Her wig *à la Bérénice* draws everyone's eyes. In the evening, when the sun has gone down, she is Diana in a kilted skirt striding along the paths of the chase, a crescent of diamonds sparkling in her false, perfectly black hair, bound by a simple ribbon in a snood at the back of her head. At the Opéra, she seeks the eyes of some ambassador, of a minister (*not* of religion), or the admiring gaze of a Greek or a Turk. One can almost hear people say, as she passes: 'She's out for big game.'

THE PLEASURES OF THE NEWLY-RICH

In Paris, indeed, the newly-rich, the profiteers and all kinds of dishonest speculators abounded; they were making enormous profits and leading lives of great luxury. Some sold provisions to the army, others bought up foodstuffs, others were content to speculate with stocks and shares, playing on the fall in value of the *assignat*. Their activities had such bad effects that a golden louis' rate of exchange was 3,950 paper *livres* on December 14, 1795, so that the government, panic-stricken, decided to close the Bourse de l'Eglise des Petits-Pères. But it reopened clandestinely at the entry to the Palais Royal, on the Rue Vivienne side, and the swell mob went on filling its pockets.

This world of shady profiteers, and their intermediaries and middlemen who were ready to do any kind of dirty work, is the scourge of any country at war, as we know from our own recent experience. But it is also a godsend to gambling houses, night spots, restaurants, amusement quarters. It was this world which could be seen every night in the salons of the former Hôtel Richelieu, and its members who made free with the pretty streetgirls promoted to female pimps and who were paid, when the violinist Rhodes drew the final chord from his quivering strings, with Pantagruelian suppers of a splendour that was revolting when the rest of Paris was starving.

Others preferred the mysteries of private rooms and heaven knows the Palais Royal was able to pander to their exigencies. In a famous restaurant there was a room with a ceiling that opened up. Then one saw descending from the heavens a chariot drawn by doves and bearing a young beauty who resembled the queens of Olympus only in name and in her revealing costume. She might be Aurora, or Diana . . . Whoever she is supposed to be, Endymion would open his arms and the Metamorphoses of Ovid were enriched by a new chapter.

But it was not everyone who had the wherewithal to sport with goddesses. For the client of modest means a good dinner was in itself a luxury at a time when life was so difficult, so it was something of a miracle to see that a great number of restaurants were always full. It is true that certain customers tried to reduce their outlay by quietly slipping forks and spoons into their pockets. One evening at Naudet's one of these prestidigitators was spotted by the waiters, and when they presented him with his bill, it included this item: 'Cutlery . . . 54 francs.' He paid up without a murmur, saying merely: 'How dear things are getting these days!'

THE DANCE CRAZE

Just like the restaurants, the twenty-three theatres, large or small, which gave regular performances, had excellent takings; it seemed the public would rather go without its dinner than without its play. But there was one passion which surpassed all others: dancing.

Within a few weeks, scores and then hundreds of dancehalls opened all over Paris – Ruggieri's, Lucquet's, the Tivoli, the Paphos. There was not one deserted garden, not one abandoned dwelling, not one convent emptied of its nuns that was not dedicated to Terpsichore. There was dancing at the Hôtel de la Chine, at the Noviciat des Jésuites, at the Carmélites du Marais, at the Filles de Sainte-Marie, at the Séminaire de Saint-Sulpice, in half-ruined chapels and even on the worn flagstones of cloisters.

Organizers of this type of pleasure set up dancehalls to fit all purses. There was one where the admission fee was so low that 'even servants can go in'. Others are fitted out in the greatest luxury for the sort of young ladies you might expect in such places, while others, more decent, were for honest bourgeois families looking for husbands for their daughters. Others were for working-class couples, for soldiers on the spree, for the porters of the Quai Saint-Bernard. All classes of society were seized by the same frenzy; the lowliest teacher of the quadrille and the polka made a fortune and the poorest of musicians earned, for scraping his violin or squealing on his clarinet, six crowns or six *livres* a night, together with three litres of wine.

Every evening, as soon as eight had chimed, the streets were filled with women in white going off to dance with their gallants. One of the most curious features of this universal passion was that it was spiced frequently with macabre associations. They danced on the souvenir of the guillotine, as they danced six years before on the ruins of the Bastille. Perhaps a certain amount of exaggeration crept into the tales of those famous Victims' Dances given in the Faubourg Saint-Germain and where only authentic parents of those executed by the guillotine were admitted. On the other hand, the Victim Mood was within the reach of all women and a good number of them never went out without a death-pale face and a blood-red ribbon round the neck, marking the place where the guillotine fell. It was one way, among many others just as macabre, of brightening up Parisian night-life.

Rather morbid, for example, was the feeling that infected a whole generation, a need to remember that it had once been afraid and to multiply the extravagance of its memories in order to prove to itself that the nightmare really was over. Few examples are more edifying than that of the dancer confronting a strange woman at a Carnival rout and shouting at her in tragic tones:

'You buffoon! They've killed my father!'

'Killed your father?' the woman replied, pulling out her handkerchief.

'Yes, they killed him!' And the man began to caper about, singing:

> 'Zig-zag, fork and spoon,
> Dance to the tune of the rigadoon!'

The life of Paris had certainly undergone a change since the days of Robespierre.

THE COUNTRY IMITATES PARIS

The same thing might be said of provincial life. We find the proof of this if we take at random any big provincial city, for example Bordeaux.

In the ancient Girondin city, the merchant-class aristocracy which was slowly being ruined by the war with England, was being replaced by a handful of newly-rich who owed their fortune to speculations on national property and on army supplies. Their wives, whether legal or not, were bound to copy the modes of the capital or rather the antique fashions of Athens.

At the start, at least, modesty decreed that they should only be worn in the evening. In the city, even in Year IV anglomania was still strong, and with it went the shawl, the frockcoat and the spencer; it was only at balls that one met the *Merveilleuses* in their flowing robes of lawn, their legs bare, and rings on their toes, bracelets on their ankles.

But it was not long before they were seen in the streets and during the daytime. From that winter onwards, their gauzy nudities appeared on fashionable walks, and as it was very cold the Bordeaux disciples of Aesculapius built up a charming clientele among these martyrs to fashion.

The offensive became even more powerful in the Year VI when fine weather returned. One day in fact the Allées de Tourny were the scene of a slight scandal. Two ladies appeared there with tunics so transparent that a crowd gathered and forced them back into their carriage. It was a second performance of Mme Hamelin's adventure in the Champs-Elysées. But the audacious young ladies soon had many imitators. Within a few months, Bordeaux had become a Grecian colony; the children were called Arisitide or Leonidas, boudoirs became gynaeceums, schools prytaneums; and the women, forever frozen stiff, were certainly as cold as antique statuary.[2]

As for the life of pleasure, there were the same tendencies as in Paris. There were concerts, races were held, fireworks set off; Talma was applauded when he came on tour to the Théâtre de la République. But above all there were endless balls at the Société Philharmonique and at the Hôtel du Gouvernement. It was a life of continual pleasures in a country where nine out of ten people complained of having no money, where the rich of yesterday were almost poverty-stricken and the rich of the moment would perhaps be destitute within a month or two.

When we move from the big cities to the small rural centres, again we find almost everywhere the same lack of money. The peasantry still managed to survive, as the earth supplied their needs, but with the financial anarchy that was growing day by day, what was to become of people with small private means, petty functionaries paid irregularly with bits of paper that were worth nothing?

A letter written at the end of 1795 by the municipal council of Vouneuil to the administrators of the Creuse region tells us a good deal about local distress. Everything was lacking in those wretched offices: no wood for heating, no candles for illumination, no registers, no writing-paper. Each employee had brought to the office whatever he had at home, but now there was nothing left; all they had was urgent work.

How could a district be properly administered – births registered, deaths recorded, citizens married, taxes imposed, decrees written up, the life of the community kept going, if all there was to sit on was a block of stone and some broken benches; when the only table was a few planks, and stationery was reduced to a single miserable sheet of paper? 'Added to which,' continues the author of this report,

> there is a complete lack of staff, as no one wants to leave the towns to live in the country, working at this sort of grind and at the same time encountering insuperable difficulties simply to keep body and soul together . . . Among all the agents for the communes in this district, only one could write correct French; although his sight is seriously affected, as he found our administration without a secretary and unable to do a single thing, he flouted his infirmities and took on the task of secretary.

Small as it is, this piece of evidence is revealing. How many small communities in France must have found themselves in the same position as Vouneuil, unable to function normally because disorder was general, because the State had no more money, because neither the good will of the administrative authorities nor the efforts of the central powers were able to grant the modest requests of a simple country council office to send them a secretary able to write and some paper for him to write on!

THE LOVE MARKET OF 'PETITES AFFICHES'

What with costly follies on the one hand and poverty on the other, there is a great temptation to see here the operation of the laws of cause and effect. This is why the Directory has a bad reputation. But we must examine the evidence and ask ourselves if this epoch's ups and downs, its licentiousness, its profligacy and debauchery have not been over-exaggerated.

It is quite certain that the populace of the big towns for four years spent too much time dancing, that a certain number of adventurers and courtesans led a gay life throwing to the winds their own money and that of others, and that virtue did by no means reign supreme. But to assume from this that the evil was general would be unjust. A handful of chronic carousers, a few hundred or perhaps a few thousands of parvenus in the worlds of finance and politics do not represent an entire country. In the capital alone, Paris should not be confused with what is fondly known as *Tout-Paris*, that narrow little world of snobbery and privilege.

Within the government itself, men like La Revellière-Lépeaux, Carnot, Letourneur and Rewbell led quite bourgeois existences. The only exception was Barras, and even in his case a legend may have been created round his 'orgies' at the Luxembourg. If we are to believe Jullian, these were most often quite simple meetings attended by Mme Tallien, Joséphine and a few other women in the same circle:

> We would meet between seven and eight; we split up into groups: those who did not play cards indulged in conversation in other rooms; sometimes Barras gave balls, but

the small size of his apartments limited the number of guests. We often played children's games; we were at ease and happy; there was neither etiquette, in the stricter sense, nor constraint. Yet it was these simple, peaceful meetings of friends that were given the name of 'orgies', and sometimes even more scandalous appellations.[3]

Jullian should probably be considered as a somewhat biased witness. But what do the police reports say, and what do the newspapers tell us about the morals of the populace? That gambling-houses are full of gamblers, that streetgirls have brief romantic episodes in the galleries of the Palais de la Révolution, from which Chaumette's vigilance had once banished them for a while: nothing very serious, in fact, and in any case fairly localized, not widespread.

There were indeed in certain papers small advertisements which scandalized more serious folk. 'The *Petites Affiches*,' one critic writes,

> are thronged with pretty girls from eighteen to twenty-two, of a most clinging nature, with the most agreeable physiognomy; they are fortunate in *knowing a little of everything*, and their most ardent desire is to find *a position with a single gentleman*.

One lady of fifty advertised herself as having 'accommodation, money and a not too ravaged appearance'. Another promised her heart to anyone who truly deserved it, whereupon three citizens immediately sent her their addresses.[4]

Obviously such literature is not to be recommended, but the fact that it raised indignant protests proved that it was still not widespread. It was to grow more prominent later.

THE MORAL DECADENCE OF FRENCH SOCIETY IS ONLY SKIN DEEP

What it is important to remember is that the Directory generation for the greater part, despite its somewhat loose fashions and behaviour, was at bottom honest. The epoch only seems immoral to us by comparison with the periods which preceded and followed it – the austere Jacobin twilight and the Napoleonic dawn. But considered in itself the period was neither worse nor better than all those we encounter in history immediately after violent upheavals have taken place.

Since the end of the Terror, a younger generation that had known no joy in life wanted to taste to the full of sweet intoxication of living life to the full again. It cast itself upon existence with the splendid voracity of a Gargantua after Lent, and the women lavished all those kisses they had been saving up so long. Though the young rascals who paraded with them were sometimes queer customers, these, we must repeat, constituted only a tiny fraction of society.

The rest of the country, leaving idlers to their gambling and their mistresses, stayed clear of the contagion. Recovering a little from its mania for politics, it went on working, confident that better days were to come: its moral health was intact.

The proof of this is that soon this enormous mass of ordinary folk was soon able to make one of the biggest and longest efforts ever demanded of a people. The France of the Directory was to become the France of the Consulate; order was re-established as a matter of course because national common sense had not degenerated.

Then daily life was to take on again its normal course, moving towards new destinies, and giving fresh meaning to this wise man's saying: 'Yesterday is a corpse and tomorrow is – something else.'

NOTES

CHAPTER ONE, THE PARIS OF 1789

1. The curious relief-map at the Musée Carnavalet showing the square as it was in 1830, with its irregular shape, its absence of convenient outlets, its one side dropping down to the river, the gothic details of certain houses and the tiny proportions of the Hôtel de Ville de la Renaissance, give us a reconstruction of the site more or less as it was during the Revolution

2. Pierre de Vaissière, *Letters from Aristocrats. The Revolution described in Private Correspondence*, pp. 300–301, Paris, 1807

3. L. William Cart, *Three Weeks in Paris during the Revolution. Impressions of the German Traveller Campe*. ('La Révolution Française', 1910, pp. 114–115)

4. L. William Cart, *op. cit.*, pp. 44–45

5. Pierre de Vaissière, *Letters from Aristocrats*, p. 166

6. *Idem*

7. *Idem*

8. *Les Révolutions de Paris*, No. 95, April 30 to May 7, 1791

CHAPTER TWO, THREE DEPUTIES AT THE STATES GENERAL

1. *Letter from the Abbé Barbotin* (1741–1816), deputy at the Constituent Assembly, ed. by A. Aulard (Société de l'histoire de la Révolution française, 1910)

2. Letter of May 10, 1789

3. Letter of June 26

4. Letter of October 26

5. Letter of August 13

6. Letter of January 6, 1790

7. The Marquis de Ferrières (1741–1804), deputy of the nobility at the States General. Private correspondence (1789, 1790, 1791), published and annotated by Henri Carré (*Les Classiques de la Révolution* Paris, A. Colin, 1932)

8. Letter of October 21, 1789

9. Letter of September 25, 1789

10. Letter of July 9, 1790

11. H. Taine, *Les origines de la France contemporaine*, Vol. I, p. 5, Hachette

12. C. Leroux-Cesbron Lofficial (1751–1811), deputy of Deux-Sèvres at the Constituent Assembly (*La Révolution Française*, 1920)

13. June 1789

14. July 6, 1789

15. Letter of July 21, 1789

CHAPTER THREE, DAILY LIFE IN THE PROVINCES

1. A. Aulard, *Taine, historien de la Révolution française*, p. 329, Armand Colin, 1907

2. Claims for redistribution of land. (Translator's note)

3. Minister of Justice,

corresponding to the Lord Chancellor in England. (Translator's note)

4. Nicolas Rogue, *Souvenirs et journal d'un bourgeois d'Evreux*, Evreux, 1850

5. Raoul Rosière, *La révolution dans une petit ville*, pp. 32–35, Paris, 1888

6. O. Boustanquoi, *Les souvenirs d'une femme du peuple*, Senlis, 1920

7. Archives Nationales, D. XXIX. Lettre de M. Briand-Delessart (Angoulême)

8. *Moniteur*, November 8, 1791, t.X, p. 132

9. Mlle G. Rocher, *Société de l'Histoire de la Révolution française*, 1914, 1915

10. Nicolas Rogue, *Souvenirs*, *op. cit.*, Evreux, 1850

CHAPTER FOUR, LIFE IN HIGH SOCIETY

1. Member of a Constitutional Club in 1791

2. E. and J. de Goncourt, *Histoire de la Société française pendant la Révolution*, Paris, 1895, p. 7

3. L. William Cart, *Impressions du voyageur allemand, op. cit.*

4. Michel Lhéritier, *Les débuts de la Révolution à Bordeaux d'après les tablettes manuscrites de Pierre Bernardou* (Société de l'Histoire de la Révolution, Rieder)

5. *Mémoires de Barbaroux*, ed. Alfred Chabaud (Les classiques de la Révolution, Paris, A. Colin, 1936, pp. 83–84)

6. *Souvenirs de ma vie*, by M. Jullian, Paris, 1814, pp. 98–99

CHAPTER FIVE, PARIS THEATRES AND CAFÉS

1. E. and J. de Goncourt, *Histoire de la Société française pendant la Révolution*, Paris, Fasquelle

2. Docteur Cabanès and L. Nass, *La névrose révolutionnaire*, Société française d'Imprimerie et de Librairie, Paris, 1906

3. E. and J. Goncourt, *op. cit.*

4. *Le Moniteur*, 18 nivôse an II (18th of the French Republican calendar month running from December 21 to January 19, 1791. (Translator's note)

5. Emile Faguet, Propos de théâtre, 2nd series

CHAPTER SIX, THE REVOLUTION AND FASHION

1. E. and J. Goncourt, *op. cit.*

2. *Lettre de Mrs Williams*, 1791

3. P. de Vaissière, *Letters from Aristocrats*, p. 265 et seq.

4. Members of ultra-revolutionary party known as *La Montagne*. (Translator's note)

5. G. Lenotre, *La vie à Paris pendant la Révolution* (*Revue des Deux-Mondes*, February 1, 1936)

6. Lairtullier, *Les Femmes Célèbres de la Révolution*

CHAPTER SEVEN, FRENCH AS SHE IS SPOKE

1. Alfred Aulard, *La Révolution française*, Vol. XXXIV, p. 482

2. *Bulletin de la Convention*, séance du 10 brumaire an II

3. *Journal des Spectacles*, No. 23, July 23, 1793

4. Supreme executive council of France from 1795 to 1799

5. Cited by Cabanès and Nass in *La Névrose Révolutionnaire*, p. 396, Société française d'Imprimerie, 1906

6. Cf. Paul Lacombe, Les Noms des Rues de Paris sous la Révolution, in–8, Paris, 1886

7. In Loir-et-Cher

8. *Petites Affiches*, July 1792

9. Twelfth month of the Republican calendar, August 18 to September 16. (Translator's note)

10. De Coston, *Origines, étymologie et signification des noms propres*, p. 41, Paris, Aubry, 1867

CHAPTER EIGHT, REVOLUTIONARY LIBERTIES

1. There were five numbers

2. Friedrich Schulz, *Ueber Paris und die Pariser*, 1790

3. August von Kotzebue, *Meine Flucht nach Paris in Winter*, 1790

4. E. and J. de Goncourt, *Histoire de la Société française pendant la Révolution*, pp. 228–229, Paris, Fasquelle

5. *Les nouvelles amours*, comico-lyrico-tragico farce

about the women of the Palais Royal, Paris (n.d.), p. 13

6. *Le Courrier d'Egalité*

7. *Journal des Spectacles*, October 1793

8. Certain youthful works of poor Boilly himself were criticized, and he was only able to redeem his reputation by exhibiting his last picture: *The Triumph of Marat*

CHAPTER NINE, MARRIAGE AND CHILDREN

1. *Annales patriotiques*, September, 1792

2. *Journal de Perlot*, October, 1792

3. *Goncourt*, p. 392

4. *Petites affiches*, November, 1790

5. *Goncourt*, p. 382

6. Stéfane Pol, *De Robespierre à Fouché, notes de police*, pp. 68–71, Flammarion, 1906

7. Madeleine Schnerb, *Primary Education in Puy-de-Dôme* (Annales de la Révolution française, 1936)

CHAPTER TEN, THE PARIS CLIMATE DURING THE TERROR

1. Albert Mathiez, *La Révolution française*, Vol. II, p. 27, Paris, 1924

2. *Souvenirs de ma vie*, by

M. Jullian, p. 144, Paris, 1814

3. L.-S. Mercier, *Le nouveau Paris*

4. *Moniteur*, August 15, 1792

5. Boustanquoi, *Les souvenirs d'une femme du peuple*, Senlis, 1928

6. A. Schmidt, *Tableaux de la Révolution française*, Vol. I, p. 203, Leipzig, 1867–1871

7. Pierre de Vaissière, *Letters from Aristocrats. La Révolution racontée par des Correspondances privées*, pp. 300–301, Paris, 1907

8. French paper money used from 1789–1797. (Translator's note)

9. Paul Mautouchet, *La population parisienne et la crise de l'alimentation sous la Terreur* (La Révolution française, 1917)

10. *Journal de la Montagne*, 15 ventôse an II

11. *Archives Nationales*, Report of 5 germinal

12. *Archives Nationales*, same dossier

13. *Papiers inédits trouvés chez Robespierre*, etc., Vol. II, p. 380, Paris, 1828

CHAPTER ELEVEN, RURAL FRANCE DURING THE TERROR

1. Wilhelm Bauer, *Un Allemand en France sous la Terreur, Souvenirs de Charles Laukhard*, p. 71, Paris, 1915

2. P. Caron, *Rapports des agents du ministère de l'Intérieur*

3. Mirepoix (Ariège)

4. The elegant name for potatoes. (Translator's note)

5. J.-P. Brissot, *Mémoires*, published by Claude Perroud, Vol. II, pp. 219–220, Paris, 1910–1912

6. P. Caron, *Rapports des agents du ministère de l'Intérieur*

7. B. Combes de Patris, *Procès-verbaux des séances de la Société populaire de Rodez*, pp. 204–205, Rodez, 1912

8. See p. 32

9. See p. 30

10. *La Feuille Villageoise*, No. 18, April 18, 1793. (Such a pretty name for a paper! It might in English be called *The Village Vine!*) (Translator's note)

11. *Correspondence de Maximilien et Augustin Robespierre*, published by G. Michon, Paris, Alcan, 1926

12. Address to the Club des Jacobins, I frimaire

13. Address 21 frimaire

CHAPTER TWELVE, HOSTESS TO ROBESPIERRE

1. Edouard Lockroy, *Journal d'une bourgoise pendant la Révolution*, Paris, 1881

2. One of these little sticks, carried as a sign of authority by police officers, can be seen on display at the Musée Carnavalet

3. Letter to her husband, August 15, 1792

4. Letter to her son, August 21

5. Letter to Marc-Antoine, February 10, 1793

6. Here Edouard Lockroy seems to be guilty of a slight error when he gives this menu as that of February 2. Robert Lindet did not attend the first dinner.

7. Archives Nationales, AF-II 45 (*Police Reports*, May 20, 1793)

8. It was Marc-Antoine who, during a trip to Nantes, had Carrier brought back to Paris after the excesses he had committed. The mission given the young man was defined in a document drawn up by the Committee of Public Safety, dated September 10, 1793: 'Marc-Antoine Jullien, commissioner of the War Office, shall proceed, in the quality of Committee representative, to Le Havre, Cherbourg, Saint-Malo, Brest, Nantes, La Rochelle, Rochefort and Bordeaux, and shall return via Bayonne, Avignon, Marseilles and Lyons, gathering information about the state of public feeling, awakening it to new life in those places, enlightening the people, encouraging the People's Societies, keeping watch on public enemies in the interior, foiling their plots and keeping the Committee of Public Safety accurately informed by correspondence.' *Signed:* Prieur, Barère, Carnot. (*Receuil des actes du Comité de Salut public*, Vol. VI, p. 397)

9. Letter of June 8, 1792

CHAPTER THIRTEEN, A BOURGEOIS FAMILY DURING THE TERROR

1. Louis de Launay, *Une vie de famille pendant la Terreur* (Revue de France, January 1 and 15, 1935)

2. As he had been in public office under Royalty, he had been dismissed at the beginning of 1793

3. *Journal de Mlle G——*, January 28, 1794

4. *Idem*, February 12

5. *Idem*, February 26

6. *Idem*, February 18

7. *Idem*, February 26

8. *Idem*, February 10

9. *Idem*, February 10

10. *Idem*, February 24

11. *Idem*, February 24

12. *Idem*, March 5

13. *Idem*, April 25

14. *Idem*, March 10

CHAPTER FOURTEEN, A PARISIAN WORKING GIRL

1. O. Boustanquoi, *Les souvenirs d'une femme du peuple*, Silens, 1928

2. French paper money used between 1789 and 1797. (Translator's note)

3. In fact, she was almost sixteen, as she was born on October 4, 1777

4. This grandmother had saved two hundred *louis* and had wanted to share them during her lifetime with her nineteen grandchildren: ten *louis* each and twenty for the youngest granddaughter, who had only one arm

CHAPTER FIFTEEN, CALENDAR FEASTS AND FASHIONS

1. It began, as every schoolboy knows, on September 22, 1792. At that time of the year, the days and nights are of exactly the same length, so that a contemporary might well remark that 'egality was demonstrated in the heavens at the very moment when civil and moral egality were proclaimed by the representatives of France'

2. J. de Launay, *Une vie de famille pendant la Terreur* (Revue de France, January 1 and 15, 1935)

3. O. Boustanquoi, *Les souvenirs d'une femme du peuple*, Senlis, 1928

4. *L'Antifédéraliste*, No. 28, 2 Brumaire, Year II

5. Le. de Cardenal, *La société populaire de Monpazier* (Comité des travaux historiques, Vol. X, 1924)

6. Archives communales de Boulogne-sur-mer. Registre des délibérations du Conseil général de la Commune, Year II, Folio 31, ed. by M. Dommanget (Annales historiques de la Révolution, 1924)

7. Nicolas Rogue, *Souvenirs et journal d'un bourgeois d'Evreux*, Evreux, 1850

8. Hippolyte Buffenoir, *L'image de J.-J. Rousseau dans les Sociétés de la Révolution* (La Révolution française, 1918, p. 52)

CHAPTER SIXTEEN, ÉMIGRÉS IN THEIR OWN LAND

1. M. Jullian, *Souvenirs de ma vie*, pp. 150–152

2. *Mémoires de Mme de Chastenay*, Plon-Nourrit

3. Quoted by Edmond Pilon in *La Vie de famille au XVIIIe siècle*, Paris, Jonquières

CHAPTER SEVENTEEN, DAILY LIFE IN PRISON

1. *Souvenirs de ma vie*, by M. Jullian, pp. 164–166

CHAPTER EIGHTEEN, IN TIME OF WAR

1. H. Poulet, *Les volontaires de la Meurthe*, p. 75

2. *Souvenirs du baron Pouget*, p. 7. Quoted by A. Mathiez, *La Victoire en l'an II*

3. Mortimer Ternaux, *Histoire de la Terreur*

4. A. Mathiez, *La Victoire en l'an II*, pp. 74–75

CHAPTER NINETEEN, LETTERS FROM SOLDIERS

1. Lorédan Larchey, *Journal de marche d'un volontaire de 1792*

2. One-tenth of a franc. (Translator's note)

3. Xavier Vernère, *Cahiers d'un volontaire de* 91, Gerin-Roze, Paris, 1910
4. Gabriel Noël, *Au temps des volontaires*, 1912
5. *La Révolution française*, 1926–1927
6. *La Révolution française*, 1914, p. 282
7. Published by Caron, *La Révolution française*, year 1934
8. *Idem*

9. Misspelling for *l'Aisne*. (Translator's note)
10. *La Révolution française*, 1907, pp. 555–556
11. He obviously means the Constitution of Year III. Consequently the letter must have been written on the 12th Fructidor, Year III (August 29, 1795) and not Year II

CHAPTER TWENTY, DAILY LIFE ON THE ROADS

1. Edmond Poupé, *Lettres de Barras et de Fréron, en mission dans le Midi*, Draguignan, 1910
2. Jouve and Girard-Mangin, *Carnet de route du Conventionnel Goupilleau en mission dans le Midi*, Nîmes, 1905
3. Jouve and Girard-Mangin, *Lettres intimes du Conventionnel Goupilleau (de Montaigu) en mission dans le Midi après la Terreur. – Ibid. Correspondance intime du Conventionnel Rovère avec Goupilleau (de Montaigu) en mission dans le Midi*. Nîmes, 1906 and 1908

CHAPTER TWENTY-ONE, THE HONEST FAMILY OF A DISHONEST DEPUTY

1. *Lettres inédites de J.-S. Rovère, membre du Conseil des Anciens, à son frère Siméon-Stylite, ex-evèque constitutionnel du département de Vaucluse*, published by Victorin Laval, Paris, H. Champion, 1908
2. Female fops, of an extreme affectation, under the Directory, 1795. (Translator's note)
3. *Lettres de La Paige* (Annales de la Société d'Emulation des Vosges, 1909)
4. F. Vermale, *La vente des biens nationaux dans le district de Chambéry* (Annales Révolutionnaires, 1909)
5. Letter of October 13, 1796
6. Letters of February 18 and 22, 1797
7. February 28, 1797
8. March 16
9. Letter of November 14, 1796
10. March 24, 1797
11. Had he 'gone native', we wonder? (Translator's note)

CHAPTER TWENTY-TWO, MME HUMMEL'S ACCOUNT BOOK

1. Gaston Martin, *La vie bourgeoise à Nantes sous la Convention, d'après le livre de comptes de Mme Hummel* (1793–1795) (*La Révolution française*, 1933, p. 243)

CHAPTER TWENTY-THREE, THE TEMPER OF THERMIDOR

1. Philippe Sagnac, *La Révolution de 1789*, Vol. II, p. 352, Les Editions Nationales, Paris, 1934

2. Alphonse Aulard, *Etudes et leçons sur la Révolution française*, 5th series, p. 6, Félix Alcan, 1907

3. Aulard, *Etudes et leçons sur la Révolution française*, 5th series, p. 13, Alcan, 1907

4. H. Taine, *Les origines de la France contemporaine (La Révolution*, Vol. III, p. 537, Hachette, 1885)

5. G. Lefébure, *La Révolution française*, Collection Peuples et Civilizations, Alcan, 1930

CHAPTER TWENTY-FOUR, BESIDE THE SEA-SIDE

1. Claude Perraud, *Cinq lettres de Fanny, l'amie d'André Chénier* (*La Révolution française*, 1797)

CHAPTER TWENTY-FIVE, MEMOIRS OF A DERANGED YOUNG MAN

1. Louis de Launay, *Un mariage sous Le Directoire* (*La Revue de France*, October 15, 1933

2. *Journal*, August 7, 1798

3. *Idem*, October 14, 1798

4. *Idem*, October 17, 1798

5. *Idem*, October 19, 1798

6. *Idem*, January 30, 1799

7. *Idem*, April 21, 1799

8. *Idem*, April 24, 1799

9. *Idem*, September 18 and 19

CHAPTER TWENTY-SIX, IN THE DAYS OF THE 'MERVEILLEUSES'

1. *Bordeaux sous le Directoire* (*La Révolution française*, 1917, pp. 32–33, G. Caudrillier)

2. *Souvenirs de ma vie*, by M. Jullian, Paris, 1814, pp. 220–221

3. *L'Abréviateur universel*, 6 Ventôse, Year III. Quoted by Aulard

4. *Journal des Nouvelles, d'indications et annonces pour Paris et les départements*, 2 Ventôse, Year III. Quoted by Aulard

INDEX